The Game of Life

How To Play ★ The New Way

Heidi Hosking

To my dearest actors, Anthony, Hayden and Declan.

You squeezed me until I came to these messages and you supported me with all the love, whilst I made magic for others, from this…

Copyright © 2023 by Heidi Hosking
ISBN 978-0-646-88951-1

All rights reserved. No portion of this book may be reproduced, stored in a retrieval system, or transmitted in any form or by any means - electronic, mechanical, photography, recording, scanning, or other - except for brief quotations in critical reviews or articles, without the prior written permission of the publisher.

Contents

Welcome to the Game of Life 1

You are it 18
...*you direct your life from your inner universe...*

What is 23
...*what plays out is our only reality...*

Seed of Intelligence 34
...*your soul path is encoded within you...*

Divine Timing 45
...*you are energetically pulled to the path encoded within you...*

Soul Agreement 72
...*you cannot change who you are...*

Life Themes 84
...*every scene of your day is an experience for YOU to embody...*

Your Actors 113
...*those in your external reflect what is there to be felt in your internal...*

The Emotional Blackbox 123
...*feeling cannot be turned off...*

Lava Lamp Effect 135
...*the state of your inner universe dictates everything in the external - not the other way around...*

Monkey Mind Nets 155
...*you behave from your rising emotions...*

Snow Globe 177
...*when it's time to explore the Heart energy, our emotions surface whether we like it or not...*

The Cone 186
...*your recurring challenges continue until your soul lessons have been realised...*

Inner Universe 207
...start here, to make sense of your life...

How to Play summary 220

The Tip of the Iceberg 222
...the little opportunities to feel will become the chaos
that forces us to crack...

Seasons of Life 232
...the harmony is between two poles...

Canvas of Life 247
...your life at any moment in time,
is a canvas that you can co-create with...

Yearnings 255
...your inner universe and external challenges
show you what you are encoded to yearn for...

The Titanic 273
...we must face what is not, before we become the version of 'what is'...

The Rainbow 279
...allow your yearnings to show up in good time...

Red and Green Lights 287
...your divine path always gives you hints internally and externally...

Playing Cards 307
...you can only play the game of life from 'what is'...

The Fairytale 315
...heaven on Earth starts within us...

Glossary of The New Way terms 319

Glossary of the The New Way energetic laws 325

How to Play summary 328

Acknowledgements 330

Welcome to the Game of Life

To my wondrous reader,

It is time to learn how to play the game of life, like never before. The New Way is to understand the utter perfection of our existence and to co-create *with* this. It is to know that everything that happens to us, good or bad, light or dark, is for a very good reason. There is no more need to pathologise ourselves as humans. As we understand and live life by the energetic concepts that govern our existence, we can play from a place of power. We intuitively see the reasons for our challenges, and we can confidently play with our experience.

At this point in time, women like you and me are in the thick of it. We see and feel our big challenges. We do our very best to stay afloat, to stay on top of the surfboard. Many of us however, only just climb back on before the next wave hits. Some barely have a hold of their leg strap, as the surfboard seems to pull somewhere into oblivion, their only life line.

The thing is, society continues to point out where our children are too loud, too chatty, too shy, too detail-focused, too unintelligible, too powerless, too questioning and well, just too much. Society also points out where our children are not enough. Everyone, in general, expects an answer out of us mothers. All fingers are pointed at us with immense pressure.

Meanwhile, at home, we deal with our own experiences of our child being too much and each family member's reactions to them. We constantly leak energy as we attempt to hold onto any family harmony that we can. As a result, we lose sight of our child's magic. At the same time, those in the external world still expect that answer, that therapy, that apology or that result, to change our child. We spend even more of our precious energy as we feel we must respond to these calls, as the mother.

Us mothers have lost ourselves. We spend so much time, energy and money, in an attempt to fix our family's problems. As a result, we lose track of what is important to us. We allow everyone's fears to distract us from our deep yearning for heart connection with and between our family members.

We have done it all backwards. We forget to first seek heart connection with ourselves as we chase after the cracks in the family bubble with masking tape. We salute the daycare, school, doctors, therapists, media and our well meaning partner, friends and family, as they pull our attention to our children's so-called problems. We lost our connection with our soul the day our own intuition was drowned out by society.

Our day to day scenes give us red lights as we take this path. We unknowingly build resentment as we ignore these signs. We leak it as we yell, control, huff, over-eat, swallow it down or burn energy to control the inner chaos. We turn a blind eye to our inner universe, our connection to our divine guidance. Our emotional body calls us.

The red lights continue. We suffer health issues ourselves. Our menstrual cycle falls out of sync. We play out fatigue. The migraines, cold sores, back pain, tight jaw, constipation, insomnia and sore throats arise as our physical body speaks up.

The red lights continue. We can't be present with our children. We interrupt our friends. We glaze over when our partner speaks. We can only manage to get through our days. It all feels hopeless, yet we drain more energy as we try to bring our heart's cheer anyway. Our mental body cries out.

The red lights desperately continue. Our relationship with our partner feels lifeless. Everyday we dread the next issue that arises within our family. As one person, we are just about out of the masking tape to hold the family bubble together. We use the rest of our energy to ignore the elephant in the room - WHAT ABOUT ME AND MY SOUL PATH? Our spiritual body screeches.

Whether you have seen your red lights across your emotional, physical, mental or spiritual bodies, are you ready to switch gears and play the game of life, The New Way?

....

We have reached the point in time where us mothers are invited to make sense of our own path. We feel the dread and the drain of mundane parenting tasks. We seek more than surface level chats with other mothers, let alone old world jobs that don't fulfil us. We want to be understood for our life's challenges and triumphs. We feel the call to move into our soul purpose and to stand on our own two feet. We naturally yearn to discover and embody our uniqueness.

We are also at the point in time where us mothers are invited to explore family harmony. As the central point of the family, we hugely feel the effects of disharmony, not only within the family bubble, but also with our extended family, friends and our children's peers. We have become aware of the cost of this elephant in the room - the issues and hurt feelings that have been ignored for too long.

Us mothers feel a desperation to strengthen our heart connection with our family members and others. We even feel called to finally honour the heaviness that our heart has carried, as we have witnessed disharmony unfold throughout our lives. We are the generation to say a huge 'YES!' to these yearnings.

Do you yearn to find your own uniqueness as a soul and to seek harmony in your connections?

Let me introduce myself...

There is no relevant part of me that relates to this book. It's because my life is an ongoing unfolding, like it is for all of us. This book is the glorious by-product of my inner work and my family work - from the challenges that have arisen for myself and my family. On that note, let me introduce you to my loving husband, Anthony; my two wondrous sons, Hayden and Declan; and our love heart dog, Bounty.

When I was young, I used my empathic skills to deeply understand people, to the minute detail. I was often bored in school. To cope, I connected dots with anything around me and I drew all sorts of conclusions. One time I played with 'if I stare with enough intention at someone's toe, they will move it'!

It's like I've lived my life backwards. By the time I read a book, took a course or even went to university, I'd often already worked out the key concepts and principles in other areas of my life. It's like I had already noticed the seeds that were planted for me by my soul path, at earlier times.

I followed my conditioning, which taught me I had to learn from others, at school, university and other professional development courses. I took the few golden keys from each experience and connected those dots with what I figured out on my own.

It wasn't until after my first son, Hayden, was born that I reconnected back to more of my own intuition. A man called Paul activated me. He hosted the 'Energetic Anatomy of a Yogi' workshop, yet he planted seeds about the ego, astral projection, the new children and more.

After I met Paul, I was straight onto my 'shadow work'. I looked at how I attempted to control my world by perfectionism, martyrdom, victimhood and more, to cover my inner hurts. From this inner work, I realised I never wanted to show up from my ego self, my monkey mind, my shadow side, my disempowered self or what I call my 'little old human self'.

* My gut wished it could erase the words I said to a girl in primary school. I told her 'you can't play with us', when she asked to play handball with my friends and my new ball.

* I felt out of control when I had a tantrum at my Mum, as I got in the car from a hot day at school.

* There was a part of me that got really annoyed when I talked negatively to others about my partner, Anthony.

* I was embarrassed at myself when I yelled at my children in front of others or huffed when they put their little painted hands all over the house.

* A part of me felt like it died when I gave my power to the hospital staff at my childrens' births.

* My soul screeched as I allowed the school staff to hint they knew my children more than I did.

* I tried to give advice to others, yet could feel it wasn't received well - I caught a reflection of my ego self.

* Down the track, my neck tensed up as I judged others.

* I felt the squirm of the darkness when I showed up from my shadow side.

There are so many examples but that's enough. The more I became aware of my shadow side, the more I didn't like this expression of myself. I desperately wanted to show up as better. I felt the pull to be that amazing partner, the most dazzling version of a mother and let alone a willing team mate with others in life, whether that was the checkout assistant, my friend or another child.

I wanted my power back. Since I was born, I knew I had often been pulled by my inner knowing. It allowed me to intuitively reach all of the answers I ever needed and to create the life that my heart had always yearned for thus far. I was forever called to express more of my true self however, rather than express myself from the shadowy behaviours, such as those I listed above. I wanted to play the game of life with even more confidence. I wanted to know the rules to it all.

But how? Who was I? What about my fears, doubts and shadows? How would it look if I showed the world even more of my true expression? On my quest to embody my best character of 'being Heidi', my subconscious questions were answered. It's led me to the most amazing connection with the divine, to understand the energetics that guide us every day and to understand truth in revolutionary ways. It's also connected me with other soul families, who have been nudged to 'embody their best character' and 'take back their power' too.

I assume you're also here because there's a part of you that wants to understand how to work through your challenges with confidence and unlock how to play the game of life?

Let me take you into the bright world of The New Way....

The New Way series

This book is the first in a series of The New Way books. Throughout this book, we will look at why our challenges arise, the energetics at play and how to unravel our challenges with others who play the game of life, The New Way.

As you will soon read, this book covers the basic rules of the game of life. These rules are energetic laws which play out *all of the time*, not just when we are happy to accept them! If we play by these laws, then we can move past the old ways of life that stem from disempowerment, ego and what our 'little old human selves' think is best. These old ways pervade deep into our everyday beliefs, thoughts and actions, often without our knowing. Instead, when we play by the perfectly orchestrated energetic rules of life, we completely upgrade our human being.

Many, many women have nudged me to 'start with the practical stuff'. They are *desperate* to wave their magic wands and flip their family and personal challenges overnight. It is so hard to accept that life might play out imperfectly. Every time I have gone to do this over the years however, the message only got louder, 'you must go within first and commit to self-responsibility before you can solve your external issues!'. If I bring practical parenting ideas first, women try to fix the external problem and avoid self-reflection, where the root cause of every life challenge begins. Hence, this book's primary theme is to understand the energetic concept of 'you are it' and to embrace 'what is'.

The New Way calls for us to unravel from the old way of superficial approaches, opinions and quick fixes. Instead, we are invited to turn to deeper and much more powerful changes. It starts within us first. As we practice mastery of our inner work, we come into our heart. When we are in our heart, *we know* what to say and what to do. We don't need advice, support or guidance from anyone else. This goes for our children and even partners too. The adventure is to remember the details of how to do this. This book will guide you through all you need to know.

The New Way

The New Way is a new consciousness. I define that as 'a revolutionary, complete turn-about in how we think, believe, act and do human life, let alone how we *be* human'. From conception, we have carried energy from our ancestors within our cells. Since birth, we have perceived our existence through the intentional and incidental teachings from our parents and every other person we have ever engaged with. These interactions and the energy we were born with brings preconceived ideas, behaviours and beliefs in how we should live life. This old consciousness has brought us our problems - emotionally, mentally, physically and spiritually.

Throughout The New Way series of books, we will turn upside down much of how we were brought up. We have not been shown a different way and it is time to insist that we go The New Way. It is time to move from disempowerment to empowerment. As we flip this way of being, we change the result. We end up with people who know themselves inside and out. They reclaim their inner knowing and they express themselves from empowerment, that is, power from the inside. Eventually, we no longer need to seek our answers through others.

As more women practise The New Way, they feel energised, fulfilled and powerful. They reclaim their intuition. Their life flows. This reclaimed inner peace means children and partners then begin to reflect this too, as the woman's energy infiltrates the family bubble.

The whole family shifts forward in their trajectory as the woman seeks empowerment. She finally finds respect from her family. She gains even more clarity, confidence and motivation to follow what she yearns for. The energy behind this work fuels her to call in her soul purpose, what truly lights her up. As she does, her daily scenes respond with opportunities, answers, the right people and above all else, heart connection with herself, her family members and beyond.

In general, it is you, the woman in the family, who has signed up to go first in The New Way, or one of the partners if it is a same-sex family. Your children are there ready and your partner will follow you in their own unfolding, as you stay focused on your own game play. Although you are the leader in your family, you are not alone. Your children simply wait for you to embody The New Way and they will rise to it. Your partner responds with resistance, to force you to step into the power within yourself even more so first. Excitingly, there are masses of women who feel the call to embrace The New Way with you.

The New Way is a new consciousness and a movement. Will you join us?

Looking into the future of the woman with her family going The New Way

The family members have realised their interconnectedness and the power of the energetic 'bubble' they exist within. They are meant to co-create together. They are exponentially more powerful than either one of them alone. They no longer feel they must separate for much of their week at school and work, then face their challenges or sweep the elephants under the rug when they do reunite. They accept their clashes as invitations to do their inner work and to face their feelings responsibly.

The family bubble continues to unlock itself as they come to more and more harmony, through every challenging experience they share. This inner work then activates each member's gifts, which complement each other perfectly, even the children's. As they acknowledge energetics in their family life, the concepts of 'parenting', 'education and learning' and 'health' transform.

'Parenting' is instead where the family team is nurtured in an empowered way. Everyone is respected equally as a wise being. Partners are seen as the ultimate team to prod and activate each other - inner work starts closest to home! Adults and children practise their unique ways to feel and to speak up about their issues in a self responsible manner. As children unfold life from their true essence, rather than their inner hurts, parents simply become teammates to guide their children where needed. Parents get on with their own soul path.

'Learning' is replaced with respect for each family member's innate gifts, which are activated as they follow what lights them up, even as toddlers. These gifts incorporate intuition and uniqueness which hasn't previously been revered. Self-fulfilment becomes a more powerful driver than money or qualifications. The more each family member activates their own gifts, the more they energetically unlock matching gifts in other family members. Everyone co-creates together as a perfectly orchestrated family bubble.

Adults *and children* seek others who match with their affinities, so they can more deeply explore and activate them. They find their matches either within or outside the family bubble and on specific interests, such as local birds, the concept of death, intuitive dance or the statistics in gaming. They trust the connection with their own soul path and play by the energetic rules of the game of life. As a result, they don't do anything they aren't called to or because someone says they should. They also don't follow curriculums or prescribed processes from others.

'Health' is seen as primarily energetics. As the family members shift the rising energies within them, they shift their physical, emotional, mental and spiritual health issues from the root cause. Through this inner work, they sensitise themselves to their own medical intuition and see nudges from their divine connection as to what supports their being. The more each adult and child shifts the stagnant energy within, the more they shift corresponding patterns in other family members and across generations. This path finally moves them away from the reactive health systems.

The New Way from empowerment

The energetic rules of The New Way explain how to play the game as individuals and also the exponential power of our interconnectedness. As we work with the sensations of our inner universe, we find the power to shift not only ourselves but others around us. We realise that we are called to finally 'have heart' for our life's challenges. We claim 'you are it'. That is, every challenging behaviour of those around us reflects another piece of ourselves to have heart for. When we do, it brings miraculous outcomes. We will go into this in more detail in chapters, such as You are it and Your Actors.

As we focus on our own character, we realise we have much work to come back to the expression of our true essence, rather than from our ego. We claim self-responsibility. We know we need to deal with our inner hurts first rather than try to fix or blame our external reality when things are not up to our expectations. Some examples are:

* when our children don't thrive, behave or fit in here on Earth
* when our partners or family are seemingly unsupportive
* when the healthcare, political or schooling systems let us down

Of course, we have had to play out the old way to realise that this approach literally drains us of our energy. It has helped us to see that we only make superficial gains as we try to fix others or give our power to anyone else. It is not to say that we move to complete self-responsibility overnight.

At this point in time, we still judge each other, even those closest to us, all day long. We judge the authorities and systems that are created on control, yet we as individuals are still to be further humbled on this. Us parents, and others, unwittingly distract our children from their intuitive connection when we control them through guilt, shame, martyrdom, spiritual ego and the much more subtle traps that we can fall into. Our children lose their focus when others in their lives project their hurts, fears, doubt and worries onto them. They cannot then thrive and follow their innate intelligence to live out their unique soul agreement. Despite our imperfect human history, it was all meant to play out like this.

The New Way is to finally come back to what has been lost and forgotten over the eons. It is also to bring in many new truths that we are ready for, particularly to work consciously with our soul agreement *and* with the interconnectedness of each other's. Let me now explain the background to the analogies I use in this book and the exciting energetic concepts that correspond to them. Please take a look at the Glossary whenever you aren't sure about a term that is used.

The analogies

This book covers the analogies that I see and have talked to my clients about for many years. I underestimated my work for a long time, as far as what I had tapped into. Each time I worked through my desperate emotions as big family challenges came up, I saw things more and more clearly.

I saw recurring patterns. I saw things in pictures. I saw the energetics at play in everyday concepts, such as a lava lamp. From this, I was able to remind my clients of how these energetic laws mirrored the issues they faced in their day. It showed them the bigger picture and explained it clearly. The more I saw the analogies, the more I realised the amount of detail needed to re-order and review every angle of our life through these energetic laws and concepts that I saw.

One day, Hayden and I watched a show on Einstein's life and it made me feel very emotional. I watched him tirelessly try to prove his work. He knew that he was onto something but others rejected the importance of what he saw. The documentary visually showed the layers of pictures Einstein intuitively saw as he 'came to' certain pieces of his work. I cried out to Hayden, 'That's what I get when I realise my analogies, oh my goodness!'. Inspired by Einstein, I even started to map energetic laws to my analogies, yet my work still felt very insignificant compared with the concepts that Einstein discovered because I didn't work with equations.

Fast forward a couple of years and my friend Johanna exclaimed, 'I just love your analogies! You are the queen of analogies! It makes it so clear'. I started to realise that my work really was designed to be explained by analogies, as you will soon read.

A year or so later, I was drawn to a book of my stepdad's, called 'The Elegant Universe' by Brian Greene. I started to read the prologue and yet again tears sprinkled my eyes. The author wrote about his skill where he took energetic concepts and put them into analogies so laymen could understand them. That is exactly what I did!

I had a big realisation. I sensed the energetic laws my work related to, yet I was not a scientist. My work however, wasn't to prove what I saw through scientific papers to scientists. My work was to help amazing families to understand the energetics of life through analogies. These analogies could help them to remember these truths and to practically make changes in their day-to-day scenes. Einstein and scientists made discoveries in the starry realms, for ideas and research. I made them more in the earthly realms, for practical use, as well as the heart realms, to bring us back to existence in the energy of love.

As I realised this, I allowed myself to receive the big claims I make in this book. That is, how we have seen life through the lens of the ego instead of through energetics. The concepts are here for you to 'feel truth' rather than to 'be proved'.

How to make magic from this book

Before we get started, I need to show you around. Picture I have just walked you into the most enchanting forest, called The New Way. You don't even give the world outside this forest a second thought as you take in its indescribable beauty. You see the most breathtaking trees. You smell the exquisite fresh forest steam. You delight in the enchanting wildlife and the calm sounds of nature. You feel a big 'ahhhh!'.

There is a lot to take in, particularly as I could give you a guided tour of each for many days. The new 'trees', 'animals', 'smells' and 'sounds' in the forest represent the terms used to describe The New Way. Like with anything new though, our natural tendency is to take a glance around, to get a lay of the land.

We can take a look at all of the aspects of The New Way in any order. They are all interrelated and I will need to mention the trees as I talk about the smells and I will mention the smells as I talk about the wildlife. Everything you need to know about this new way does not roll out in a linear fashion. It is interconnected and you will be drawn to different parts of it at different times and in a different order to other people.

Here is my beautiful motif. This represents how we step into The New Way in a circular and yet unique nature. Enter where the leaves open and go through the golden triangle. As you stand in the middle, you glance around at the different golden triangles on offer. You can read any part of this book that calls to you because there is no end and no beginning to all there is to remember with The New Way.

For the sake of linear time and space however, I have written it to be read from cover to cover so that you are taken on a journey. Do remember, some parts may not feel as useful to you at the time you read it. Trust that the pennies, or 'golden keys', as I call them, will drop when the time is right, in your unique day-to-day life.

Each chapter explains an energetic concept, an energetic rule for the game of life. As this is an adventure into a new consciousness, I have written why you want to know about each one, so you can stay focused on why this information relates to you.

I use many practical examples throughout the book which are common storylines for more families than you might realise. Of course, many of the examples are also mine. We are here to play out such similar storylines and to support each other on this! *Remember, there are many others like you that feel called to embody The New Way.*

There is so much complexity in our existence, yet The New Way wants to be seen for the simple, underlying energetic laws, which explain the game of life. It does take investment of your time and energy to remember and practise The New Way. Once you have learnt the energetic concepts however, it is simple to understand life and how to work through your challenges. This investment will pay you back exponentially with harmony, respect, ease and fulfilment for yourself and everyone you have an effect on.

The New Way terminology

To go forth towards empowerment, we must be ready to acknowledge that our beliefs, old way systems, how we live and even terminology need to crumble. We must use new terminology as we switch to life The New Way. The old world has placed so much conditioning, connotation, ego and 'old way' energy into so many of our words.

To understand The New Way, we need to smash down so much of what we thought we understood. Terms such as 'school', 'autism', 'mindset', 'emotional regulation', 'choice', 'limiting belief', 'the collective', 'higher self', 'karma', 'high vibe', 'ascension', 'values', 'fear-based', 'heart-centred' and 'manifesting' are instead explained through a new lens.

The New Way guides us to truly split from the mainstream and new age spiritual worlds, where disempowerment still lurks. We will go through more about this as new terminology is revealed in the book. It can upset us to turn words on their head, which have been embedded in our reality for a long time. We are still free to use whichever terms we most resonate with at any time and change at any time. In empowerment, do go ahead and use the words that come specifically to you as you talk out loud to your family and friends about what you have discovered. We are invited to make a gradual shift and to stay open towards The New Way.

Don't forget to access the glossary of The New Way terms at the back of this book at any time, to 'remember the language'.

Defining your truth

As we will remember throughout the book, we all have a very unique soul path. We are all on a different path to the same kinds of places - freedom to be our unique self, to live a life of most fulfilment, to have dazzling health and to nurture this for those around us too. Yet if you turn to any three people in your life, you will surely eat a different breakfast, exercise differently and have at least slightly different ways that you deal with an inner tantrum! We are not supposed to be copies of each other, yet we play by the same energetic rules.

By default, this means that parts of this book will resonate with you and parts may not! It is your role to honour how you feel about each part and to then be curious to work out what feels true to you each step of the way. If you feel to reject an idea, take it as an opportunity to feel into it and to understand why. What do you deem to be true instead? Can you stay open to both sides and trust you will unfold more of what feels true to you as you go about life? Know that it is powerful to sit in your own truth. It is also powerful to spy on which concepts make you feel uncomfortable, which may cloud you from further truth too.

To go The New Way is a practice and an unfolding, not something to rush or achieve. This book explains the highest truth - that is, how we can live life *if* we could play the game by these energetic rules 100% of the time, with a snap of the fingers. Please let us all honour that this is not possible. As you sense the truth in anything you read, check in for what you feel is an easy next step and aim to focus there first.

Let's now step into The New Way and perceive it through analogies, stories and examples.

You are it

...you direct your life from your inner universe...

2020

When we first got our Border Collie, Bounty, I went through some inner tantrums in 'one more thing to do'. The role of Dog Mum was much more involved than the role I thought I had signed up for! Some days I called Bounty to the gate to go for a walk and he was already there or soon sprinted over. On other days, I called and he didn't come at all. He was busy in the garden. I got frustrated. 'Come on, do you actually want to go for a walk? Fine, don't worry. I won't worry then. You miss out.'

The energetic pattern was clear. When I was in good spirits and ready for a nice outing with the boys and Bounty, he responded well. When I did it because I 'had to', Bounty stuffed around. To see this pattern, I had to get honest about how I truly felt each time I prepared for a walk. It would have been easier to simply blame my dog for the times he played up. Instead, I noticed that I had an internal reality and an external reality and that both were energetically linked. Of course, it's not just pets that energetically respond to our inner universe but also our children, partner, friends, the postman and anyone else we happen to interact with on any given day.

Let's play.

Imagine that your life right now is you in a hologram-type virtual reality game. You are the only player. Your soul plays the game of life through the avatar of the human body you chose. Everything you see in front of you is projected there, which you perceive through your senses. What you see in your day to day scenes, the good, the bad and the ugly, I call your 'canvas of life' or your external reality.

You are the 'Creative Director' of this canvas of life. You are it. The other players in your life energetically respond to the swirling energies within you at any one time. You also match energetically with them and their inner universe, as they play their virtual reality game too.

> ## ENERGETIC LAW
>
> 'You are it' - the scenes in our external reality reflect the state of our inner universe.

'You are it' means that your inner universe attracts *everything* that ends up in your external reality. There is no turn-off point for this energetic law. In other words, you are the director of your virtual reality in every scene of your day, no exception. If you feel grumpy, then your external reality will show up scenarios to help you to feel this grumpiness within. If you feel excited, your external reality will show up in matching scenes too. If it's time to explore how it feels to stand up for oneself, you will attract those people that will test you in specific ways.

> External reality - what you see, touch, hear and smell through your senses.
>
> Inner universe - what you perceive as emotions and sensations within you.

To really paint this picture, let's consider that one day you are a movie director on a movie set in your virtual reality game. You are the director - you are it. How the day plays out comes back to you. If you show up distracted in stress that day, the actors will inevitably bumble about or begin to chat on the sidelines. If you show up in the highest of spirits and bring your most congenial self, the actors will reflect this by being punctual and helpful. Their acting skills will likely be the best they have ever managed, in reflection of your inner universe.

> Actors - the people that show up in and interact with us in our day-to-day scenes, who reflect how we feel within, 100% of the time.

Of course, you cannot bring a shiny, upbeat inner universe to the director's job every single day. You can fake a smile but you cannot hide the state of your inner universe at any one moment. The old world has taught us to control our emotions and think positive thoughts to affect our external reality. However, no matter how much we smile on, we will inevitably face life challenges. In fact, our 'actors', including our children, will reflect the true state of our inner universe, no matter how much we try to kid ourselves. In the coming chapters, we will unfold how we are and aren't in control of what goes on within us and how we can play out our life scenes as director, in the most successful way.

When we own that we are the Creative Director, sovereign being or player one, [insert your own fun title here], we see that we are responsible for how our life plays out. Everyone else is an actor in our movie as we embody our soul's chosen journey. The actors in our day's movie scenes respond to the 'directions' we project from the rising energies of our inner universe. There is no exception to this. We will cover this in more detail soon.

> Player one - assume you are the only player in your virtual reality game. Everyone else is a non-player character.

When we point the finger of blame at others or try to fix, advise or control them, for *any* reason, we have forgotten to play by the energetic law of 'you are it'. We play by disempowerment, as we try to find power in our external reality, instead of from within. Similarly, when we seek answers from others through external help, advice and teachings, we have also forgotten to play by 'you are it'. As we tune into our inner sensations instead, we claim self-responsibility and step back into the empowered director's role.

> *You can only shift your external challenges, no matter what they are, as you shift your inner hurts that land you in these scenes.*

Summary

- ✱ 'You are it' is fundamental to The New Way.
- ✱ It is the only way to tune into your uniqueness and find your answers.
- ✱ It is the only way to create true harmony within yourself and with others.
- ✱ We seek empowerment through self-responsibility, as we own our inner state.

To play with ...

- ♦ Which of your actors do you tend to point the finger of blame at?
- ♦ Notice the inner sensations they make you feel. Spend a present moment with this same sensation each time they make you feel it. The more you can notice and then release this emotion, the more you play by empowerment.

What is

...what plays out is our only reality...

2009

I was pregnant with my first son, Hayden! I felt my yearning to breastfeed. It was something I wanted to do. I didn't realise that I had created pictures in my mind, snuggled with my new baby and relaxed in the experience together.

Fast forward past Hayden's premature birth, and I found myself at home without him. I pumped through the night whilst he was in special care for three weeks. I dealt with excess milk, a baby that didn't have his suckle reflex and instead, I poured milk down a nasogastric tube.

The day Hayden got his suckle on, the hospital gave me one night, together in our own room, to see how we went. I was terrified as he struggled to latch on after we had relied on the nasogastric tube, yet I wanted to get my baby home. It continued like this, as Hayden and I struggled to get him onto one particular side in the first few nights at home. In the end, he fed from just one side for our entire breastfeeding journey.

Whilst Hayden struggled with breastfeeding in the first few weeks at home, he also didn't sleep easily. I was anxious and beyond exhausted to get him to sleep, after every two-hourly feed around the clock. Anthony suggested we look at bottle feeding. I flatly refused as I couldn't bear to feed Hayden formula, and I didn't want to pump ever again after the first few weeks of hell. At the time, I never admitted to myself the utter disappointment our breastfeeding journey felt like.

Through this breastfeeding experience, I saw 'what is' very clearly. My rosy view of breastfeeding was not how it played out because I had only felt my yearning in the light. There were too many factors that needed to be explored in the shadows, for myself and for Hayden, to have a perfect breastfeeding experience for *our* soul path. My divine path landed me into those challenging scenes. This allowed me to explore 'what it feels like to be unable to feed my child with ease' and the emotions that came with that as a mother. We will look at this further in the coming chapters on the Seed of Intelligence, Soul Agreement and Life Themes.

How breastfeeding played out for me was not what I thought it would be, not what I would have liked and certainly not what 'they' told me it should be. Energetics however, played out 'what is'. The only thing I could do was to be honest about how I felt about that.

> What is - the divinely orchestrated scenes of our life that *actually* play out, which show us 'what wants to be', 'what is' or 'what wanted to be'. These can be quite different to how we try to steer our lives or the parts of our lives that we ignore.

Bias towards the rosy view

More often than we realise, we mistakenly see ourselves through the rosy view of 'what we'd like it to be'. We try to portray our life, in general, to others in the light. We tell them about everything that is positive in our life. Our social media feed confirms this to everyone. We stay focused on our grand plans for the future. Of course, it is vital to notice what flows in life and to celebrate this. If we only observe our reality through the light however, we create a false version in our mind of our character's expression and reality here on Earth. We will unravel the cost of this in further chapters in the book.

For most of us, we don't often spend *present time* with 'what is'. It can be difficult to acknowledge the day-to-day scenes that make us feel uncomfortable within. It can be upsetting to take a look around and realise the scenes we find ourselves in don't always match up with what we value or dream of. It can be tricky to admit that we don't tell others the whole truth of our existence, and we suffer behind closed doors. It can be even harder to admit to ourselves that many of our grand plans haven't eventuated or at least not as quickly as our little old human self promised. Then there are the challenging surprises on our timeline which really remind us of what we'd like to turn away from.

> Shadow expressions - any behaviour that is not of our true essence, instead driven by our emotional charge.

Despite our inclination to only notice our light side, we have just as many shadow expressions. It can be extremely painful for us to consider that we are nowhere near perfect. It is just as painful to consider how the *actual* expression of our character is perceived by others, particularly our loved ones. Our little old human self distracts us from this as it judges others and justifies and rationalises our own shadow expressions.

> *If we watched a replay of our life, like a 'recording' of our soul's time here, we would see 'what wanted to be', not what we tried to make happen or what we would have liked it to be.*

The lower humble road

It is like we drive on the lower road in an older car and yet see ourselves in a fancier car up on the brand new bigger, better, super highway. We try to give off the sense that we live in the fancy car world, yet when we observe all of the scenes of our life and 'what is', we realise we still drive on the humble lower road. What actually plays out and how our actors perceive us, is different to the version of our character and our life which we create in our mind.

Here is an example of how mothers can perceive themselves as different to what plays out.

Many mothers, who are called to The New Way, yearn to play their mother role well. They notice the effort that they put into their child's clean diet, lovely activities and even their emotional wellbeing. They like to think that everyone in the external notices them as this too. Despite this, they also turn away from the daily scenes where they nag, convince, bribe or yell at their children. Although they like to see themselves in the fancy car up on the super highway, 'what is' reminds them to come back to the humble car on the lower road.

We have been conditioned to turn away from our external challenges which has disconnected us from the sensations within our inner universe. We are afraid to feel discomfort. As we will continue to unfold, our ability to change the displeasing scenes of our life and our connection to our true essence ironically lies within the discomfort.

To play by 'what is' we must continue to stay present with each scene of our day, even the uncomfortable ones. If we don't, we miss the nudges of where we are supposed to direct our focus, to be in sync with divine timing. We will cover this more in the chapters on Divine Timing and Red and Green Lights.

Here are some examples of when we ignore 'what is'.

* *We tell everyone our life is grand. We ignore 'what is' - the scenes where we are stressed by money, our child refuses school or we don't feel true joy.*

* *We take our children out to lots of fun places. We ignore 'what is' - the scenes where we feel anxious before each outing because the children are constantly chaotic in front of others.*

* *We tell others how healthily our children eat. We ignore 'what is' - the scenes where the children need to be bribed to eat well or when we dismiss their wishes to try some junk food.*

- *We sign up to a new business opportunity where lots of people earn great money. We ignore 'what is' - the scenes where, months and years later, we haven't received this type of money.*

- *We set aside time to work on our new business idea. We ignore 'what is' - the scenes where the computer doesn't work so we spend hours trying to fix it.*

Each of these examples shows us that what we tell ourselves or others, does not quite match up with the scenes that play out. Each scenario involves some 'push', to try to make it happen, which hints that our little old human self is at play.

When we get honest, we might:

- *talk honestly about the great parts of our life and also that we seek more joy or that we struggle with money.*

- *see that despite our desire to be seen as a fun mum, the scenes do not support this to flow.*

- *realise our children feel deprived or behave in disrespectful ways when it comes to food.*

- *sit with how we feel about false promises and our energy expenditure for little return.*

- *see that the computer glitch is a nudge that it's more important to take a break or get the groceries done.*

We have been conditioned to think that we need to drive the perfect straight line to where our little old human self would like to go. Divine timing steps in to take us on winding paths through the shadows and back again, until we finally arrive in the scenes of what we truly yearn for. We will see this in more detail in the chapters on Yearnings and The Cone. In the meantime, our little old human self either gets frustrated with or ignores all that doesn't line up perfectly with where we think we want to go.

> *Divine timing orchestrates the scenes of our life. How they actually play out and exactly how we express ourselves is 'what is'.*

Often, we are on track to what calls us, yet our little old human self can push this too much, too soon. From the previous examples, it's clear to see what each mother yearns for but instead has pushed for.

* For *life to feel easy and peaceful, without the problems.*
* For *my children to remember we had fun.*
* To *have healthy children.*
* To *make decent money to support my family's life.*
* For *me to move forward with my soul work.*

As we focus on how to drive the car straight to 'what we'd like it to be', we miss all of the divine invitations to sit with 'what is'. To sit with 'what is', is to honour the path of our soul agreement and the experiences we actually signed up for, such as my challenging breastfeeding scenes. The chapters on the Soul Agreement and Life Themes will explore this further.

To play from 'what is', we must humbly let go of our little old human self's goals, expectations, intentions and rosy view dreams. We can then expect surprises, an understanding of why we had to go through the shadows and miracles that we could not have dreamt of ourselves.

> *'What wants to be', 'what was always going to be' and 'what is' remind us that we are drawn to that which is on our soul agreement. It is to accept 'what is' and seek 'what wants to be'.*

Why you want to know about 'What is'

Once you acknowledge 'what is', you start to realise where you try to do life from the fancy car up on the new highway. In other words, you see where your little old human self tries to steer yours and even others' lives to the more perfect scenes it can devise in parenting, health, schooling and beyond. Of course, our little old human self doesn't know what is perfect for each of our unique paths.

Here are some examples that highlight our little old human self's hidden agenda when it tries to push us to certain things that actually don't flow.

* *Maybe you stress yourself to earn extra money to afford the private school you believe your children need.*

* *Perhaps you exert a lot of energy to convince your child into the benefits of soccer, school or a different outfit, despite their resistance.*

* *You might try to push your child into more nature time or with other children, although they just love to game at home.*

* *Maybe you find yourself in arguments with your partner when they eat food you don't approve of or spend too much time at work.*

It is important to remember that despite what you envision and dream for, the divine version of 'what is' will always play out. 'What you'd like it to be' or 'what you think or believe it to be' stems from your little old human self. It limits the potential of what miracles can actually play out when you let go.

> *'What is' links with divine timing and how our scenes need to play out for our soul's experience. Our divine path is not perfect.*

To let go however, is to feel. As we've been conditioned to expect and attach to outcomes, we then have to feel emotions as life plays out differently to what we thought it should be. Let's remember however, as humans, we cannot help but dream. It is constant work to make peace with 'what we'd like it to be' and to stay open to 'what wants to be' instead. As we allow 'what is', we feel old emotions rise. This is the old energy that our inner child swallowed down when adults tried to push 'what I'd like *you* to be', 'what I think it should be' or even 'what my parents told me it should be' onto us.

Our emotions continue to rise, which we will see in the chapter, the Lava Lamp Effect. They highlight where we still need to surrender to our divine path rather than take further action from our little old human self. Our actors tell us when we try to drive the fancy car on the too-good-to-be-true highway when they give us resistance in our day-to-day scenes. Maybe we try to take a too-perfect stance on parenting. Maybe we try to come from a place of superiority. Maybe we interfere with someone's path. Our actors' negative responses tell us 'uh uh', come back down to the humble highway and play out these scenes right here first.

Rather than push, stop and feel.

To let go is also to flexibly change directions. An example is when our children resist us. This is a cue to step back and look at 'what is'. Is their resistance an invitation to slow down, to take a moment for yourself, reconfigure the day or maybe to speak up about something?

Working with 'what is'

In place of goals and intentions, we are invited to notice our emotions and to get excited to understand what we truly yearn for. When we feel passionate about something, we can be sure this yearning comes from a divine place and that we will be guided to it, in divine timing. We will look further at this in the chapter, on Yearnings.

Rather than so much push, we need to do the inner work. We must humbly accept all that is on our soul path, including the shadowy parts of our dreams. As we face our inner discomfort, we more confidently accept that each phase of our life is to drive the humble, less fancy car on the authentic road. We know this road is exactly where we are supposed to be.

We find true fulfilment and happiness as we allow everyone's path to play out. We feel the magic it brings as we allow the divine timing of 'what is'. To get to this place, we must let go of 'what I'd like it to be' and allow the emotions that inevitably rise. To play the game of life, The New Way, it is fundamental to own 'you are it' and to embrace 'what is'.

Summary

* We don't have control over how each scene of our day actually plays out.
* We must acknowledge that what does play out is divinely orchestrated.
* We have been conditioned to allow our ego or little old human self to think it is in control far more than it is.
* We will have emotions arise as we surrender to our character's shadowy expression and the less-than-perfect scenes we find ourselves in.

To explore ...

- Which scenes of your life *do* match up with what you dream of?
- Which scenes in your life *don't* match up with what you truly yearn for?
- How easy does it feel to accept your shadowy expressions?
- How easy does it feel to accept the parts of your life that don't match with your dreams at this point in time?

Seed of Intelligence

...your soul path is encoded within you...

2020

One day, the boys and I planted seeds they had collected in Woolworths giveaways. I asked them, 'How does this seed become a basil plant, whilst this seed becomes a violet?'. They stopped and looked at me with an expression of 'I have absolutely no clue!'.

It was like a download and mini life lesson just poured out of me. I explained to the boys, 'It's the energy in this seed that tells it how to grow and what to become. It also even directs it to grow upwards in the dirt, to find the sun. All we have to do is plant it mindfully with love. We must be careful not to stamp the dirt on top with too much force or it won't grow how it needs to. Then we provide it with water and sun. The rest is up to the plant! We don't have to do ANYTHING else! It just unfolds to become what it was always meant to be!'.

My passion grew on the spot for this amazing process. I wondered how many of us have never sat with this magical concept and drawn any conclusions ourselves, particularly our wise children. We have not been encouraged to question the energetics of life which has disconnected us from the divine.

'It's a seed of intelligence!', I announced. 'It is connected with the divine, the universe, the stars. It then connects itself into the earth to grow and transform. Did you know if we spend time with it and give it love, even without words and just energetically with our heart, it will grow up stronger and in better energy? An energetically stronger plant doesn't attract the bugs, just like we don't attract the bugs if we feel loved and keep our energy strong too!'

I could not help it. Everything I saw in my external reality, I brought back to the reflection for myself. What was the significance of this realisation? I scanned intuitively whilst the boys continued to drop the peat everywhere as they planted dozens of seeds in our ill-prepared nursery.

'It's like we are the parents and the little seed is the child. If us parents come in and continue to press down on the soil each day, the plant won't grow well. It's like when parents control their children too much. If we decide the sprout doesn't look right as it pops up and we do something to change it, I don't know, like we trim an important tiny sprout leaf, we interfere with its seed of intelligence. Its own intelligence can't perform its magic to become the plant it was encoded to be. When us parents try to change our children or don't allow them to be exactly who they are, it's like we press down on their ability to grow freely and towards who they were encoded to be. We lose track of the innate intelligence within us all which attempts to guide us to our own unique expression.

'You know how plants feel too? Well, if we change something about it as it grows, that little seed feels our energy. As we interfere with it, we hint that it isn't on the right path for what it is to become. It would feel so much sadness because it ultimately wants to make us delight in it when it has grown into tasty basil or a beautiful violet flower, *even if it's not perfect*. It would also feel ashamed to need to be changed by the very people it wants to delight. Its seed of intelligence simply guides it to develop into what it was always going to become. It doesn't make choices along the way to be like that.

'This is the same for each of us! We have a seed of intelligence. We must have! That's why we are literally drawn to certain people, interests, foods and everything. It's also why we are repelled from certain places, activities and clothing. That's why we feel upset when people hint we did something wrong, when actually we just followed the pull of our seed of intelligence. It's energetics. It's our connection to the divine.

'Even when you crave lots of chocolate, Deccy, it's your seed of intelligence that pulls you to it. For many reasons, you were meant to experience it, even if that was to explore the effects of sugar. That's why you get so mad at us when we try to stop you. We interfered with your seed's unfolding. We doubted the magic within you, even when it seemed like you did the wrong thing. We thought we knew better.'

As I pondered this concept further, a question came to me. I asked the boys, 'Would you say your seed of intelligence makes up your expression as you grow, like your height, your hair colour, the sound of your laugh, even the types of ailments you get… or is it already decided?'. 'Already decided', they instantly responded in unison.

What is your instant response to this question?

> Seed of intelligence - the energetic intelligence within you that dictates what you are pulled to and repelled from, to realise your soul's path.

In those few moments where this all poured out of me, we realised we had tapped into something pretty cool, if we connected all the dots. We must have a seed of intelligence. It must be connected with what I call our soul agreement and the experiences we agreed to. It also drives us to how we look and express ourselves, our true essence.

Our seed of intelligence has some amazing pulling power. It makes sure we fall for the dangling carrots, to go down the path of the experiences we need to have. We can say no at any moment and yet the experience simply shows up in a different way, with a different storyline, but lo and behold, the same theme. You could even say that each time we think we make a choice, it's also our seed of intelligence in action.

How does it feel to consider that energetics pulls us far more than what we have been led to believe?

Why you want to know about the Seed of Intelligence

It is important to remember, and also remind our children, that our seed of intelligence drives us to our unique expression, just like a flower's seed guides it to express itself as a rose or a daffodil. It is like the aim of the game of life is to connect back to our seed of intelligence so that we naturally express ourselves from our unique true essence. As we do this, we drop the pull to people please, follow shoulds and traditions or extinguish our true desires.

Turning away from our seed of intelligence's expression

Many of us express our character as versions of ourselves that are quite a way off our true essence. As we grew up, we were made to:

* keep quiet.
* hide our uniqueness that made others uncomfortable.
* sign up to what our parents wanted for us.
* behave how society wanted.
* …. and/or didn't have the opportunities available to express our true essence at that point in time.

As a result of this less-than-fertile 'soil' for our unique seed of intelligence, our character's expression is often a result of interference with our seed's unfurling. Despite this, our true essence is evident when we are magnetic or do something with ease, as we will see in the Soul Agreement chapter.

Although we may feel upset with how much we are disconnected from our true essence, remember that our magic is activated as we own 'you are it' and embrace 'what is'. On the contrary, if we feel that we have embraced all of our potential, let us not forget that our true essence, fully expressed, would be blinding! We always have more to reclaim.

The more we pull away from the expression of our true essence, the more we suffer from physical, emotional, mental and spiritual health opportunities. We also suffer when we try to snip at another's seedling unfurling. These are signs of our ego's expression.

Here are some examples of how you might turn away from your seed of intelligence.

* You grind at a job that your soul despises.
* You sign up to an intellectual university degree, although your true desire is to paint.
* You go out for a women's dinner, although you would feel relieved to stay home.
* You save your money, although you feel called to take a holiday.
* You keep your opinion to yourself to keep the peace, although you know what you'd like to say.
* You eat the salad leftovers because no one else will, although you don't feel like it.
* You hold your tears in despite your shaky voice and trembling lips.

Allowing our seed of intelligence to guide us

Our seed of intelligence gives us the whispers of how to move forward from where we are now, to play life on our divine beat. We sense it by what we feel called to. It does not take us on a direct, perfect, light path. Oh no, it does not! Remember, sometimes we feel called to paths that are perceived as 'wrong' however, there is light there too.

> Divine beat - to land in each scene that 'wants to be' and explore this, rather than pull towards what your ego thinks it should be or to race ahead of time.

Our seed of intelligence is ultimately our intuitive voice, which we can learn to tune into. Its whispers are often tied to our uncomfortable inner sensations and thus, we must move through our fear of these feelings. The Emotional Blackbox and Lava Lamp Effect chapters will continue to explain how our seed of intelligence guides us into challenging scenarios which match the experiences enlisted on our soul agreement, for that point on our timeline.

As we accept that we have an energetic intelligence within us, we realise it dictates our physical expression, interests and challenges. We can then understand that we will be pulled to 'what was always meant for us' in a good way, as well as our more displeasing scenes. These are our invitations to feel what it feels like to go through the triumphs and challenges of our earthly experiences.

The concept of the seed of intelligence also means that we can't convince someone off their path, unless they are to play out 'what it feels like to have someone interfere with my seed of intelligence', which many of our children do experience. When we try to convince our child to take off their jumper in summer, to eat broccoli or that school *will* be good, we need not give it too much energy. At that point in time, if it's not for them, it's not for them.

If we continue to interfere and attempt to control how they think and feel, we only weaken our child's heart connection with us. It is more useful to come from a curious perspective and trust that they are pulled to this behaviour for a reason. We then allow them to freely unfold their seed's soul path without the need to stomp down too hard on the soil, where their seed of intelligence wants to pop through. Of course, this is much easier said than done!

Old parenting styles hint that if you allow your child to follow their own path, you are a weak parent and your child will grow up with a sense that they can get away with anything. From the angle of The New Way, it is a fine balance as we tune into the whispers of our seed of intelligence as a parent. At the same time, we must trust our child's divine path and their consequences as they explore that path. As we do, we begin to let go of 'the need to be a perfect parent'. We also start to let go of the old energy that us parents are 100% responsible for every way our child expresses themselves and how they turn out. We will continue to go through more examples in the coming chapters.

Do you sense where your children or partner give you the 'get out of my way, I need to explore this' energy? How do you feel about others who try to convince you into or out of things that you just feel called to? Do you recall times when things haven't gone to plan, despite the best of intentions? This is the time to honour that our seed of intelligence lands us into particular scenes to get us to feel and experience certain themes on our soul agreement. It comes with the pull to do it despite other's best arguments. We will explore this further in the chapter, Soul Agreement.

To play the game of life, The New Way, is to allow ourselves to be pulled more to what feels good and right, which syncs us with 'what wants to be' on our soul agreement. To follow our seed of intelligence is to trust our feelings and to notice where we judge our thoughts and decisions. Instead, we can explore *why* we landed into these scenes with curiosity.

Here is an example of why you don't need to question what you feel called to.

Let's say you know you can't afford to have takeaway but the idea won't leave you. As you go out to collect the takeaway, you meet up with a long, lost friend who ends up as a vital actor in your life in the near future. It was an important reason to follow your calling to get takeaway despite good intellectual reasons not to. At the same time, you also had to go through the pain of less money that week because you overspent on the takeaway. There is light and dark in any path we travel.

There is light and dark in any path

We must catch ourselves when we judge what we are energetically called to. Instead, we can curiously follow the path, to see why it called us there. Just because it is a challenging path doesn't mean it is incorrect. A path into the shadows invites us to have an experience, so we can find the light on the other side. You know how much stronger you are because you went through a life challenge? It can be easy to miss the light that occurred as you went down this tricky path, such as how others opened their heart to you when they saw you struggle.

We really can't get it wrong. If we feel called to get the takeaway but instead save our money to 'be good', we will still be pulled into the same themes. Maybe we receive a speeding fine to still have to face 'what it feels like to hand over money as I try to save'. Quite likely, we will still bump into the long lost friend in some other way.

Rather than steer our children away from what they will likely explore anyway, we can talk to them about the ins and outs as they experience this particular path. We can offer them stories of how we struggled our way through something similar and also what we got from it. *For example, as much as I tried to steer our children away from lollies, there was a point when I said to Anthony, 'what lollies were your favourite when you were younger?'. We had a fun conversation and chose to remember that there is light in this topic. This helped us to let go of the need to keep our children on the perceived perfect path.*

In the coming books of The New Way series, we will also go through how to guide your children to make decisions from their heart, which includes *our* inner work, when they take things too far. It certainly does not mean we simply let go and allow what our inner feelings say a 'BIG NO' to. For now, we can remember that the more we create fertile soil for our children's seeds of intelligence to earth into, the more magical their expression will be.

Nourishing soil starts with heart connection. Heart connection is less judgement of the unfurling of our children's expression. With this heart connection, they then listen and respect us when we feel our seed of intelligence's pull to guide them. What else do you see as important for your family's seeds to flourish in?

As we accept the seed of intelligence concept, we might consider the guilt we feel about how we played out certain scenes of our life. These storylines were all supposed to play out how they did. We were supposed to hurt that person so that they left our life, because that was the end of the season with them. They were supposed to go through the specifics of being hurt like that. We were supposed to be 'unperfect' with our babies, because otherwise they would have no 'scar points', which give them challenges to unlock in their game of life. We were supposed to fail in school or never finish anything, so we could eventually see our invisible magic was the exact opposite of where we spent our time. Whilst the guilt is actually unnecessary, we feel this emotion because we have been made to think we did something wrong at the time. As we will soon see in more detail, this emotion *is* still there to process but on the other side is a deep knowing that we have never shown up as 'wrong'. It was our seed of intelligence all the way.

Summary

* Our seed of intelligence is energetically encoded with our true essence's expression.

* We need far less input from the outside world to find our uniqueness than we think we do.

* We must connect with the whispers of our seed of intelligence that pull us to where we are supposed to be.

* Although we may judge where we are pulled, there will always be light from this experience.

* We suffer when we turn away from our seed of intelligence's pull

and/or when we try to control the energetic unfurling of someone else's soul path.

✷ From childhood, we turned away from many angles of our true essence because of feedback from our external reality.

To play with ...

Notice any scene in your day where you feel the pull to go a different way than what you think you should or someone else tells you that you should. Follow your seed of intelligence's pull with curiosity!

If you struggle to feel the pull of your seed of intelligence, play with these sentences:

- 'If I had nothing to lose, I would ....'
- 'If I was a rebel, I would ...'
- 'If I didn't have to explain myself to others, I would ...'
- 'If I had one month left on this Earth, I would ...'
- 'If I had all the money in the world, I would ...'

Divine Timing

...you are energetically pulled to the path encoded within you...

2005

I finished my Speech Pathology degree and it was time to apply for a job. My dream job, or so I thought, was to work in community health with children. I soon applied for a community health position in Sydney. I ignored the part of me that didn't want to live in Sydney and went for the interview because it was 'my ideal job'. It was my first interview and I wasn't in the most private location to focus when they phoned. The pressure was too much and I stuffed it up. I didn't get the job and consequently felt like I'd never get one if interviews were like this.

Soon after, I went for an interview with Education Queensland, to work as a school speech pathologist. It was the next best thing to community health and at least it was paediatric work. My confidence however, was shot from my first interview and my mind went blank as I spoke to the Education Queensland interviewers. I stuffed it up again. I got a rating of three. A rating of one was something like 'highly rated'. Two was something like 'a good option'. Three was merely rated as 'employable'.

With a rating of three, I was given the last choice of positions. It was a permanent job in Miles, a tiny agricultural town about four hours west of Brisbane *or* a temporary position in Cairns, the tropical city on the Great Barrier Reef. For me, it was an instant 'yes' to Cairns as I had been there before and everything about it called to me. At the same time, I did feel nervous to take a temporary job and my dad insisted it was a crazy move to decline a permanent one.

The next year, I moved to Cairns and I thrived there. I caught tiny planes to beautiful Far North Queensland to service the schools in the First Nations communities. I shared my passion for children with disabilities as the speech pathologist in early childhood special needs. I earned my scuba diving licence and I happily guided all of my visitors to Cairns' tourist attractions.

That year, I met my Anthony as I joined the local gym. I also reinterviewed particularly well and took a permanent job that came up in Education Queensland. I felt like I had won the game of life because I had listened to my inner nudge to move to Cairns.

I look back on this point of my life and consider how I would never have met Anthony and known what it was like to live somewhere I truly love, if I had taken the permanent job in Miles. Not only had I played the game of life, but Anthony had too. There were also a trail of factors that led him to move to Cairns that year. We were supposed to collide. It was all divine timing that played out in front of our eyes. Divine timing played out for every scene we landed in then as well as every scene we would land in, into the future. I wonder if you have considered all of the factors that have perfectly landed you where you needed to be, to set you up for future scenes of your life too?

2022

We realised it was time to sell our house of nearly 12 years. By this time, I was well aware of the concept of divine timing and to allow ourselves to simply be pulled to 'what wants to be'. I talked out loud to the family, 'The house we end up in is already decided upon and it's waiting for us to find it. If it's not meant to be, then it won't be'.

Despite this announcement, we still played out 'what we'd like it to be' until we were spat out in the direction of 'what was always going to be'. We thought we wanted acreage. We thought we wanted no pool as the pool we already had was more maintenance than it was worth. We thought we wanted to live north of where we were, in an area we thought was nice.

For the many houses that we inspected, at least one person in the family was keen and one person insisted they wouldn't live there. We walked out in arguments as we tried to convince the others to like it. Occasionally, we were all *okay* with a particular house but we couldn't even make an offer because we hadn't sold ours. It was all in perfect orchestration.

We decided to sell at auction and we calculated the timing of when we would move by the auction date. We assumed we would sell on this day. At the very last minute, our best prospect pulled out of the auction. We didn't sell due to low offers. We were certainly stalled, and this was the divine at play, to make sure we collided with the house we were to buy at the exact point in time to make it happen. Despite this, we still felt our disappointment at our little old human's expectations being dashed. I even felt the frustration that we had fallen into the trap of 'what we think it should be'. In the meantime, I attended an auction event and saw many properties sell and also get passed in.

A week later, we sold. It was perfect timing that we declined a less-than-attractive offer at the auction. The people who bought our house were international buyers and weren't legally able to bid at auction. The disappointment at the auction turned out to be the blessing in disguise for the great offer that they put forward.

Next, we started to open up to the idea of a smaller house on a big enough block rather than the bigger houses on acreage we thought we wanted. This gave us a sense of relief as we thought about smaller mortgage repayments and more finances to travel. With that, we found a more humble property we thought we could get for a better figure. We put in an offer, sure that this desperate owner would sell. We were surprised when the agent told us that after months on the market, someone else had randomly put in a higher offer at the same time. We had to move on and follow the path to 'the house that was always going to be'.

Through events at that time, we started to realise that ahead of acreage, no pool and other factors on our wishlist, what became important was a nice suburb for the boys to find other children to play with. Homeschooling made me yearn for this over space and privacy. We surprised ourselves as we put in an offer on a tiny block with a nice house, in a family friendly suburb, because it was in the 'Lego land' I said I'd never live in. We were surprised yet again when our decent offer was declined!

Next, we started to realise that possibly the biggest priority for us was 'to keep the mortgage as low as possible' so we had far less financial stress than ever before. We came to all sorts of things as the weeks and daily events played out. For the first time, we noticed houses in suburbs to the west, exactly where I had said I would *never* live, because they were extremely good value.

The house we finally bought was the first house that the whole family was happy about. It wasn't acreage but certainly not a tiny block either. We had less privacy but it also came with a pool that would be more usable than our last. The property had somehow been passed in at that auction event despite the great price we got it for. Divine timing made certain the owners were ready to take our lower offer and probably not a moment sooner, if we had sold 'on time' at our auction.

We had finally travelled our path to find this house. There were so many factors out of our hands that closed doors on us, to be sure we didn't end up in certain places. As we looked at houses, we had daily experiences to force us to feel our emotions. These experiences guided us to our priorities at that exact point in our lives. It wasn't what we thought it would be. The acreage was clearly in the future and we reached for it too soon. The pool was clearly not something to let go of and sure enough, we all used this pool much more than the last one for various reasons.

Before long, Declan announced he wanted to have a different experience to homeschool and that he 'just wanted to ride to the local school'. For many reasons, it was the perfect school for him. It also brought many positive experiences, in contrast to the negative experiences he and the whole family had endured at his first school. The divine factors of why we were supposed to be in this house and area had already begun to unfold.

In hindsight, I felt frustrated by the energy we had spent on houses that were never meant for us. We didn't listen to Hayden's nudges of, 'I don't want to go. I don't like those houses'. We truly exhausted ourselves and yes, made ourselves agree that to sell and buy a house is one of the most stressful things you can do (if you do it the old way)!

Through the process however, we learned where we didn't pay attention to our inner sensations. So many times, we forgot to look at all of the factors and get honest about how we felt about them. Instead, we tried to create 'what we'd like it to be'. The financial factor was always, deep down, the most important factor to us but at times our little old human self distracted us from this. Our exhaustion reminded us that to play the game of life with divine timing in mind, you must feel first, *then* take action. We were still novices!

> Divine timing - the perfection of our existence and divinely timed scenes that play out so that we can experience the life themes on our soul agreement - despite our ego's attempt to change this.

Wasting time deciding

I said to Anthony, 'We think there are so many options in life! We almost love to challenge ourselves to find an answer from an overwhelming buffet of so-called choices. But actually, despite all of the seemingly endless options in front of us, for each of us there is only one true option at any one point for any one thing. Most choices in front of us are not real options, like we saw with the houses that we couldn't buy. We kid ourselves all day long!

'If we sat back until we felt the answer that we knew deep down, we wouldn't be so exhausted! We would have time to relax and do everything we say is important to us but we never get to. Then it would be like we played the game of life on the beat of divine time.'

I continued my passionate speech as I imagined how we might feel first, then take action. "'I need new shorts but I know I want them in this type of shape and made of natural fabric". I wait patiently. BOOM, the exact ones land in front of me at the right point in time. I took the time to sense all the factors of what I wanted and I knew them when I saw them.

'Next, "I wonder what to do about my child's crooked teeth." I consider the options in front of me. As much as I ache to get started on some type of treatment, none of them feel right. My child says no too. Wait, wait, wait, wait. BOOM, someone drops the name of a dental approach that is just right for us. I can *feel it!* Meanwhile, as I wait for my shorts and my dentist to come into play, I take notice of what else I'm in search of. "I'm after a doula for my baby on the way. I'm not in a rush because I know how this game works. I'll take some time to feel exactly what she will be like." BOOM, down the track, I meet her. She's not an experienced doula but she matches up with all of the characteristics I felt would be just right for me.'

As I talked this out loud, I already knew where I didn't play the game of life like this. There were times where I entertained less-than-perfect choices, even when I knew deep down they weren't quite my golden answers. I didn't trust myself to wait for 'what wanted to be'. Also, at this point in my life, I was very fatigued. I had to face the emotions that arose from how long I had turned away from my seed of intelligence's whispers. I had burned so much of my precious life force as I took action from my little old human self. I saw how much we waste time, energy and money when we don't feel for our answers first.

> Golden answer - the option of 'what wants to be' which we find as we tune into what feels right on all accounts. Also called 'our dots'.

Finding our golden answers

I started to see that at any point in our day, we have many dots in front of us. The dots represent the endless 'choices' of what to eat, what to do on the weekend, which friend to call, which school to send our child to, the best option to improve their immunity, whether to renovate, which online course to take, whether to hang out the washing on a cloudy day and on and on. It takes energy just to process the thought of all of those choices!

Amongst all of the dots and dots of 'options', there are actually only a few that are bolded or have our name on them. They are our golden answers which link with the path of our soul agreement. They are 'what wants to be' for every move of our day. Yes, there is even a golden answer for what to do about the washing! Although we as humans often face indecision, our seed of intelligence knows 'our dots'. The game of life is to feel for 'what wants to be' rather than think through the loud chaos of perceived choices.

We, as humans, have not been taught to tune inwards for 'our dots', the golden answers, that are just right for our unique path. Instead, we have been conditioned to come up with our answers from external sources, whether they are our unique 'dots' or not. Some examples are:

* what the doctor says
* what my mum always does
* what my dad believes
* what the magazines, media, high profile figure touts

* what my best friend swears by
* what the astrology says

'Our dots'

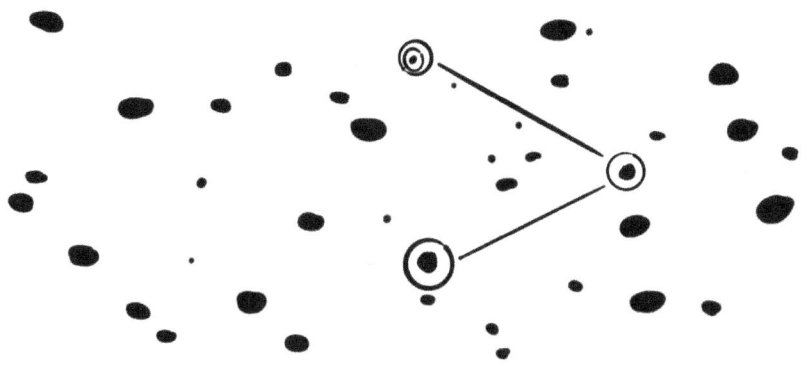

*When we leap from one golden answer dot to another,
we play life in divine timing. When we play out 'what wants to be',
life is more harmonious.*

When we neglect to play by divine timing, we see life as busy chaos. We often take action when instead we need to tune in first. This approach penalises us in the game of life as it drains our precious life force. We waste time, energy and money until we get spat back out to land on our golden answer dots, sometimes decades down the track.

Think about how often we dive in and take action without any reverence for 'what wants to be'. We go out and buy the thing and then discover it's not for us. We sign our children up to activities and then discover it doesn't suit them. We go out and socialise with people until we realise they are not for us.

When we don't tune in first, our seed of intelligence has no choice but to land us in chaotic scenes, to virtually hit us over the head, to realise it wasn't a golden answer. Sometimes, this can take many hits over the head, which we will look at in the chapters on The Cone and Red and Green Lights. As we get hit on the head, we can scan for where our little old human self jumped in.

We may have taken action from:

* what I'd like it to be.

* what I believe it should be.

* what I think is easiest.

* what saves me energy, confrontation, meltdowns or other discomfort.

* what my husband prefers.

* what pleases my parents the most.

* what makes me look like the more perfect woman/mother/daughter/friend.

* whatever - I didn't care, I just took the default option or someone made the choice for me.

Feeling for the golden answers and in the right timing

As I realised the concept of 'our dots', I also realised another factor about divine timing. Not only must we feel for our golden answer dots, we must also feel for when they want to be chosen. Although we might see all of our golden answer dots in front of us, there is a certain order in which 'our dots' want us to see them too.

Particularly for those who are the visionaries in the family, we can try to reach for all of 'our dots' at once, because we can see them. We know we want family harmony. We know we want our family to eat healthily. We know we want to do our soul work. We might feel travel, chickens and amazing veggie patches are for us! Each of these dots however, aren't to be grabbed at all at once, or again, we drain our energy.

> *Some people are happy to just take the first option they see and some over-research. Instead, it is to feel for and wait for what it wants to be.*

We are ahead of the beat of our time if we rush in and claim any old dot before the golden answer dot appears. *For example, we sign our active child up to soccer because the neighbours recommend it, although the golden answer of gymnastics was about to appear a couple of months later.*

We are behind the beat of our time if we sit back and miss the golden answer, which leaves us to pick from so-so dots. *For example, we leave it too long to go back and get the beautiful top we saw and it's now out of stock. We have to buy something else that doesn't have the same magic.*

When we play out life by divine timing however, we feel first, then take action. Here are some examples.

* *We ask our child and they tell us they don't want to play soccer. A couple of months later they mention gymnastics, where they thrive for years.*

* *We see the beautiful top and we get honest that it ticks so many boxes. Although we are late to get home, we take the moment to try it on. It becomes a most loved top.*

The conversation with our child about soccer and those few extra minutes at the shops feel priceless.

Not only do we leak precious energy if we reach for dots that aren't our golden answer, we also leak energy when we reach for our golden answer dots too soon.

Here is an example.

A keen mother wants to have children who grow up on a property, who are homeschooled and know how to grow their own food. The parents however, strain to keep up with the landcare as well as time with their daughters. The girls eventually request to try out school. The parents agree as they bit off too much and feel exhausted. Down the track, the girls request to come out of school and it all works much better then as both parents have much more time and energy on their hands.

> *It's not time to make a decision until it's time to make a decision.*

What it feels like

We must *feel* for the golden answers in our life. Instead, we have been conditioned to jump in and follow our little old human self who makes choices from factors that aren't at the core of our divine path. Internally, the golden answer will feel like a big sigh of relief, even though there may be some less-than-ideal factors or things that make you feel nervous too. *For example, I did feel nervous about my decision to take a temporary job and I did have to cry some tears about our lack of privacy in our new home, but they both still felt like 'this is it'.*

Sometimes we have to feel frustrated, disappointed or other emotions first, to be able to see an answer that may be just to the left of us. It takes practice to remember to feel and to be able to see past the seemingly obvious answers in front of us. It also takes patience to wait when we can't see the golden answer. We must throw all of the options into the air and then feel for what *feels like* 'ahh yes' on the other side.

> *If it's not the time, then it won't* feel *easy or like it actually is the time.*

The void

To bring a challenge to the game of life, usually our golden answers appear just after we reach for a less-than-perfect 'dot' or choice. We reach for other dots too early because we feel 'the void'. We sense when change is about to occur and it can feel very uncomfortable to trust that the very best option will land in our lap in good timing. The game of life is designed this way to make us work to have full faith in our seed of intelligence and divine timing!

Most of us like to move through change like the moves we do on monkey bars. We prefer to hold onto the old option (one monkey bar) and not let go of this until we have our hand firmly on the next option (the next monkey bar). *Examples are when we continue to catch up with a draining friend until we find another more resonant friend or when we keep our child at a less-than-perfect sport until we find something better.* The ultimate in the game of life however, is when we sense the old option is no longer for us and we let go of it. We sit in the void (or swing through the air monkey bars style) and trust that the next option (or monkey bar) will come before we 'fall'.

> The void - when one season of our life has come to an end but another hasn't yet started, such as when our child clearly doesn't belong at school but we don't know the next best place for them.

Flowing instead of structuring

As we play by divine timing, at every moment in our day we feel into 'what wants to be' next. As we allow our seed of intelligence to guide us, we eventually throw to-do lists and routines out the window. Instead, we rely on the timing and the agenda of our day through the intelligence of our inner seed.

If we tune in, our seed of intelligence nudges us with 'YES!' and 'NO!' feelings all day. Often we override the 'NO!' feelings and thrash ourselves with chores or take our children to a social outing when we don't feel like it. We do this because we are still to play out the life theme of 'what it feels like to disrespect my inner whispers and ultimately, my soul'. As we work through this life theme, on the other side, we yearn to respect our inner state first, above all else. We will look at how to work through our life themes in many of the coming chapters.

Of course, whilst many of us still have to make appointments and routines forced by the structures we live by right now, we sometimes have to go against our seed of intelligence's nudges. In time, we will all be called to live more freely so that we can honour our inner guidance. For now, we can continue to practise connection with our inner sensations of 'YES!' and 'NO..'.

Here are some examples of how our seed of intelligence can guide us if we give it space to.

> ★ *I used to get worried when I hadn't regularly cleaned the bathrooms, vacuumed the house or washed the sheets. Interestingly, the less routinely I did these chores, the more I found myself pulled into them through divine circumstances. One day I offered to pay the boys to vacuum the house but they never got to it. The very next day, I smashed a jar of honey onto the floor. Immediately, I was pulled in to mop and vacuum!*
>
> *As I vacuumed, I felt myself energised to do it because it was now so necessary.*

The time was ripe. The boys had missed the beat of divine timing and my seed of intelligence landed me into the scene to do it instead. My little old human self had other tasks planned for me that morning but it was easy to see that the vacuuming was what 'wanted to be' that day. I realised how the other tasks weren't as necessary as my little old human self had touted them to be. I was on the beat of divine timing.

★ *The old me got a slap down when I didn't play by the beat of divine timing. I used to routinely change the bed sheets. Often, the day after I washed the sheets, the boys wet the bed or brought sand into their bed and I was forced to rewash them. The same types of scenarios happened if I vacuumed too much. Someone inevitably gave me a reason to get the vacuum out again straight afterwards. Each time, I despaired, 'I just vacuumed yesterday!' and even, 'Oh why did I push myself to wash the sheets yesterday?'. I started to feel that I was ahead of the beat of time and these incidents were my penalty. It was my little old human self that thought I needed to do them more regularly, which burned my energy as I tried to keep up.*

The New Way will rock us until we let go of structures created by our little old human self and 'what I think it should be'.

Waiting to feel energised

I started to play the game of life from a pretend 'hammock'. I only got up and took action when I truly felt called to, like you would only get out of a comfortable hammock on a lazy holiday when you were truly energised to. There were often day- to-day tasks that didn't excite me, but I knew I had to do them, such as book my car in for a service. As long as I kept these tasks in my periphery and stayed connected with my inner universe, lo and behold, something always energised me to get up out of my hammock and do it! For *example, one day Anthony and I talked about whether to sell my car or not. By the end of it, I realised at that point in time, I was more energised to save for a holiday than take on another car loan. I became energised to take care of my car and the first thing I did was book it in for a service.*

The more I played the game of life this way, the more I trusted that everything that needed to get done would literally call me there, in good timing. When I played out divine timing, everything went much more smoothly. It was the key factor. *For example, my car was serviced on the day they had the part it needed or the boys didn't let the wet dog in the moment after I cleaned the floors.* Think about the countless factors that are at play when we land in a scene even five minutes earlier or later than 'perfect timing'.

I only put myself behind any part of my day when I felt truly energised. As I felt pulled to lie on the grass with Hayden and Bounty, I did this until I started to feel into 'what wants to be next'. I only got up from my 'hammock' when I felt the 'YES!' energy. At first, it took some time to scan the buffet of *all of my options* to see past my to-do list, ego's pull or usual daily routine.

'What wanted to be' was often not what I usually chose to do. I slowed down and enjoyed my family. I realised I craved passionfruit. I focused on my drawing. All the while, I heard my monkey mind tell me about a to-do list, what I should eat instead or why drawing wasn't the best use of my time.

On the days I felt energised to do a lot, I went with this wind. I sailed through more than I would have if my monkey mind had whipped me to do 'just because' on a different day. This concept matches with how we are energised to clean the house when visitors are imminent and we do it efficiently! When I couldn't bring myself to lift a finger on life however, I went with this too.

Before long, I clearly sensed when I felt energised to do something and when I felt my little old human self whip me to do it. When I hit the nail on the head of 'what wanted to be' with my time and energy, I felt satisfied. I found satisfaction not only in traditionally pleasing activities, such as self-care or family time, but even in chores. However, when I obeyed my to-do list, tried to stick to a routine or did 'what I said I would do, although it doesn't feel right anymore', I couldn't find the same satisfaction.

When I didn't find satisfaction with where I put my energy, my little old human self whipped me to stay with the activity even longer. *For example, when I researched something for hours or I chased down another item on my to-do list.* The problem was, when I took action from my little old human self, I never felt the same satisfaction. Instead, I felt whipped to do more, to try to get a quick hit of this false satisfaction. Again, I was penalised by this approach with drained energy. I often took it out on my family through huffs and complaints of not enough help.

Divine timing through our actors

We can get off course when we don't listen to the resistance of our actors. Our child may drag their feet as we leave the house, which hints to check whether they want to be social that day. If we go anyway, this often leads to the day where the children fight, have an accident or no one can really decide what to do. We feel less-than-satisfied with our social date as we leave. Instead, we missed the golden answer to just relax and take it easy with an emotional child.

Our partner may resist our big ideas, such as when we want to rent out a space to start our new healing business. Firstly, we need to consider them as energetic brakes on our idea. Maybe we need to be paused so we can collide with the golden answer, which puts less financial pressure on us. Perhaps a friend then moves into a new house with a healing room we can use for free.

Alternatively, perhaps our partner's resistance is a hint that it's not quite divine timing for our soul work. Instead, our energy is best spent on our family challenges so that we can sync in with the clients that will soon come towards us, with their own family challenges. We change as a person from the inner work it takes to move through these family challenges. This serves our soul work in exponential ways.

> *The resistance of our actors is often the divine brakes put on us. It can also be a red light to our ideas and a clear signal to check in with where the golden answer actually lies.*

Deciding as a group

We often make decisions with others without the intention to find 'what wants to be'. We have been conditioned to take care of number one and to fight for what our little old human wants or to give in and go with what someone else would like it to be or thinks it should be. It is a process that takes communication and patience, to find what wants to be. We go back and forth until the golden answer arises, where everyone feels the big 'YES!' together. The key is to patiently check in with each person, who ideally checks in with their feelings and 'what wants to be' themselves.

As a group, the golden answer sits in the middle of us and hints, *'this is actually what it wants to be'*. It is different to a compromise as this concept means one person gives in to another. To find what wants to be, we must be prepared for an unexpected answer and not necessarily in the timing we think it should be. *Like with the search for our house, we all had to feel for it and we all had to wait for it to appear too.*

Insisting on the golden answer

Through this practice, I realised there was *always* a divine golden answer, for myself or in a group. If I jumped in and went with an option that was less-than-the-golden-answer, something always went wrong. *For example, when I bought polyester leggings because they were cheap although I yearned for more expensive bamboo ones. Afterwards, I realised the polyester leggings were too uncomfortable. I had wasted even that small amount of money and now owned another piece of clothing I felt like I 'should' wear.* The golden answer was to wait and make sure I really wanted the bamboo leggings and that it wasn't a different pair of leggings or pants that awaited me. I knew the day the bamboo leggings were on a very good sale that they were the golden answer. I felt it. I learned my lesson and bought them.

A group similarly pays the price if they do not come to the golden answer. *For example, the restaurant that one person chooses willy-nilly is closed when everyone arrives. Another example is when the whole family sits in silence at the cafe. They didn't see the golden answer was to stay at home because everyone was moody.* As a group, it is each person's responsibility to feel into it and speak up if it doesn't feel right. We must listen to anyone's hesitance or resistance, including our children's.

Letting go

As we honour our seed of intelligence's pull to 'what wants to be', we must let go. We must surrender what we think it should be, would like it to be, have been brought up to be or even what *others* think it should be. It will bring up emotions as we have to let go of the dreams and expectations our little old human self has planted within us. We also have to appreciate that there is an intelligence that pulls us to the scenes where we were *always meant to be*, which means our thoughts do not affect our reality how we have perceived them to.

When we come back to 'what is', we trust there is order and a process to what we yearn for. We cannot skip ahead to what we want it to be, mostly because we don't usually factor in the challenges we must face to achieve our dreams. There are countless factors that need to collide, to ensure we arrive at the exact point in time and space for everything our seed of intelligence is encoded to play out. It is a journey to be at peace with the unique timing to this.

Sometimes divine timing lands us in challenging storylines, such as 'If I hadn't gone today, I wouldn't have crashed my car'. As we find the courage to acknowledge there is light and dark in any path, we trust that we were meant to be at that exact point in time and space. We always change from any experience, be it 'good' or 'bad'.

As we live with respect to divine timing, we *will* have to make less-than-perfect choices, like when we have to do something we don't love to do, for money. This will also lead us to divine timing of the experiences we need to have, albeit sometimes in the shadows. We will look at examples soon.

Current challenges around divine timing

We land in many challenges because we haven't been aware of how to play by divine timing. When life doesn't work out, we pathologise ourselves. For those who often play behind the beat of time, they whip themselves for procrastination. For those who often play ahead of the beat of time, they shame themselves for their lack of success or blame the actors that stall them. Instead, it is to change course and play by divine timing. The chapter on Red and Green Lights will guide you to do this.

It can be easier said than done to play by divine timing. We are overscheduled because we are conditioned to add more on our plate, even if many of these things are not 'our dots'. The aim is to sense every 'dot' we have on our plate, which doesn't actually have our name on it, and find the courage to let it go. This usually starts with conversations with family members as to what they really want and more importantly to check in with our 'YES!' and 'NO...' feelings. There may also be some 'dots' to add *onto* our plate, such as what we have forgotten we truly value. In the Titanic and Rainbow chapters, we will look at why it takes time to move towards life by divine timing.

We can never truly play by divine timing if we don't honour the energetic concept of 'you are it'. We often ignore our own soul's red lights when we continue to put our children or other people before our own inner nudges and wellbeing. In contrast, children and men, *in general*, are more inclined to first do what is best for them. As we go The New Way, we are invited to not only pay attention to our inner 'YES!' and 'NO..' feelings but also to act on them and speak up to others unashamedly.

Why you want to know about Divine Timing

As you play the game of life, there are bigger and smaller decisions to make, such as whether to pack the toys up for your child, what to make for dinner or whether you should stay in an unfulfilling job. Your little old human self reminds you of the seemingly endless choices to distract you from the whispers within.

You can feel relieved and confident to play the game of life, once you realise your answers are already out there. You just need to tune in and wait for 'your dots' to appear. Life choices only feel chaotic because the dots for *all* players in the game of life are out there. You just need to know what you resonate with and patiently wait for it, to play from this more peaceful place.

> *As you go The New Way, you will continue to land in scenes to practise mastery of how you use your time, energy and money.*

Syncing with divine timing

When you play the game of life by divine timing, it is like you are at a sushi train. You can take the first option you see and it *could be* the golden answer. You will feel it if it is. Often however, the sushi that will satisfy you the most is still to come. You want to be at the right place at the right time, in order to be ready to take that sushi as it comes towards you on the tracks. It is not a bad strategy to sit and watch the sushi options go by so you are sure and ready as it comes back around.

If it's meant for you in life, it will come back around but of course don't play from behind the beat of time either. Remember, when you realise your answer too late, it was actually never meant for you. You may need to land in 'what it feels like to make the wrong choice and miss my golden answer' time and time again so that you yearn to play the game of life by divine timing instead. In time, you will easily know what will satisfy you in any daily scenario and you will be ready to grab it as it arrives. You will take nothing less as you trust the void and wait for the perfect option.

> *Take extra time to tune inwards to 'what wants to be', the golden option, despite what you might want it to be otherwise.*

Syncing with your actors

Take the time to check in with yourself and/or the other actors you need to decide with. If you ever feel rushed to make a decision, it is an alarm to give it some space. Like the sushi train, trust that whatever is meant for you will become known in good time. If any actors involved in the decision with you, including children, show hesitance or resistance, there is something else to be considered. Trust that despite your frustration with them, you are not quite yet on 'what wants to be'.

Playing by divine timing

With practice, you find the golden answer more easily. As you find the golden answer within yourself you become far more empowered. That is, you trust your own divine wisdom more than you trust the advice or opinions of others. You start to speak up in a group when you sense it's not the golden answer.

There becomes a point where you no longer need to seek answers externally. Instead, you are in tune with the answers that arise from your inner work and the clarity with which you spy your answers in your day to day scenes. We will go into more detail of how to do this in the chapters on Life Themes and the Cone.

As you become more in tune, you start to feel the disrespect of your own innate intelligence if you enlist professionals, healers or psychics. This also goes for advice or wisdom from well-meaning friends, family and teachers. It also begins to include books, podcasts and realms that include rules, dogmas, protocols and frameworks. You are always more connected to your unique answers when you connect back to your inner universe.

To find the golden answer at any point in your day, you might :

* *Take a moment to recognise your exhausted state and consider an easier meal to cook that night. Otherwise you may have spent extra time in the kitchen and ended up too tired to respond with patience when your children rejected the meal at dinner time.*

* *Cry it all out so you feel certain that you need to move cities for your husband's job offer. As you let go of what you have now, you realise your soul craves a rest from your job and that this move will give you that. Otherwise you might have stayed and blamed your partner for the financial stress on the family when they couldn't find a job whilst you still felt exhausted from your job.*

* *Take the time to talk to your child when they don't want to go to school. Even though you are late, you then realise the answer is to talk to your child's teacher, which alleviates your underlying stress on how you can afford to change to a more expensive school or to homeschool. You otherwise might have tried 'I don't have time for this' or 'I know it's hard but you have to go anyway' with your child, which weakens their heart connection with you.*

Divine feedback

Your challenging situations hint when you haven't quite hit on 'what wants to be'. If you take these challenges as a red light from your seed of intelligence, you know you need to tune in further for the golden divine answer. The red lights *do* happen as we have never been taught to take the time to feel into the divine choice nor has it ever been modelled to us. You can probably recall many times when you've been burned for your less-than-divine choice. Remember, it is a practice to play the game of life, The New Way.

As you are the first one in your family to play by divine timing, keep in mind you may upset others as you tune into your seed of intelligence. We are not used to last minute cancellations, especially if it's for reasons such as 'it just doesn't feel right for us today'. Remember however, if it's not right for you, ultimately, it's not right for them.

> *When we meet in divine timing,*
> *it is exactly right for* **both** *parties.*

If your child requests to cancel their piano lesson at the last minute, in the long run, it is important to honour your child's seed of intelligence. It is to trust that it was not 'meant to be' for the other party either and often they just hadn't seen it. At times, in hindsight, the other party will be able to see that your call actually suited them too. Maybe then they acknowledged their growing headache or perhaps they realised it gave them time to get to the shops to pick up food they needed for dinner. When the other party doesn't realise they are invited to play on divine timing however, it can bring up feelings of frustration and anger. They may feel the old conditioning of 'but you can't just do that', 'how unreliable' or even 'you're not teaching your child to stick with what they have committed to'.

Sometimes, your child may still have to go to the piano lesson, for many reasons. Maybe you feel too embarrassed to cancel at the last minute. Maybe you sense your child needs to face 'what it feels like to go to my lesson when I haven't done any practice'. Then afterwards, you come back to 'you are it'. You work through your feelings and also your child's. You come to the heart of the matter on whether they want to continue piano or not. The next time your child doesn't want to go, you may say yes to divine timing and cancel at the last minute. You have less charge on this topic and you can see they have had tricky times with friends at school that day. In a coming book of The New Way series, we will go into further detail on Mother-Child Team work.

As more and more of us begin to honour the pull of our seed of intelligence, we understand the need for much more flexibility in our schedules. We still feel irritation as others test our rigid plans and ideas but when we understand this is an inner work invitation, we realise it's also an invitation to play by divine timing. If someone else cancels or changes plans, it means we missed the nudge to cancel it ourselves. We know we are in tune when both parties ring to reschedule at the same time!

Scene by scene, you must listen to your inner feelings, to stay connected to your divine whispers of when to act and when not to.

The benefits

As you play by divine timing, you are awarded with a goodie bag! Some examples are:

* extra energy, time and money

* immense satisfaction and increased intuition, as you use discernment to consider all factors and trust your feelings on your choices

- respect from your actors when you notice they are your divine brakes or questioners rather than just actors who give you grief
- heart connection with yourself

To do it well, you must be in tune with your inner universe, to feel the 'yes' and 'no' sensations and to problem solve with patience. This takes inner work, to release the frustration that was hidden as you allowed your little old human self to make your decisions for decades. You also begin to work as an interconnected team with others. You insist on communication much more than you ever have to play to the beat of your soul agreements.

As you master the game of life in divine timing, you start to land at the right point in time and space far more often. Like a perfectly written sonata, you can feel the harmony as you land on the divine beat of time.

Summary

- Every scene of our life is divinely orchestrated.
- Sometimes it seems like we are pulled because of a 'bad choice' but it was actually what wanted to be.
- When things work out for us that was always going to be too.
- The emotions we feel about the scenes we land in match the climate in our inner universe.
- When we play life on the divine beat of time, we take the time to feel into 'what wants to be'.
- Our actors can give us resistance as a form of 'divine brakes'.
- The aim is to sync more and more with our golden answers which bring more harmony.

* If we take action from what our little old human self thinks it should be, we can waste our time, energy and money.

* We can allow our seed of intelligence to pull us to what feels best and feel our way through the light and dark of each experience that comes from that.

For you to ponder on ...

From now on, notice every scene that you land in where someone gives you resistance. Take this as a divine sign to reconsider your next move.

Soul Agreement

...you cannot change who you are...

2016

I felt the call to leave my mainstream speech pathology career as I realised I was expected to wave a magic wand at children's issues. There was no space to look at the root cause with the child's mother. The more I tuned in holistically, I saw not only the child's issues but also the bigger family stressors at home. There were many elephants tucked under the rug when it came to school, sibling, financial and partner issues, let alone the mother's inner disharmony too. I realised the superficial nature of my job and that the speech issues were the tip of this iceberg.

I finally came across a health coaching certificate, and I was excited to leave the allied health system. I did not realise how horribly challenging it was about to become as I started my own business and then later, brought forth this work. My seed of intelligence attracted scenes that made sure I stayed humble. It did not allow me to earn too much money and stop there in 'success mode'. As a result, Anthony and I went through the stress of a shrinking bank account and the thought that I may have to return to my speech pathology job. Sure enough, I did need to go back. We had to vaccinate our Declan under duress, to afford daycare. I also had to swallow my pride as I pushed myself to act as a speech pathologist, although I ached to do it all my way.

I cried and cried. I let it all out and then pointed the finger at the universe, at any guides, angels or ancestors out there that could help me. I swore at them and I stomped my foot. I was able to see beyond the allied health system and yet I felt so frustrated that I had to stay in my government job for money.

I let so much out that I started to think outside the box. 'If only I could go and be a florist! To just work with flowers all day and come home and watch some mainstream television without a care in the world....' Yes, I have now realised that a florist job can be really stressful but I didn't see that at the time.

I told Anthony that I had bargained with the universe, to leave me in peace and to get me a job as a florist. Anthony had said for a long time, 'just go and get an easy school hours job, and save yourself the stress'. Although it seemed like a good idea, I saw where the florist idea would lead me. The fire burned again within me.

'You know what would happen? I would go and work in a florist and my colleague would tell me about her child and their issues. I wouldn't be able to help myself. I'd talk her through it, I'd create courses and mentorship offers in my head. I'd find passion again. I HAVE NO CHOICE! WE THINK WE DO! We are literally 'yes sir, no sir' to what we have signed up to be, if we want to have a nice life.' I rocked and cried some more, as I realised how much the divine literally had me in a position. I have also then come to the fact that it has nothing to do with wanting a 'nice' life but once you have realised your soul mission, it is grindingly hard to back out!

I knew too much about the energetics of children's development and the energetic connection with their family. No matter where I went, this realisation followed me. I had activated the passion within me. It was huge and I knew it could really change the world. I could not hide from it, no matter how many challenges were in front of me on this path. It was what I had agreed to, somewhere, somehow. It pulled me, as I kicked and screamed!

At this point, I hadn't realised the seed of intelligence concept. I could just see that we had certainly signed up for particular experiences. I connected the dots. I started to gaze at everyone through the eyes of, 'What have they signed up to experience, like a calling, for the good and the bad?'.

I could see the pull and passion for each person. Sometimes it was simply 'to make a point of connecting with others', like for my Mum. Sometimes it was 'to find adventure and travel and all that goes with it', like for my Dad. The more I tuned in, the more I could see more than one thing for each person. My Mum certainly signed up for travel too, but she did a lot of it through her work as a flight attendant, whereas my Dad did it through solo travel after overseas work. My Dad did not sign up to connect with others so much. In fact, it has been one of the trickiest points of his life, as he refuses to be a people pleaser, to change himself for others or even see things from someone else's point of view. When I realised this, I could see that even this challenge was something he would have agreed to explore. It was an experience that he chose to have, like he chose his travel adventures that came easily to him (but certainly not without stories too!). Like all of us in our experiences, I know that my Mum and my Dad could fill books with what they have come to, just through these experiences and how it all felt to them.

I realised how much my parents, and every other human, are energetically pulled to follow their passions, and then experience the challenges that inevitably unfold as they do. We are encoded to persist, even in the darkest of times. Despite the cost to our physical, emotional, mental and spiritual health, there is a part of us that wants to stay and play the game of life when it gets tough. Most of us however, have never connected to this when we have been in those times.

Tune in now. As we own the concept that topics, places, people and foods usually attract or repel us, we can sit with the wonder that something is energetically programmed within us. With energetics, it's all or nothing. We either chose all of these experiences and our existence is energetically organised or we chose none and we play out random chaos. We can also consider that our seed of intelligence can't choose to energetically pull us to some scenes of life and allow our human mind to choose others. It's all or nothing. Let's look at this further.

Often, we question the concept of energetics when we consider our big challenges. We claim that surely these experiences were random or that we wouldn't have chosen them. In this case, our response is driven by the emotions that we felt through these challenges. We lose sight of our power to move through big challenges, to at least survive if not thrive. As we own our experiences, we immediately sit up straighter and start to ponder on 'Why?' and 'Who actually am I?'. Then we come back to the energetic law that *everything* is divinely orchestrated. Our big challenges are fundamental to the game of life because we grow so much from them.

I considered how I was pulled to continue my work with The New Way. I saw how my parents were pulled to have certain experiences. If we were pulled to all of this, we must have been pulled to far more, even the smaller details of our life. All or nothing. I could see the divine order to it all.

I realised the concept of the 'soul agreement'. I felt called to name it this, to remind us that we agreed to these experiences, because there is *always* goodness that comes from our experiences. It is our human work to also have heart for the challenge of it too.

> Soul agreement - our agreed life path, which includes *themes* we are to explore, which connects with what we are drawn to and repelled from.

To bring this concept to life, I visually saw the soul agreement like a ridiculously long scroll. It enlists each theme we are to experience throughout our whole life. Once I realised the concept of the seed of intelligence, I then saw the analogy that the information from our soul agreement is encoded into our seed of intelligence. It's like someone scrunched up this scroll and 'zhoom', all the information energetically transferred to this seed. The seed of intelligence is our pulling force in life and our soul is the one to drive it, to claim 'you are it' and play the game of life from this empowerment.

> Empowerment - To find your power from within. To be able to stand on your own two feet as a sovereign being. To own the energetic law of 'you are it'. To know you can only shift your external reality as you *firstly* shift your internal reality.
>
> (This definition is different to the usual way we have seen empowerment - 'Since I've been suppressed all these years, I will unapologetically get up and do life however I please'.)

The energetic concepts of the soul agreement and seed of intelligence remind us that we are here to play out our soul's path, and *no one else's*. The people in our life have their own soul agreement, seed of intelligence and soul path, including our children. We have experiences with others, not to interfere with their paths but to make sense of it, from our soul's point of view. You are it.

So, what is and isn't on our soul agreement? We have included what I call 'life themes' to explore and embody during the day to day scenes of our life. That is it. We all play out similar life themes, but through countless different storylines. These storylines come back to the same types of themes, such as 'being misunderstood', 'having a kind friend' or 'having little support as a mother'. We will look at the concept of Life Themes in detail, in the following chapter.

Why you want to know about your Soul Agreement

The life path we chose, with all of its details, is extremely unique. Most of us have not made sense of this uniqueness. Instead, school made it feel like there are only so many subjects or sports to be good at, and there are only so many pathways with which to use these skills. Society mostly only reveres gifts and talents that come under the school banner. Parents have generally continued from this perspective, in how they see and nurture their children's gifts.

From our early years, we were conditioned to put ourselves into plain boxes. In primary school, we were taught to categorise ourselves under simple labels of black, brown, red and blonde hair. We missed the magnificent shades and varieties of hair and how these correspond with our family lines. We either came from a typical family or a split family. There was no talk of 'my Mum had two miscarriages before me', 'I was adopted' or 'my grandparents live with us'.

We were also taught to categorise ourselves as sporty, academic or 'other', rather than marvel in the exponential gifts we all carried.

Here are some examples of the invisible magic that was not revered in school:

- those that could make others laugh with a quick wit
- those that could spy the agenda behind a curriculum
- those that could easily make a dollar
- those that could see people's auras
- those that could problem solve and create with their hands
- those who cared for animals
- those who could see adults who lie, leak their stress or treat others unfairly

> *Invisible magic - the gifts encoded within us, that no one externally can teach us to do any better, often not revered at school. Also referred to as 'magic of magic'.*

As children, we immediately narrowed our magic of magic as we were asked single-focused questions, such as 'what's your favourite subject at school?', 'what do you want to be when you grow up?' or 'what sport do you play?'. We completely lost sight of our most amazing gifts and became an identity of something like 'my hair colour + my family structure + my favourite sport'.

On the contrary, from the early years, when we expressed our uniqueness that wasn't so accepted by society, the world quickly gave us 'no' responses. There may have been loud responses, such as those children who were bullied for their dramatic skills or given a suspension, because they tried their art skills through graffiti. There were also subtle 'no' responses.

Here are some examples of when we sensed our magic of magic was not received or was 'wrong'.

* The child who drew pictures in fine detail but was signed up for sport instead.

* The child who loved being in the garden but was told 'that path won't make you any money'.

* The child who was interested in aliens but their teacher responded with 'there's no evidence in that, let's look at NASA rockets instead'.

* The child who could see how to hold space for their parents' arguments but was told 'you don't need to worry yourself with this'.

Our uniqueness even includes how we play out the details of the day to day scenes of our lives. We are all quite different in how we stack a dishwasher, which muscles we use when we sit down and the tiny details of how we make sense of the concept of money. By the time we list off every last gift and challenge that we have experienced, are experiencing or will experience and how we play out our day, we start to understand that no one else could have signed up for anywhere close to this too. This is our extreme uniqueness, yet we've been conditioned to see our identity as very simple.

Our uniqueness is underexpressed and barely celebrated. Instead, we have been taught to judge each other if it's not something that school would award or even if it is something school would award. As we do so, we miss the magic in the many angles of our expression. It is no wonder that our society struggles with the physical, emotional, mental and spiritual effects of this type of existence.

Our uniqueness is more than our gifts and untapped magic. It is also about the challenges and struggles we agreed to, which hold golden keys to more of our magic. We will get to more on our agreed challenges in the upcoming Life Themes chapter.

The New Way means we understand that we are likely to be very different in how we approach any situation and what we do and don't prefer. This also goes for how we hold space for our children to express their uniqueness in the finest of details too. It is powerful to firstly take the time to understand what is on our soul agreement, so we can then have compassion for everyone else's chosen experiences. Theirs will be *very different but divinely orchestrated* too.

Understanding the Game of Life

Our soul agreement, along with our seed of intelligence, remind us that there is order to our life and what we experience. The soul agreement is the 'heart', which gives us passions and skills to nurture. We are also encoded to have the desire to persist with our challenges, which are literally obstacles to move through, to fuel our passions even further. If we didn't have a soul agreement, we wouldn't have any reason to be our character and would end up as lifeless robots who simply copy each other. Yes, most adults and children have somewhat lost connection to their seed of intelligence and as a result do copy others more than they realise. This book, and those of The New Way series, will guide you to connect back to your seed of intelligence and true essence more of the time.

We perceive information from the scenes of our day and it is supposed to be filtered through our inner feelings. This then creates our own angle of truth. For most people however, we have lost connection with our feelings and hence, we simply copy and paste from what our brother did, the news reported, our mother modelled, the kinesiologist told us, the podcast announced and/or the professional prescribed.

Instead, The New Way is to remember how to feel (heart), so we can reconnect with our intelligence (star), to draw our own conclusions from our day to day scenes with our unique factors. We then bring our uniqueness to life as we place ourselves behind what is important to us (earth). Here, we find joy and fulfilment that eludes so many of us right now. Anyone who teaches rigid curriculums, processes and step by step approaches, stamps out the invitation for another to perceive the information, make it their own and create from there.

Our soul agreement allows us to co-create our lives with the divine. This is a huge turn-around to our upbringing, which focused us towards what the authorities, systems, curriculums, traditions, religions and shoulds told us to do. They can be distractions that take our power, wherever we aren't strongly connected to our divinely orchestrated seed of intelligence. They can, of course, be guides to what we needed to come to but with our own inner discernment.

Understanding you cannot change who you are

As we resonate with the concept of the seed of intelligence and soul agreement, we come to an important energetic law - 'you cannot change who you are'. Our seed of intelligence is within us, like an energetic microchip of what we, our human character, is about in this life. It is encoded with our soul agreement. As much as we may try to avoid what we agreed to explore, our seed of intelligence continues to attract curly storylines. This ensures that we experience our agreement and that we really feel it.

Think about the implications of the energetic law 'you cannot change who you are'. How much do we try to change each other, especially those closest to us? How much do we judge each other for how we express our seed of intelligence, even when it's from our gifts? What about when we express ourselves through undesirable reactions to our valid challenges? How much did our parents reject our unique expression, often unknowingly? What about school and university or any teaching facility's perception of our uniqueness? How much have we judged our children or witnessed others judging our children's uniqueness? Society as a whole judges us too.

The very sad thing is that, from our childhood, we have been conditioned to judge our own precious, magical and perfect seed of intelligence and how we express our unique essence too. We may reject our physical appearance. We may detest our particular shadow expressions, such as when we yell or bite our nails. We may even turn away from a particular gift, such as singing. We have been so conditioned to judge and pathologise our behaviours that we aren't even aware of all of the magical pieces of ourselves that we have tucked away.

Allowing divine timing

As we play the game of life by divine timing, we can remember that our soul agreement wants to unfold to a specific beat and in a certain order. We must catch ourselves when we interfere with others' paths, for example, when we offer advice, try to convince others or help too much. We must also learn to see where our little old human self interferes with what wants to be, on our *own* path too. We will soon look at why we are drawn to interfere with our seeds of intelligence and how to instead surrender to our unique unfolding.

Summary

* Our soul agreement is the energetic reason for our lives.

* It is encoded in our seed of intelligence which pulls us to every life scene we need to land in.

* We have agreed to all of our experiences because even the challenges are for good reason.

* Our soul agreement has recorded our uniqueness down to the details of what and who we are drawn to and repelled from.

* We must reconsider any ways of life that confine our uniqueness or judge it.

For you to ponder on....

- Can you name at least one of your 'magic of magics'?

- What can you do easily, without trying, often that others cannot?

- Now ponder on your family members' invisible magic or ask your children what they sense theirs are.

Life Themes

...every scene of your day is an experience for YOU to embody...

2019

My Hayden has a lot of what I call 'Star energy' integrated. That is, he can be super wafty and disorganised when he's in the shadow of this energy. When he's in the light of the Star energy, his memory is unbelievable, his concept of maths is far beyond his years and he blows your mind with his stories of astral projection and the galactic realms.

So far, Hayden has enjoyed his experiences of the light aspects of the Star energy. The shadow aspects have been much, much trickier for him. When Hayden spaced out and didn't hear or follow through on directions, people yelled or grabbed him, to snap him back to reality. I did too. It was clearly awful for him to experience as he couldn't help but waft off, particularly when he was little.

As the years went by, I got upset, frustrated and completely exhausted by this shadow aspect of the Star energy, which Hayden experienced. By this stage, I allowed myself to flow my emotions so I didn't take it out on him one more time, even though I did this less than perfectly. I was then able to have heart for my Hayden and what it must be like for him to go through this.

In the flow of my tears one day, I started to hold space for myself. 'It's tough for him, but actually it's also tough for me as his mother!'. There, I said it and boy did I feel it. I allowed myself to realise how challenging it had been on me too. All this time, I had hardened myself so that I didn't feel my underlying emotions, so I could get on with the role of his mother.

As with the soul agreement concept, it was clear to see that Hayden had agreed to experience what it was like to waft off and frustrate people with his behaviour. At the same time, I also experienced it as 'a mother of a child who wafted off and frustrated people with his behaviour'. I felt disappointed and frustrated with him, and yet, I also struggled to see others disappointed and frustrated with him. There were many angles to explore as a mother of a wafty child and yes, I could tell you all about this experience I was here to embody.

Along the way, I saw Hayden was hardly able to help it and I found even more heart for him. The trauma of his early experiences, and his starry nature, made sure his seed of intelligence pulled him into tricky scenarios. I tried to stand up and speak up for him with many other upset people in his life, however, I copped a lot back. Whilst I copped it from others, I also had to drive back home when he forgot his shoes on important occasions, remind his 12-year-old self to eat breakfast then clean his teeth and other mind-blowing scenarios.

My experiences were my experiences to own. They weren't Hayden's fault. I must have agreed on my soul agreement to explore the Star energy in the shadows, from this angle. The common factor was the theme we both explored - 'what it feels like to have or be a wafty, disorganised child'. Hayden played out the angle of the character. I played out the mother. We had different experiences, but they were interconnected. My experience was just as valid as his, and it linked to how I felt about what I went through with Hayden.

As I connected more dots about our linked experiences, I realised we both experienced the Star energy in the light too. Hayden's unbelievable memory reminded me of how I remember my credit card numbers, primary school teachers' number plates, each child's name in my primary school and more. Later on, as I realised Hayden was intuitively 'tapped in', I began to open up to my intuition too. We continued to experience the Star energy in the light, through our intuition, intellectual skills and creativity. We will explore not only the Star energy but also the Heart and Earth energy in coming books of The New Way series.

> We will cover more about Star, Heart and Earth energy in the chapter, Snow Globe. For now, you can scan the code to take the quiz to find out more of your True Essence Profile. Do you and your family members hold more Star, Heart or Earth energy?

Hayden and I explored the Star energy in parallel and also many other themes, as mother and child. We both explored the concept of premature birth. Hayden was the child born premature, and I experienced the mother angle. To this day, we continue to explore how we felt and still feel about the repercussions of this event. Another theme we both explored was the school system, Hayden as the child and myself as the mother, which reflected my own experiences in school too.

Honouring your soul's experience

What did this all matter? Well, the day I felt my own frustrations in 'being a mother of a child who is wafty and disorganised', I had an epiphany. I had finally honoured my own soul's experience, as I allowed the emotions to surface. As I went within, I didn't race out to try and change or fix my child and his life challenges in such a hurry. From this inner work, I became more calm, clear and ready to open my heart to my son and his experiences. He felt my patience and compassion with the shadows he explored, and we moved through our challenges as a powerhouse team, albeit far from perfect! These experiences were as much a part of my soul path as they were his.

Most of us mothers haven't considered our own experience as 'a mother of a child who explores certain themes on their soul agreement'. *If we turn away from our own soul's experience, to only hold space for our child and their experience, we miss a big piece of the game of life.* We forget 'you are it'.

As I realised this concept, I saw the energetic law of 'we are all energetically connected'. Not only did I have an experience of Hayden's experience but so did everyone else that observed or heard about his challenges. Each person had the opportunity to connect inwards, to note the sensations they felt from their angle.

> ### ENERGETIC LAW
>
> 'We are energetically connected' - we have an emotional effect on each other, which drives change in a ripple effect, if we embody our life themes.

> We 'do' our mother role as we address our children's daily needs. Not so many 'be' the mother, that is to *feel* what it is like, to embody the mother role in our unique scenarios with our family.

From here on in, I began to play the game of life from the angle of 'what is my experience of this very scene I find myself in?'. As I did this, I then played from what I could control and how I felt about it. It honoured the energetic law of 'you are it'. The more I played this way, the less I needed to try to change, blame, fix and advise others. I didn't need to interfere with others' paths nearly as much and I gained respect and heart connection from my actors as I did this. In turn, many problems I used to have with my actors fell away.

As I named 'this is what it feels like to be a mother of a child who .....', I honoured my own angle of any experience and remembered I had valid feelings about it. I also felt the magic as I played out a theme that must be on *my* soul agreement! The term, 'life theme', rolled off my tongue as I explained this concept to my clients.

> Life Theme - every scene of our day lands us into a theme we agreed to explore, to make sense of this experience as a human. A life theme starts with, 'what it feels like to ....'. Whenever you feel thrown by a challenging scene or an actor in your day, make it your priority to name the life theme you have landed in. As you say it aloud, your soul begins to feel acknowledged for its experience.

On my soul agreement, it is clear that I enlisted the life theme of 'what it feels like to be a mother of a child who is wafty and disorganised'. Of course, this is not the only challenging life theme I experienced or would experience as a mother. As I sat with *any* scene of 'being a mother of a child who...', I allowed myself to feel my valid emotions. As I did this, I then found clarity, passion and an energy that drove me to take inspired action, instead of action through emotional charge. I also didn't turn away from 'what is', by emotional suppression.

Here is an example of how I responded differently as I honoured my own emotions.

When Hayden did something embarrassing at the park, I responded to him with more compassion, if, on the way home, I flowed my stress through tears. 'I'm just feeling judged by those mothers that expected me to have a more perfect child and that I could have done something to stop your impulsive action'.

My children exponentially changed in reflection, as I responsibly honoured 'you are it'. We will go into more detail of this Mother-Child Teamwork in a coming book of The New Way series.

> *Have you sat present with what it is like for yourself as a human to go through your challenges?*

Reading your soul agreement

Soon, I became curious as to what other life themes I had signed up for on my soul agreement. It wasn't hard to work out the ones I had already played out. I scanned my childhood. Life themes explained my whole existence here since point zero.

What it felt like to:

- be the oldest of two girls.
- have a best friend throughout my primary school years.
- pick my favourite colour as fluoro orange to be different to everyone else.
- play netball and the piano.
- go to a catholic girl's high school, although I was not religious.
- have parents who divorced when I was 12.
- go on exchange to Brazil.
- eat a bag of chips off the road with a friend for the fun of it!

These experiences alone were life themes that I could fill pages on. As I scanned my experiences of these themes, I realised the many angles I had embodied. I was technically an 'Earth expert' on what it was like to have a sister, play piano or be an exchange student!

Just when I thought my memories told me I'd had a great time for years in a successful netball team, I realised the many scenes I had buried. It was stressful to be a shooter, particularly when the team needed me to get that goal in. I felt like I had failed my family, who supported me, when we lost. I felt heartbreak as I missed out on the school A grade team. As I remembered these scenes, all the unexpressed emotion surfaced.

The challenging scenes I had been through were real. My heart felt relief and peace as I was freed of this swallowed down stress. It was a green light to continue this inner work. As I embodied the emotions of these experiences, I then carried a different energy about me when it came to these topics, such as feeling pressured in sport. This then rubbed off on how I held space for my boys in their activities.

Not only were my bigger experiences life themes to embody but every single scene of my day was also. The good, the bad and the ugly scenes!

I played with:

- 'what it feels like to have someone honk their horn at me whilst driving'.
- 'what it feels like to sense my partner stressed about his day'.
- 'what it feels like to have unexpected money show up'.
- 'what it feels like to have a child reject a meal I made with love'.
- 'what it feels like to be hugged by my child'.
- 'what it feels like to realise a friend had unfriended me on social media'.
- 'what it feels like to remember when I told a girl in primary school she couldn't play'.

I was the actor in these scenes and I could tell you what was challenging, exciting, disappointing, stressful, satisfying, frustrating, heartbreaking and guilt-inducing about each of my experiences. With some time, I bet you could do this with all of your life themes too.

Doing life from your inner universe

As I tuned into how I felt in each challenging scene I found myself in, the external actors and events that played out became far less of a focus. In fact, it was like the scenes magically readjusted to much better looking ones when I felt into my life themes. People who were hard work in my life started to have reasons to not be a part of my life anymore and faded away. My boys got along better, gave more hugs and spontaneously revealed more of their gifts. Anthony started to have far more compassion for me and my life challenges and became more supportive. I found this space for him too. It's not to say it all magically changed and we lived happily ever after. Heck no. In the upcoming chapter, The Cone, we will go into more detail of what happens energetically when our challenges resurface.

As I saw the magic of inner reflection, I knew I could not continue to point the finger of blame at anyone for how they showed up. In practice, I found out how tricky it was to embody! Despite this, I knew it was not the priority to fix or try to change anyone else. The magic came from the inner work. The external problems literally shifted in ways that I couldn't have thought up myself. This was the start of my road to empowerment and self responsibility. It was magical to co-create with my seed of intelligence rather than my ego's life choices.

Feeling is the key

What I realised is that we are here on this Earth to *feel*. The light bulb went off as my seed of intelligence literally pulled me to be in certain scenes, at certain times. When I forgot something, ran into a long lost friend or my child refused to go somewhere, I realised how divine timing was more in control of my reality than I was. I also realised I had feelings about each of these scenes.

There was an energetic link between the scenes I landed in and the feelings within me. The scenes I landed in were the life themes I could choose to feel into. They forced me to feel 'what it feels like to {insert the exact experience here}'. In other words, as it was time to explore certain life themes on my soul agreement, I found myself in day to day experiences and challenges that corresponded with these themes. To embody these life themes, I had to feel. I had to feel without judgement and notice the perfect order to it all. There were still, however, many, many scenes of my day where I did not feel.

We 'read' our soul agreement as we notice our life themes. We can easily miss 'what is' when we try to do life by what we think it should be or when we race to help or fix others.

Naming life themes

To get clear on the life theme my clients found themselves in, I guided them to start with 'this is what it feels like to…'. Sometimes it was 'what it feels like to be a mother of…' and sometimes it was 'what it feels like to be a woman/partner/daughter of…'. Sometimes it was 'what it feels like to be a child who..', as we felt back to those early scenes. Sometimes it was straight to the scene, such as 'what it feels like to feel cold'.

Here is an example of how a mother might explore her angle of the life theme first and what happens when she doesn't.

Let's say a mother is worried about her child's speech. She circles in on, 'this is what it feels like to be a mother of a child who is misunderstood'. When she names the life theme, as the child's mother, she more easily feels her valid feelings. Immediately, the tears arise from the emotions she has clocked, as 'a mother of a child who is misunderstood'. From this inner work, she can then be present with and hold space for her child, when they face their communication challenges. As the mother feels with her child, reflections for herself around the life theme of 'being misunderstood' start to surface. They occur in her current reality and she also remembers scenes from her past.

If this mother doesn't work to focus on her life theme and 'you are it', she instead gets caught up in her own worries or the concerns of the child's teacher, father, family or friends. She ends up flustered about whether to take her child to speech therapy or how to fix the speech issue if her child refuses to participate in therapy. The distraction to look like she has done something about her child's speech, ensures she misses the life theme she has landed in. She then misses the golden answers for these scenarios that are borne from her inner work.

To put your finger on your own life themes, you can start with the first scene of your day, 'what it feels like to wake up'. You might explore 'what it feels like to wake up… with a sore neck' or 'to wake up… and feel nervous about something that day' or 'to wake up… and be busting to go to the toilet' or 'to wake up… with a hug from my partner'. Each scene causes you to feel very differently!

Perhaps, however, you experience 'what it feels like to wake up' life themes, in the night. Beneath this overarching life theme might be, 'what it feels like to wake up… to my child in the middle of the night', which overarches 'what it feels like to wake up to my child in the middle of the night… because they wet the bed' or '… because they had a nightmare' or '… because they cried to be breastfed' and so on. These are just some life themes of 'waking up in the night because of my child', let alone 'waking up in the night for any other reason, such as a storm'. It is a practice to note how your inner universe honestly feels as you experience these life themes, rather than simply take action.

You can choose any life theme in your day to explore further. We usually get pulled to explore the most challenging ones, where we desperately seek an answer. Look no further for help than your angle of the life theme you landed in.

Why you want to know about Life Themes

It is important to take some time to understand the energetic concept of life themes and why they are on your soul agreement. Remember, you explore life themes in every scene of your day. It is just to remember to take the time to be present with them and to own the power of this. This is key to self responsibility.

As we explore our life themes, we come to our 'soul lessons'. As we make sense of our life themes, we unravel our inner hurts, trauma and old conditioning, energetically creating more inner peace within us. This more harmonious landscape within us begins to attract more pleasing scenes in our external reality. In good timing, as we have embodied all that we need to with that life theme, we take the soul lesson with us and no longer attract scenes of this exact life theme.

> Soul lessons - what we come to, as an empowered outcome of the experience of a challenging life theme. For example, 'no more overgiving to my partner, in areas where they actually don't want my input'.

Here is an example of how our seed of intelligence lands us in challenging scenes until we come to our soul lesson.

Let's say a woman sells a product with a Multi-Level Marketing (MLM) company. Over several years, she experiences many scenes of her day to day life, as she explores 'what it feels like to sell a product via an MLM approach'. She experiences the light side, as she makes new friends, brings in income for her family and even teaches her children about the product. She also experiences the shadow side, as she spends substantial time on the business or away from her children. She feels through her guilt and makes changes, to find more work life balance.

The rules of the company however, force her to do things that go against her. Bigger feelings arise as she feels trapped and inauthentic. She suffers headaches and insomnia, as she eventually acknowledges how stressful it is to have to do something that doesn't feel right, for money. She cries her tears and feels her frustration.

From this release, she finds clarity to finally leave the company. Her seed of intelligence had pulled her towards this experience and particular scenes, to explore the corresponding life themes. Some of these life themes were 'what it feels like to be busy with work and less available for my children' or 'what it feels like to work for a company that makes me do something I don't want to'. Her soul lesson had been to express herself with more integrity than she had been able to, within the confines of someone else's creation. In fact, if she had not moved on, she would have attracted curlier storylines to ensure she felt the pull to leave. The life theme of 'what it feels like to sell a product through an MLM company' was embodied.

> *A life theme is an angle of life we agreed to explore, to embody what it feels like to be a human who experiences this. By default, we better our external reality through this process.*

Working with your soul agreement

Life themes explain your experiences every moment of your entire life. They are in your face if you look! They always begin with 'what it feels like to…..', which is also exactly the way you can tune into and work through them. Life themes can feel positive or negative, light or dark. They will however, always bring both sides and in fact *many angles* to experience, over and over again, until you have.

We leave many life themes unexplored until the right time, such as those who go back to make sense of their childhood in adulthood. Life themes appear and overlap each other in perfect timing and in conjunction with our actors' life themes too. *For example, it is no coincidence that we land in scenes* to explore 'what it feels like to stand up for myself' at the same time we explore 'what it feels like to have a nervous tummy'.

> *We are not meant to notice and embody every life theme of our day but to use this approach to work through our challenges when we feel called.*

We can try to avoid our life themes, particularly the challenging ones we have chosen, however, our inner universe will eventually attract a storyline to swing us back to experience it. *For example, when I realised I was unable to escape my soul work.* As we say 'yes' or 'no' to particular storylines, we experience the very life theme we need to, even if it feels like we've made a mistake or have avoided something. Each scene you land in is no mistake.

We can notice and feel our life themes at any given point, to literally read and co-create with our soul agreement. Our life themes spell out where we need to focus our attention, to best play out our divine path. They guide us to find our soul lessons of which we will go into more detail in The Cone chapter.

Here is an example of how our day-to-day scenes invite us to feel the life themes we land in.

Let's say we plan to vacuum the house but our child falls and hurts their knee. We can see this scene has pulled us to spend time with our child instead. We can then take this divinely-timed scene to feel into 'what it feels like to have a child who has injured themselves' and all that this divinely-timed injury calls for. At first, it may bring up frustration because we have to let go of our little old human's plans to vacuum. It may bring up worry, if they cannot make their sporting event that afternoon, or any other feeling depending on the circumstances. Ultimately, it is an invitation to allow our inner universe to indicate how it actually feels that day.

As we hold space for our own experience, we can then hold a more empowered space for our child. If we don't feel into these life themes, we are likely to respond through huffs, martyrdom or any other emotionally-driven expression. We will look at emotionally-driven expressions in the Monkey Mind Nets chapter.

Here is an example of when we find a soul lesson in our life theme.

Let's say we want to encourage healthy eating for our children. We soon land in the scene of 'what it feels like to have a child who rejects my meals' so that we feel through the messages of this life theme. We may experience soul lessons on why it's important to allow intuitive eating and surrender what we think is best for our child. We don't know our soul lessons until we have embodied our life themes.

Noticing your soul purpose through life themes

Life themes also link us to our soul purpose and constantly nudge us to see the magic of 'who we really are'. Many women of The New Way search for their soul purpose, as they often feel they haven't achieved enough or have lost track of who they are. Their life themes however, tell them otherwise. It is easy to overlook the scenes of our life that don't appear to mean much but continually show us our true essence.

Here are some examples of how you may have overlooked your 'invisible magic'.

* Perhaps you have been in many scenes since childhood, where you were a leader of others, even if it was naughty. You were landed into scenes to practise leadership, in the light and the dark.

* Perhaps, throughout your life, you found yourself in scenes where you magically connected with the fine details of nature or realised how easily you connected with animals. You were landed in scenes where you intuitively connected with elements of the Earth.

- Perhaps you were always prepared to look at yourself and readily owned where you made a mistake. You were landed into scenes to practise self-responsibility.

Our invisible magic are our gifts we barely notice, because they are so innate to us, yet aren't listed on a curriculum or revered by everyone. At any point, we can retrace the life themes we have experienced but never consciously noticed and explored. This reminds us that our soul purpose has been hidden in 'what is' all along.

Feeling your way through

We have been conditioned to suppress our feelings and thus we have disconnected from much of the sensation within us, our power. Because of this, we often get to the end of our day and haven't noticed our inner universe's whispers or even tugs at us. As a result, we play out our life themes quite unconsciously because we don't acknowledge or feel them. Our busyness with life conveniently distracts us from feeling. We also forget to embody our life themes because it is not second nature to us. This is a result of our conditioning to only go out and 'do' motherhood rather than 'be' the mother internally too.

> *The magic is to allow ourselves to feel our experience and to name it as we say 'this is what it feels like to....'. Whether it feels positive or negative, each life theme invites us to embody what it feels like to experience it without judgement.*

We are empowered when we trust that our scenes of life are there to activate us. They are there to be felt for good reason even if it challenges us. Our answers to our challenges are revealed as we work with our specific life themes, which again, are in divine orchestration for our soul path. This is in contrast to how we have been conditioned to seek advice, opinions and even psychic readings or other external input. It is also in contrast to the idea that we must stab around for where to start with our inner work or choose an inner focus that someone else deemed was next.

Initially, it can help us to seek answers externally as we learn to connect inwards. Ultimately however, we separate ourselves from our own connection to the divine as we do. As we play by empowerment, we realise no one can ever come up with the exact answers we need for our unique path better than co-creation with our own life themes.

As we go within, we solve our challenges through empowerment. We don't need to fix, blame, complain and judge, which only projects our rising emotions. Without the charge, others listen to us. As we are more peaceful within, others also feel safe to share more deeply. They get to the heart of the matter as they sense that we won't judge or project our emotions onto them.

> *To be the Creative Director of our life, we must embody our life themes and align with the divine timing of our soul agreement.*

The different types of life themes

Whether we like it or not, our soul agreement lists certain life themes that we agreed to explore at certain points on our life's timeline. *For example, 'what it feels like to be a mother' or 'what it feels like to have to take my child out of school'.* There are also life themes we agreed to continually explore from many different angles throughout our lives such as 'what it feels like to be unheard' or 'what it feels like to be a people pleaser'.

You may explore life themes as the main actor of the scene. *For example, 'what it feels like to be good at soccer'.* You also explore life themes as an observer. *For example, 'what it feels like to be a parent of a child who is good at soccer' or 'what it feels like to have dreamt of playing soccer and instead follow it religiously on the TV'.*

Whatever the scene you are in, this is the angle of the life theme you chose to explore it by. You might be the main actor, the mother of, the partner or ex-partner of, the daughter of, the worker of or any other relationship to the one who has the main experience. *Some examples of this are your experience of 'what it feels like to be the partner of someone going through depression', 'what it feels like to notice my father caring more about my brother than my mother' or 'what it feels like to be the ex-partner of someone struggling with their new partner'.*

It is just as valid to have emotions if you are the observer or 'side actor' as it is to play out the angle of the main actor(s). It is vital to honour that *your* experience is still a life theme on *your* soul agreement before you try to take any action to help, fix or change others. We are all energetically interconnected and naturally feel with others, as long as we are connected to our emotional body. We will soon look at this concept in the Emotional Blackbox chapter.

We can notice our unique angle as 'a mother of a child who experiences certain life themes', before we try to guide our children away from life themes they were always meant to experience.

Life theme in the shadows

We have enlisted gazillions of life themes on our soul agreement, to experience from many angles. At this point in time, our shadows want to be seen first, which is why many women yearn to understand how to play the game of life with more confidence. Hence, we will mostly focus on our challenging life themes in this book.

Here are some examples of challenging life themes you may have experienced or still go through. 'What it feels like to....':

* have a child who won't sleep / stay asleep.
* take my child out of the school system.
* have a partner or ex-partner who doesn't agree with my parenting visions.
* have parents who don't agree with my life choices.
* yearn for more heart connection with my children.
* be a mother who doesn't get enough support to run the house and family.
* be unable to find alone time, to do the things I love.
* do things that don't feel right, for money.
* be exhausted with life.

Our shadow life themes can be big, challenging themes that make themselves known to us. *For example*, *'what it feels like to lose a baby'* or *'what it feels like to be abused'*. They can be subtle, challenging themes that we really do have to get honest and feel for. *This might be, 'what it feels like to never really reach my potential' or 'what it feels like to always get my ideas squashed by the family'*. They might be a recurring challenge that happens sporadically or an ongoing season of life.

Life themes in the light

Life themes can be amazing experiences. *For example*, *'what it feels like to find my soulmate and love them until the day I die'* or *'what it feels like to give birth to my precious child'*. They can also be subtle light ones. *Perhaps*, *'what it feels like to never go wanting'* or *'what it feels like to always have fresh running water'*.

Life themes can be simple everyday experiences. *For example, 'what it feels like to enjoy my warm soup for lunch' or even 'what it feels like to enjoy the act of driving my car here on Earth'!*

We can also play out life themes where we haven't, as yet, had much feeling about them either way. *For example, 'what it feels like to live in x suburb of y country', 'what it feels like to run children to school everyday' or 'what it feels like to go to a certain gym, hairdresser or supermarket'.* They, of course, still bring shades of light and dark as we explore them. In divine timing, we find ourselves in certain scenes to feel the particular emotions that go with our unique experiences.

Your life themes shape you

There are countless factors that shape our expression, both internally and externally. Of course, how we feel internally, at any moment, dictates our expression. We are also an expression of the scenes and corresponding life themes we find ourselves in at any given moment. We will soon look at some examples.

Unfortunately, we have been conditioned to make judgements of each other. We believe that we have chosen, in that moment, to be annoying, boring, weak, emotional or any other 'seemingly negative' quality. We haven't realised that we as individuals haven't truly *chosen*, at any moment, to be like that. We must recognise the countless factors that shape our behaviour. This goes for adults and children.

Here are some examples that show how our expression is shaped by our internal and external factors.

* When I was young, I loved to play in the pool. I knew many pool games and I could do tricks, such as backflips, into the pool. Many years later, Anthony wanted to put in a pool. I wasn't that keen for one but I went forth, as he and the boys really wanted it. It turned

out to be the coldest pool with cold marble tiles around the edge, backed by a shady forest. We even installed a shade sail in case the sun made it hot! As someone who feels the cold easily, I only had to put my feet on the frosty marble tiles and I had goosebumps. I'm sure our friends thought I was boring as I often sat beside the pool while they came and enjoyed it. I felt boring myself. The life theme of 'what it feels like to have a cold pool' forced me to look and feel boring.

As you know, we sold our house and our next house also had a pool. This one was out in the sun surrounded by much warmer pavers. Before long, I was in there and I played games with the boys. They couldn't believe it when I enjoyed myself, let alone when I did backflips into the pool! Finally, I was able to express my fun side. The external factors and the life theme of 'what it feels like to have a warm pool' changed my expression.

✱ Although it seemed like a grand decision to one day take Hayden out of school, the external and internal factors I had felt made sure that I was activated to do so. Despite this, Anthony wasn't sure and others judged me for the 'choice' I had made.

For years prior to this however, I had felt the burn of life themes, such as 'what it feels like to be a mother of a child who was bullied, without real action taken' or 'what it feels like to be a mother of a very bright child who was understimulated at school'. I literally felt pulled to 'do something' and it became obvious that I was energetically guided to get Hayden away from school.

When I got honest, as a human myself, I still had plenty of doubts and emotions as I was pulled down this path. I never thought I would homeschool my child and at times I didn't want to. The journey however, to be 'a mother of a child who left the school system' had started long ago. My seed of intelligence had pulled me into scenes, since Hayden was at daycare, which activated me to feel and see what I needed to do as the time approached.

From these types of experiences, I realised that how I expressed myself and how others saw me, at any given moment, was a result of external and internal factors. *The cold pool was an example of an external factor that changed my expression.* The burning emotions I had felt in previously challenging life themes were internal factors that changed my future expression. *The soul lessons I realised from 'being a mother of a child who was bullied… and bored' were an example of the internal factors.* Others didn't understand my choices because they hadn't explored the life themes that I had embodied.

The thing is, we can't click our fingers and make all of the external factors change, because we decide we want to express ourselves differently. We are in less-than-perfect circumstances for divine reasons. We can, however, have compassion with how we show up each day. We can remember our expression is not always our fault or even what we'd choose. We can also remember that our family members, friends and beyond are also a result of the factors that surround them.

Have a go. How would you express yourself differently, with different external factors and life themes to play out?

* How would you be different if you always had ample money?

* How would you be different if you were given time to yourself more often?

* How would you be different if your only life's role was to honour how you felt?

* How would you be different if your children and partner didn't have their certain challenges?

* How would you be different if you weren't attached to food?

Finding the heart of the matter

As we learn to play the game of life, The New Way, it is vital that we question and feel into, 'What is my actual experience here?'. In other words, what life theme have we landed into? Sometimes it can be easy to put our finger on the life theme we find ourselves in. Remember, in any one scene of our day, there will be several life themes we could list, as we saw in the 'waking up in the night' life themes. Whatever comes to us is just right for that moment in time. We can never get it wrong. If there is another angle to be felt, another scene will appear in good timing. We will look further at the energetics of this in The Cone and Lava Lamp Effect chapters. At any point, our aim is to find the 'heart of the matter'.

Here are a few examples of how to put your finger on the heart of the matter.

* The first time I went to get in our cold pool, I experienced the life theme of 'what it feels like to be freezing cold in my new pool'. Deep down, I felt my charge that it wasn't warm enough for me, even on a hot day. I felt through two angles of 'what it feels like to be disappointed with our new pool... and let alone a big spend'. The first angle was to be disappointed with something that should be fun and exciting, a new pool. The second angle was to be disappointed with something we had spent a lot of money on.

  I then faced the next angle of 'what it feels like to be unable to join our friends'. As I told our visitors that I found the pool too cold, I sensed their disbelief that I really wouldn't get in, like I couldn't let go and have fun. My feelings led me to the next angle of 'what it feels like to be boring'. Now I was at the heart of the matter. This theme showed up in many scenes of my life at that time and was there for me to notice an expression of myself that I didn't like.

* Let's say your extended family organises a restaurant lunch. Your child refuses to put on dressed up clothes and as a result you end up

late. Here, the very scene you find yourself in hints at a life theme for you to explore. In this case, the first life theme is 'what it feels like to be a mother of a child who has a tantrum as we go to walk out the door… with a child who won't change clothes', two angles.

The first angle brings up 'what it feels like to deal with my child's tantrum', which many parents know about. The second angle also brings up 'what it feels like to have a child who resists clothes that society deems as dressed up', also a common theme for sensitive children and their parents. Although common enough, these life themes still raise valid emotions for you as the mother.

The very next scene is the next life theme - 'this is what it feels like to run late… whilst others wait for us', two more angles. The first angle is to be in a rush out the door which can happen in many different storylines. The second angle is to be late for your relatives and their expectations of punctuality. Again, both angles of this life theme bring up separate valid emotions.

As you feel into each life theme, you start to sense the heart of the matter, such as 'I felt stressed to be on time'. You realise your parents' need for punctuality puts you and your child under stress. Your seed of intelligence pulled you into this scene with a child who wouldn't put on certain clothes, so you could feel the need to slow down in life. This scene was not your child's fault as much as an alarm to slow down in your life.

As you feel through what else caused the stress, you explore 'what it feels like to be a mother of a child who does not suit restaurants that require certain attire'. This angle adds to the heart of the matter that family gatherings need to be readjusted to be less stressful.

The heart of the matter is the underlying problem of our life theme, which helps us to find our soul lessons.

To find the actual issue, most of the time we need to experience many similar scenes until we feel, surrender and see what needs to be seen, the heart of the matter. As we get to the heart of the matter, we start to see our soul lesson. In the above example, the soul lesson may have been to realise, 'I need to slow down and create occasions where my child can freely be themselves and I need to talk to my extended family about this'. The chapter on The Cone will explain this further.

We are going through similar experiences

Underneath the different storylines we play out as human characters, our experiences boil down to very similar life themes, such as 'what it feels like to be unheard' or 'what it feels like to give my power away'. Many women share even more specific life themes such as 'what it feels like to have a partner who isn't part of the family life as much as I would like'. Others share the pain of 'what it feels like to have sleepless nights with my baby and not much family support around'. Some feel 'what it feels like to realise life has distracted me from prioritising connection with my children'. As we all honour these real feelings, we are united in compassion and find energy to create change.

If we do not embody our life themes, we can be very quick to judge another's circumstances. Yet the experience we judge can actually boil down to the same life theme that we experience through other storylines. These matching life themes are our shared experiences and opportunities to appreciate how connected we are.

Here are some examples of different storylines connected to the same life theme.

- ✱ Two women wait for their yoga class to begin. One is clearly underweight and the other carries more weight than average. Before the class, they both sit and fiddle with their clothing, which hints of the same life theme - 'what it feels like to feel self-conscious in my body, when I wear yoga clothes and sit in front of a mirror'. One could judge the other as 'so skinny' or 'so fat' yet they both explore the same life theme, just through different storylines.

The life themes bring up common emotions such as shame, frustration and embarrassment at their body and jealousy of body-confident women. They both experience a deep sadness as they reject their physical body, in place of their hurts they experienced as they grew up. Of course, their unique angle is to experience what it's like to be overweight or underweight, which also brings different angles to 'write home' about.

* A couple are in an argument. They are stuck in 'my partner is wrong' or 'I need to convince them of my side' however, they both explore 'what it feels like to be misunderstood'. The heart of the matter is that they both want to be seen, felt and heard. Their behaviours reflect feelings of frustration, anger and ultimately sadness at this.

* Let's look at two women who explore the life theme of 'what it feels like to mother myself'. One lost their mother when they were little. The other's mother was too busy and stressed to take on the mother role, although she was around each day. They both feel abandonment and an overwhelming responsibility to 'keep it all together'. The heart of the matter is that they both don't feel worthy to be cared for.

* Many women experience the life theme of 'what it feels like to be unable to feed my child'. Some have breastfeeding issues. Some have fussy eaters. Others don't even have enough money to afford food for their child. Each of these mothers feel the desperation, guilt and dread of mealtimes, as they go through these challenges.

* The life theme of 'what it feels like to be an unfulfilled mother' is also orchestrated by many different storylines. One woman has a husband who earns plenty of money and drops her children to their private school each day, yet she's lonely and empty. Another

woman homeschools her children yet faces overwhelm each day because she wears so many hats. Despite her best intentions for her children, she wonders why she has no soul fulfilment herself. These two women would appear fundamentally very different in society yet they share one of the same life themes on their soul agreement and feel the same emotions.

At the core of our life themes, we all feel the same spectrum of emotions. We can so easily judge another person's experience, yet overlook that we agreed to explore the same deeper life theme in a different storyline. We can also justify that our experience or storyline is not as 'bad' as another's. *For example, the mother of the fussy eater might claim 'at least we have food on the table'.* Yet, at the core of our life themes are the energy of emotions. Sadness is sadness. Guilt is guilt. Frustration is frustration. As we connect to our emotional bodies, no one feels emotions any more or less than another. We simply feel the intensity of this particular energy through our particular storyline.

The importance of playing the game of life, The New Way

If we *don't notice* the life themes we land in every day, we may:

- ✱ live vicariously through others and forget we have a soul path too.
- ✱ point fingers of blame externally for how our reality turns out.
- ✱ literally attract chaotic scenes on others, particularly our family members.
- ✱ feel washed around by life with bigger and bigger challenges.

As we work consciously with the life themes enlisted on our soul agreement, we use our challenges to help us move into the vibrations of the unexpressed energies within us. As we feel the tension, pain, emotion or discomfort, we can release it from our inner universe. *For example, if we allow our toddler's meltdowns to have us in tears too, it is a golden key to be able to release this old tantrum energy from our childhood.* As we shift ourselves from within, we shift the scenes we don't like, which includes our actors. This is true empowerment and self responsibility. We will look further at this in the coming chapters and more about how important it is to *feel with* our children in a coming book of The New Way series.

As we embody our own life themes, we become a beacon to guide others, to the goodie bag of results that we receive in the process. Some examples of the goodies are:

* inner peace - when you don't have to turn away from any aspect of yourself

* health - physically, emotionally, mentally *and* spiritually

* self-responsibility and empowerment - you own 'you are it' and you are respected for this

* confidence - you know there is a divine order to move through your challenges

* fulfilment - the unexplainable satisfaction as you play the game of life, The New Way

* intuition - you eternally open up to more of your gifts

* energy - to speak up, make change, face another life theme

It is easy to brush over our life themes, particularly when our little old human self prefers to have our life together, sorted and pretty much perfect. It can be easy to throw our hands in the air as we feel confused about where to start with our challenging day to day scenes. Instead, we can play The New Way, as we simply say, 'this is what it feels like to....'.

Summary

* Life themes explain our uniqueness, the countless angles of human life we agreed to explore.

* The life themes we land in are divinely orchestrated and help us to 'read' our soul agreement.

* We do not even need astrology, psychics or advice to tell us what our path is about.

* We are here to feel and embody our soul's angle of each life theme above all else.

* Most of us 'do' our character but forget to 'be' it, which is to remember to feel the life themes we land in every day.

* Life themes are invitations to stay present with each scene of our day.

* They also invite us to embody our emotions as we go, rather than to hold it together, push on, and do life unconscious of the state of our inner universe.

To try ...

We can tap into our soul agreement as we pay attention to each scene of our day and say 'ahh this is what it feels like to…'. We can then connect to how we feel within our inner universe.

Go about the scenes of the rest of your day and take note:

- if you remember to name the life theme - 'this is what it feels like to ..'.

- how easy or difficult it is to connect with the sensations within your inner universe - without any judgement of them.

Your Actors

...those in your external reflect what is there to be felt in your internal...

2014

At two years of age, Declan already showed signs of his ability to intuitively read people. When I asked him to get his dirty clothes from his room, he looked me in the eye, intuitively scanned me and then responded '...NO'. It was quite a slap in the face! I was curious however, because I could tell he had tuned into me before he answered, and he was very cute to do this at such a young age!

Each time Declan scanned me, I tuned into myself. I realised I had already had thoughts of, 'I'll just do it if he doesn't'. Sure enough, every time, he told me 'no'! Instead, I envisaged he had already done the task. By this shift within, I changed the words and how I asked him. I said with conviction, 'Deccy, please go and get your dirty clothes from your room'. He turned around and did it! I couldn't believe it. I shifted within and he shifted in the external.

2015

From about six months of age, my Hayden showed up with eczema and other rashes. At age five, eczema appeared in one of his elbow creases. At that time, I also had a rash in my elbow crease, which was unusual for me. When we saw our chiropractor / kinesiologist, I mentioned how we both had skin issues in the same place. He brushed over it, but I felt a pang inside me that said, 'you didn't understand me!'.

A few years later, I asked a very psychic woman in South Africa. She simply said, 'Yes of course. Hayden mirrors your health issues. He is here to highlight these to you'. I had seen the energetic link between mother and son, and yes, this reflection continues for Hayden and myself.

2016

We visited many people to help us with Hayden's food sensitivities. The problem was, I didn't feel like we could afford their services, let alone the foods and supplements they recommended. Before long, I saw Paul, the man who activated me, and I told him about my problem. He insisted that I see an intuitive herbalist in Canada whose intuition could help us more efficiently.

I told Anthony about Dorothy and he asked me how much. I told him with a nervous tummy. He responded with doubts. I felt like I was squeezed between two panes of glass, as I knew our son needed help, yet I didn't feel like I had the blessing from Anthony to go ahead with it. I cried for the fact that I honoured my heart, the tricky financial position we were in and actually, what was important here. I went back to Anthony and spoke about how we couldn't leave Hayden's health as it was and how much I really felt the nudge to see Dorothy. He responded with, 'well, if you feel that strongly..'. I shifted within and he shifted in the external!

I started to see my family members as the 'actors' in my virtual reality of 'you are it'. You could also see them as 'non-player characters', who forever responded energetically to my inner powerhouse. My actors reflected me whether I liked it or not. Just when I thought I felt happy, one of them came in and did something that raised the emotion, which was already there, within me. The actors in my reality were like a magnet. They highlighted the emotions I had swept to the side earlier in the day or the deeper hurts I was not even aware of.

> Your actors - every person we interact with reflects something to be seen and felt within us, 100% of the time.

The more I connected with my physical and emotional bodies however, the more I felt the discomfort of these rising energies within me. *For example, I felt physically tight in my tongue, jaw or shoulder; or emotionally I felt a lurking frustration or sadness.* There were days where I felt such discomfort that I willed my actors to prod me. They did.

One day on the way to school pick up, I was beside myself with stress around my throat and jaw. Hayden got into the car and told me how they had not dealt with a child who had bullied him. It all came up. Another day, I felt sensitive and tender and Declan opened the car door straight into my tummy. I was finally in tears. As I noticed the rising discomfort within me, it was not usually longer than a day or two before something prodded me enough to release it.

Once I realised how my actors prodded my inner feelings, there was nowhere to hide but to face the elephants I had swept under the rug for so long. I had to get honest with myself about how I felt within my inner universe, and I also had to be honest with my family. I couldn't blame them for their displeasing behaviours. Their reactions nudged me to go within and honour how I truly felt, which I did not always have the energy and inclination to do. Energetics however, didn't care!

> *We are designed to own and co-create with our inner universe.*

The actors in my virtual reality all worked in different ways, at different times. Sometimes they prodded me. Sometimes they held space for me. This all happened in reverse too. I was their actor, who matched up with them perfectly and energetically for their agreed experiences too. At times I prodded them and at times I held space for them. We were divine energetic pairs.

Here is an example of how we all mix and match in how we interact.

When Anthony played my tricky actor, my relationship with at least one of the boys was easier. When it came time for one of the boys to prod me, my relationship was generally smoother with Anthony. When it felt like they were all against me, things went really well with the other actors in my life. Of course, when our whole family connected smoothly, other actors or events, such as the weather or technology, prodded me instead.

Despite the scenes and interactions in our lives that flow, we will always have scenes and interactions that reflect our unresolved hurts too.

'You are it' and 'It takes two'

This brings up two energetic laws - 'you are it' and 'it takes two'. As we have seen, 'you are it' reminds us of the magic that is possible when we shift the energy within us, which shifts how others interact and respond to us. This energetic law reminds us that we are disempowered when we try to change others, if their behaviour makes us feel uncomfortable. Their behaviour simply reminds us of the state of our inner universe.

Next, we can consider the energetic law of 'it takes two'. As we interact with another person, we are *always* a divine energetic pair. We collide with those who magnetically prod our rising energies as we do for them at the same time. If we feel irritated, that day we will surely interact with someone who will behave in irritating ways. If we feel sensitive, we will have interactions with others who aren't sensitive to our emotions, to make us feel this sensitivity. Their types of prodding behaviours also reflect the state of *their* inner universe. This reminds us that we collide with each other by the pull of our inner universes. Of course, the state of our inner universe is linked with our seed of intelligence.

> ENERGETIC LAW
>
> 'It takes two' - we always interact as energetic pairs, to land each other into particular life themes and to feel the corresponding sensations within

Here is an example of how two actors collide, according to the life themes their seeds of intelligence pulled them to land in.

Perhaps a mother has an easygoing day at home with her three children. Her husband arrives home and comments on the chores she hasn't done. She blames him for how he makes her feel because she felt fine with the children. At the time however, the mother has swirling emotions of guilt and unworthiness there within her inner universe.

The inner emotions of guilt and unworthiness energetically link to the life theme of 'what it feels like to have a husband who sees me as not enough'. In truth, she did feel guilty she didn't clean up the dishes, which prodded on her inner hurts of being 'not enough' from childhood. Her husband also landed her in the life theme of 'what it feels like to doubt myself as a mother'. Her husband himself, landed in the life theme of 'what it feels like to have a wife who appears to have it easy at home with the kids'. His unloving comment towards his wife reflected his rising emotions about this. They were a divinely collided pair.

Certain people will prod us at certain points in our lives. We can get tricked that the problem is the particular actor, however, it is simply energetics that they were the 'messenger' to prod us at that particular moment. On other days, it will be other actors.

> *As with 'you are it', our primary issue is the state of our inner universe, which we cannot run from and which attracts our challenging actors.*

If you feel uncomfortable sensations when you interact with someone else, these are *your* sensations to be explored. Yes, you may feel someone else's energy too, but essentially they reflect what is there within you, linked to your life themes and soul agreement. To claim we have picked up on someone else's energy and that it's not ours is a fallacy from the new age spiritual world, to bypass the real sensations of our own inner universe. That is, if someone interacts with us in a displeasing way, there is always something to be honoured within our inner universe. These feelings link with an inner hurt from our past. We will explore this more in the coming chapters.

'You are it' reminds us to own our inner hurts and 'it takes two' reminds us that we collide with others, in perfect orchestration, to prod the energies within *both* of our inner universes. Whilst we must own and explore the energies they prodded within us, we must also remember that they have rising energies to own and deal with too. Anyone who points the finger outwards, hasn't connected inwards to feel how they truly feel. It always starts with 'you are it'. In coming books of The New Way series, we will go into detail on how to do your inner work and then importantly, how to deal with the issue with the other person in empowerment.

There are countless factors at play to ensure that we collide with actors who reflect the state of our inner universe. Your seed of intelligence makes sure of this. Of course, the days where we feel quite clear inside, are the days we find those actors who are happy and easygoing matches too!

Why you want to know about Your Actors

Your actors remind you to feel your inner universe in every scene of your day. It's not just with your family members but with every single actor you come across in each scene of your day. They give you an emotional reaction and it reminds you that your inner state forever communicates to you.

Your actors are merely your magnetic messengers. Your inner state attracts particular actors who behave in particular ways, to land you into life themes to explore. *For example, if someone yells at you, you have landed into the life theme of 'what it feels like to be yelled at'.*

Your family members behave in tricky ways, to invite you to feel. Your children respond to your rising emotions with behaviours that challenge you. It may be in the form of resistance, shyness, overeating, overgaming, rudeness, speech issues, bossiness and more. Your partner will also respond to your rising emotions. They may allow you to annoyingly make all the decisions and have no say for themselves *or* give you resistance all the way. They may whinge, say things without heart, fail to see you, try to control you and more. These behaviours are all an invitation for you to realise how it makes *you* feel inside. Your actors reflect your unexpressed emotions every single time they show up in displeasing ways. The coming chapters will continue to unravel this concept.

> *We cannot escape the energetic laws of 'you are it' and 'it takes two'.*

Own your inner universe

It empowers us to remember that our actors' challenging behaviours remind us when to feel within, to find our divine answers. If someone gives you a 'negative response' to a great idea you've had, they invite you to connect with your inner universe. As you do, you feel the emotions and charge that need to be released before you respond, give up or back down in a more empowered way.

As you release your emotions, your calmness and clarity guides you to see your actors' resistance as your 'divine brakes' on what you may have pushed too soon. In contrast, you may feel the need to explain the strong urge you have to proceed, as I did with Anthony for the herbalist. As you proactively shift your feelings from the inside, your actors won't show up with behaviours that reflect your doubts, worries, frustration and anger, in just as annoying external scenes.

> *Your actors will behave in the most unbelievable ways,*
> *the more you ignore your inner universe.*

The energetic law of 'it takes two' means that we are always perfect energetic pairs when we interact. As you shift within, some actors may leave your life scenes. Others will miraculously surprise you with their congeniality, compassion and respectful new behaviours, that reflect your clearer inner universe. It is an energetic law 100% of the time.

You can certainly feel upset when someone makes you feel uncomfortable, however, this is your chance to remember that your actors are divinely orchestrated to *help you* feel and release the rising energies within you. Remember, to find inner peace means that you will need to and want to get prodded. I'm sure you'd agree that you wouldn't choose to put yourself in those dark and darker places yourself. We will look further at why you want to shift your inner hurts in the Lava Lamp Effect chapter.

The New Way reminds us to honour 'better out than in'.
It is powerful to face the energies within us.

They are the messenger

As you continue to release the pain from your past hurts, you start to feel thankful to these actors who interacted in these prodding scenes with you. You can picture each person as a soul, wearing a certain mask. At the end of your life, as the curtain comes down, they will remove their masks and you will exclaim and joke, 'you got me so good, you did!'.

Remember, if your child whacks you in the face or your partner talks rudely to you, it is your chance to feel the sensations *within* you rather than to primarily blame them. Your actors are the tip of the iceberg, the messengers. They invite you to feel how you truly feel, without judgement. The next step is to shift your inner state as it is useless to hold it against your actors in the external. As you allow your emotions to flow, you start to realise what is truly below it, the deeper hurts they magnetically raise. You then realise your very valid reasons for your inner discomfort, physically, emotionally, mentally and/or spiritually.

Your day-to-day actors help you to circle in towards the deeper energies from the darker places of your life. Firstly, you must feel the rising energies within you about the more insignificant challenges. These day to day prods allow you to practise how to release your inner hurts responsibly and own 'you are it'. As you allow your actors to prod you, even if it seems over the top, you start to connect inwards more efficiently. You see more clearly that your inner work is divinely orchestrated. You can simply explore your day to day challenges one scene at a time. These are the inroads to your deeper traumas, which surface as you become well practised at going within. We will explore this more in the chapter, The Tip of the Iceberg.

In the coming books of The New Way series, we will go through how to do this inner work for yourself and then how to respond and guide your family members in their challenges too. For now, we must learn more about how to play the game of life by the energetic rules.

Summary

* Your actors behave in response to the state of your inner universe, 100% of the time.

* Your seed of intelligence draws you into scenes with actors who are an energetic pair.

* Their behaviours magnetically raise old emotions within you.

* Their behaviours are also driven from their unexpressed emotions.

* You land in scenes to experience the different angles of a life theme.

* We are in empowerment when each person owns their own emotional response - there is no need to point the finger of blame.

To play with ...

In the coming days, notice exactly how you feel within, when your actors are tricky for you. Specifically, how do you express yourself as they do?

The Emotional Blackbox

...feeling cannot be turned off...

2013

At his 'Energetic Anatomy of a Yogi' workshop, Paul introduced me to the concept that our old emotions lie within our muscles and tendons. He proved it as he ran us through a Bikram yoga class. As we squeezed our inner thighs in a squat, he called out things like 'now feel the guilt for the people you've hurt'. We wobbled all over the place as he drew attention to the emotional energy that caused our weakness.

I had practised Bikram yoga on and off for four years, where we held the same 26 postures each time. It was like a baseline for me to see how my physical body felt in each pose on any given day. The practice and my physical body started to teach me.

I became aware of my reduced range of movement in my shoulder, in a particular pose. At one point, it began to feel even more uncomfortable. It was like the energetic charge within my muscles had started to surface. I hadn't noticed this charge before but the sensation at this point certainly got my attention.

As I stretched and expanded this shoulder area in class one day, I suddenly sensed how much emotion I had never expressed from my parent's separation. The energy met me in my throat and my face. I barely got to the car before I cried and cried. The big bubble of energy had surfaced. In the coming days, I gave myself plenty of space to feel it and surprised myself at how much there was. There were many angles of the life theme of 'what it feels like to be a child of divorce'. I had been disconnected from it for a long time and my physical body had numbed it.

The next time I went back to yoga, I could not believe that my shoulder had released so much. The ease with which I did the pose was like a nod from my soul agreement. The peace and flexibility in my shoulder showed me that I had done the inner work. I had felt and released the emotions I swallowed down at the time, which had been stored in this exact spot. I felt so empowered that I had been able to change myself like that.

I went on in this fashion and literally felt the energetic link between my physical and emotional bodies, as I released every emotion that surfaced. This process brought inner peace to the place in the physical that had previously felt discomfort. I used to say to my Anthony, 'I've done that tight shoulder and that left hip and it's just my jaw to go!' because that was all the tension I could feel at that point. That was, until I realised each time I moved through one place of tension, the next body part lit up. There was *plenty more* beyond what I could feel in my jaw.

I began to unravel the emotions of my life's scenes in an order that only the intelligence of my physical body knew. My emotional, mental and spiritual bodies were all tied in too. I hadn't yet seen the energetics of the seed of intelligence, which orchestrated it all in divine timing. I knew however, that I needed to allow the sensations within my body to talk to me rather than judge them myself.

As I allowed myself to feel my inner sensations, memories started to surface. I was then able to feel and remember how I felt in those scenes, much of which I had suppressed and moved on from. Before long, I realised there wasn't a single scene of any memory where I hadn't experienced emotional reactions. From yoga, my connection with my physical body showed me the exact place that these unexpressed emotions were stored in my body. It tensed up, even subtly, as I thought about the previous scenes of my life. It was a muscle on my scalp, the left side of my shin, one particular muscle within my hamstring, a muscle around my tooth or sinus and so on.

As I leaned into the emotions that were trapped in these charged up or painful places, I realised the full spectrum of emotions. My daily challenges helped me to feel the exact vibration of each emotion, as energy within me. *For example, when one son was jealous of the other, I got angry with them. I then realised, although I expressed myself angrily, it was actually jealousy that had surfaced within me. When the boys fought, it was often to do with similar themes from when I was younger.*

The more I craved to flow the discomfort out of my physical body, the more I got to know a much bigger range of emotions than I had ever been present with. There was despair, grief, disappointment, frustration, loneliness, rejection and many more. Just when I thought I was sad, tears didn't flow until I realised the exact emotion that was caught in my physical body.

My physical body was the point of truth. Although it was easier to pretend that I didn't feel certain emotions in certain scenes, my little old human self didn't get to decide what I felt. I literally *experienced* certain emotions at the time and my physical body was the 'emotional blackbox' that recorded them. I could only unlock my physical body as I stayed open to which emotions actually lay there. At times however, it felt easier to pretend I was fine or avoid the life theme I knew I had experienced altogether.

> Emotional blackbox - Our physical body has recorded our emotions in each scene of our human life, since point zero. It has tensed around and numbed much of the energetic charge we would otherwise feel.

I began to notice the signs of trapped emotion when people told me 'I'm fine' or 'I've worked through all of my emotions on that'. At the same time, they tensed their jaw, flared their nostrils, glanced away or allowed a distraction. These reactions show how conditioned we are to disconnect from presence with our inner universe. As we keep our emotional reactions to ourselves, the clever physical body physicalises it, to take the brunt of this unexpressed energy within us. It desperately hangs onto these unexpressed energies, so we don't completely flip it.

The 'emotional blackbox' energetic concept came to life as I used these exact words to explain to my clients, 'feeling cannot be turned off'. 'Feeling cannot be turned off' is an energetic law which exists 100% of the time.

> ### ENERGETIC LAW
>
> 'Feeling cannot be turned off' - We *experience* emotions in every scene of our day. We don't get to decide what we feel. We must embrace 'what is'. Our points of truth of our inner state are : our disempowered behaviours, our external reality challenges and our physical health issues.

Why you want to know about the Emotional Blackbox

Your physical body talks to you through pain, tightness, weakness or other physical issues that you know of, for divine reasons! It lets you know exactly where you have stored certain emotions from your corresponding life scenes. Discomfort is where this energy attempts to rise, yet your physical body tenses around it when you haven't released this emotion. Pain is your invitation to lean into it, to release it. We will cover this in more detail in upcoming books of The New Way series.

The physical body takes the brunt

Our physical body has stored our unexpressed emotions since point zero. For most humans, it is a typical pattern to tense and clamp down on our rising inner hurts, to 'keep it together'. We may purse our lips, tense our scalp, squeeze our jaw or tighten our back muscles in response to the scenes of our life that challenge us. We have convinced ourselves not to feel our justified daily emotional reactions, as we are not accustomed to feel this energy trapped within us. Despite this, feeling hasn't been turned off. Instead, we control the flow of our inner universe as we tighten our muscles, tendons and fascia, in many places of the physical body.

Our trapped energy explains much of what society has been puzzled by, as far as our health issues and life challenges. The schooling, medical and even healing worlds have looked for work-arounds, to explain our physical, emotional, mental and spiritual challenges. The answer however, is right there in front of us.

> *When we don't express our emotions, our physical body is forced to tense our muscles and fascia to hold onto them.*

We experience many physical side effects because we do anything to avoid expression of our vulnerable side.

Here are some examples of how the physical body takes the brunt:

- tight muscles and fascia - such as hamstring issues, back pain, tight jaw
- weak muscles and fascia - such as slumping, lack of fitness, ankle injury
- common physical health issues - such as headaches, ear infections, back pain
- bigger physical health issues - such as cancer, endometriosis, arthritis
- physical body anomalies - turned in feet, poor eyesight, bunions
- physical discomfort - ticklishness, lactic acid, cramps
- developmental anomalies - speech issues, poor fine motor control, crooked teeth

Each of these presentations indicates that the physical body is 'at limit' of the emotional energy it holds onto, in a certain place. The stored energy in specific muscles and fascia results in pain. This stagnant energy attracts disease or specific anomalies to our human expression. *An example is a child who can't move their tongue and jaw for efficient speech because these muscles are heavy with stored emotion and are already at capacity.*

Finding the root cause

Think about all of the different approaches people employ to try to deal with the above issues. Some will turn to the medical system. They seek pharmaceutical treatments or surgery, to treat the pain, kill the pathogen or cut out the issue at the site. Some will turn to alternative health approaches, such as herbal medicines or supplements, to see if this helps the body physically. Some will seek paediatric allied health professionals, who literally try to work the muscles to improve the issue. Many see cramping muscles as a sign for more magnesium or ticklishness as just 'one of those things'. None of the above approaches are incorrect, as they allow more humans to explore the ins and outs of these approaches in detail themselves.

With *all* of these more well-known approaches however, the unexpressed emotions are left within the person's being, like a weed that was not pulled out by the root. This stagnant energy either progresses the issue or attracts another life theme, in an invitation for the root of the weed to finally be pulled.

Here is an example of how a person continues to land in scenes to invite them to feel their trapped energy.

Let's look at when orthodontists use braces to twist a child's teeth into place. Before this, the child stored unexpressed emotion in the muscles within their palate and gums. This trapped energy tensed these muscles and pulled the child's teeth out of place. Throughout the braces process, these muscles are forced to relax. The problem of crooked teeth is eventually fixed.

As the child's muscles are forced to relax however, the child feels the discomfort as the energy swirls in their inner universe. If the child doesn't continue to release the trapped emotion, their body clamps down on the energy with perhaps a tighter jaw or scalp instead. They may later experience migraines or family disharmony when they have their own family. These storylines prod them to release the stored anger within their facial muscles that was swallowed down in their childhood family challenges. The braces process was merely another invitation to hold space for our child's unexpressed emotions.

If we release our unexpressed emotions, we do the work from the root cause. This literally dissolves tension, disease, pain and even reverses seemingly 'incurable' issues, such as poor eyesight and ticklishness. The New Way invites us to remember that we as 'player one' can heal ourselves, if we work with our life themes and inner universe.

> *Disease forms in the very places our physical body constricts around our unexpressed energies.*

As we comprehend the strain on our physical system, when we hold onto our emotions, we start to change our stance on emotional expression. We realise it's actually powerful to be guided by the feelings within our physical and emotional bodies. This process, by default, unravels our health issues in divine order. We then start to see the amount of energy we have exhausted by the conditioning to research, pay for and go through with sometimes challenging approaches to improve our health. Often, we then realise they were band-aid fixes or not even our unique answer. It almost feels too simple to honour our inner universe and to trust it is the answer we seek.

Our unexpressed emotions explain our character's presentation

We exist under the energetic law of 'better out than in'. Our physical body expels vomit, ear wax, snot and splinters. We consciously flow our urine and faeces. Imagine how you would *behave* if you held in a poo for a year or a decade? You would lose mental focus, creativity, patience and drive to do life, because your physical body would need to use all of its resources to hold it in. Alternatively, your nervous system may completely switch off the desire to expel this entity, which would make you feel 'switched off' too.

> ENERGETIC LAW
>
> 'Better out than in' - our body seeks to expel that which is designed to flow, including vomit, ear wax, splinters, urine, faeces and emotions. There is a cost to try and block that which wants to flow.

Whilst our unexpressed emotions drive our physical body issues, they also explain our other shadow presentations. As we are 'full up' with emotion, our mental focus starts to wobble. We cannot stay present with life and others. We lose track of what is important to us. We communicate with far less sophistication. Our spiritual health is also affected. We question life. We give up more easily. We lose track of our connection to our divine potential.

We diagnose ourselves in all sorts of ways, to explain our shadow presentations. We declare depression, anxiety, sensory processing issues, stuttering, autism, suicidal, midlife crisis, perimenopausal, pathological demand avoidance and more. We must remember that each human changes their presentation as they hold onto the emotions they clocked from point zero. Any expression that is not from our true essence is all changeable. We will cover this in more detail in the Monkey Mind Nets chapter and look at diagnoses further, in an upcoming book of The New Way series.

Our uniqueness

It is important to remember that we are *not* all here to move straight into emotional embodiment. You surely know if your emotions feel ripe to release. If they are, then continue to flow your emotions as responsibly as you can. If not, it is likely that another person in your family feels and releases emotions quite readily. If it's not you, more often than not, it is one of your children. The family bubble always seeks balance and there is always at least one person who is more emotional.

> Family bubble - the dynamic ball of energy that interconnects all family members in a family unit. As one member changes, to seek balance, the other members are drawn to change.

The person who feels their emotions the most, does best when those around them understand their pull to flow these energies. If it is another person in your family, your role is to continue to welcome and embrace emotional expression, so that they feel safe to do so. We must recognise the subtle signs we give off that suggest 'emotional expression is not welcome or an empowered thing to do'.

In the meantime, you can begin to reconnect with your emotional and/or physical bodies. Women, in general, are to explore emotional embodiment before the men. Whether it's yourself or another family member who is ready to honour their feelings, you start to see the amount of time, energy and money saved as you practise this empowering approach. You seek less outside fixes and answers. You land on 'what is' more efficiently.

If you don't sense your emotions within you, know that your energetic emotional blackbox runs subconsciously. This happens particularly if you disconnected from feeling your emotions for fear, when you were younger. The idea that our physical body holds onto our unexpressed emotions upsets those who want to put their past behind them. It can be difficult to see what is positive about emotional reactions that involve heavily shunned emotions, such as jealousy, grief or anger.

Our points of truth

Our external reality persists with challenges until we get honest about how we feel. No matter how much we try to turn away from our inner sensations, there are three points of truth that remind us of our unexpressed emotions:

* our behaviours, words and tone of voice, driven by our charge
* challenging scenes in our external reality
* physical health issues

No matter who tells you to think positively, to get over it or any other strategy to avoid feeling, remember that these people are likely disconnected from their physical and emotional bodies. Your physical body is your point of truth, of the energy that swirls within you. You cannot cry too much if the energy wants to flow out. Trust it is valid and of volume because we have clocked emotions to every scene of our life!

Our seed of intelligence is kind. We can only face so much physical, emotional, mental and spiritual tension within. We can also only play out so much corresponding chaos at any one time in the external world. Whilst some areas of our life require attention, others flow more smoothly. Whilst some areas of our physical body ache, others will be numb or at peace. Of course, life can seem quite chaotic and/or our physical body may feel the brunt of it all, because we have so much backlog to express. In any case, as we feel through our smaller day to day challenges, we circle inwards to the deeper shadows of trauma. In divine timing, we are more confident and efficient to do this. It is agreed upon and inserted into our seed of intelligence.

Summary

* We overrode our innate urge to release our emotions, as those around us gave subtle and not-so-subtle signs to stop it.

* Our emotional blackbox however, clocks our emotional reactions to each scene of our life.

* Our physical body holds onto these unexpressed energies so that we keep it all together.

* We might tell ourselves that we feel fine; however, our health issues, day to day external challenges and disempowered behaviours are the real points of truth.

* We must connect back to our inner universe, so we can change the state of these points of truth.

To explore ...

Spy on the actual state of your inner universe. Do you sense your points of truth :

- more so from within, such as physical body issues?
- by your challenging scenes on the outside?
- as your less-than-empowering behaviours?

Remember that all of these points of truth are your reminders that you have emotions ripe to connect with and feel.

Lava Lamp Effect

...the state of your inner universe dictates everything in the external - not the other way around...

2019

Over the years, I tuned inwards and allowed myself to feel the life theme of the experience I found myself in. I processed a lot of challenging scenes in my day to day life. I felt through certain parenting challenges, tough ones with friends and even with my pet. One day, I realised something big. That morning, I already knew that I felt irritated. I wasn't myself on the inside. I was short with the boys, even though I tried to stay calm. I knew it would be 'one of those days'.

Later that day, I went to do a quick trip to the local IGA supermarket. Declan heard and announced that he wanted to come so he could buy chocolate with some birthday money. Immediately, I felt my neck tense as we went around the merry-go-round on the life theme of 'what it feels like to be a mother of a child who insists on buying loads of chocolate to eat, despite wanting him to stay healthier'. I also knew it affected our heart connection if I interfered with his pull to play out this life theme, so he came.

When we got there, he decided to buy a box of Lindt chocolates at the full price of $20. My neck burned and my jaw tensed. I couldn't help it, 'No, that's too much. You already know this box is on sale at Woolworths. Can't you wait until tomorrow?'. He brought me into yet more scenes of 'what it feels like to have a child who insists on buying chocolate' and also 'what it feels like to watch your child throw money around, like it's confetti'. Of course, Declan dug his heels in and insisted that he buy it. We had a tussle in the aisle whilst he refused to allow me to leak any of my issues at him. I had no choice but to literally let tears surface, as I gave in.

We got back to the car and I let it up. He tapped somewhere deep and on a day like today, I was ready to crack. I talked 'open diary style' about the frustration in what I saw was a waste of birthday money, excess sugar and the regret that he always went through after he did this type of thing. I started to dry my eyes as we arrived home, before I saw our garden...

The new mower guy was in action at our place. Our whole front garden was cut to the ground, whipper-snippered, bare. The young native plants I had grown were destroyed, along with our herbs and pineapple head that we had tended to for ages. I could barely see through the tears that leaked from the shock of it.

I questioned, were my tears that morning about the chocolate box or the mower man? I wanted to blame something for how I felt. This is when I clearly saw, it was both and it was neither! In energetics, it's always all or nothing. I was already sensitive that morning. My seed of intelligence clearly dropped me in certain scenarios so that I cracked. Both scenes brought up the feeling of helplessness. My tears weren't really about *either* scenario. They were actually more so about the energy that had swirled within me, that was ready to express. My feelings were also related to *both* scenarios because they matched the helpless feeling that arose within me from that morning. It gave me no choice but to feel and express these deeper energies. The divinely orchestrated scenes, which I had no control over, helped me to feel the unique vibration of the emotion of helplessness.

From this, I pondered even more on the energetic link between our feelings on the *inside* and our challenges in the *outside* world. When I named the emotion my boys felt in each challenging scene of their day, it was the same type of emotion. *For example, one particular day I said, 'That would make you feel frustrated', 'argh you'd be frustrated again', frustrated, frustrated, frustrated. The scenes continued until a big enough scene was the final straw for them to really get frustrated and let it all up.*

It is like the energy within us is a ball of rising emotion. This ball of rising emotion wants to be prodded and each scene on the external is simply an invitation to lean into it. What if we could lean into and release that frustration after the first scene?

I practised it myself. As soon as I noticed swirling emotions within me, I leaned into the energetic ball I knew was there and released my tears. I felt more empowered as I didn't need to look for who or what was to blame for how I felt. When I couldn't stay present with it to release it, I used my challenging scenes to bring me back inwards, to feel those emotions. As I did this, I found inner peace and claimed self-responsibility. I noted that as I worked with my inner universe, I worked with the energetic law of 'you are it'. Every time I was challenged on the outside, it was an inside job.

For the boys and myself, the sooner we got honest about our emotional reactions and made time to feel them, the sooner our day went more smoothly. If I stewed on something or felt tightness in my jaw as I went to bed, I made the time to honour the emotions that arose within me. I then slept *much* better, woke in a better mood and the boys and I flowed so well the next day. That is, until the next energetic ball of emotion rose up to be addressed.

When I rushed and stressed, as I tried to get the boys out of the house, I allowed myself to crack over the frustrating things they did. I got honest about my rising emotions and brought it back to the life themes I found myself in, such as 'I'm just tired of doing this without much support', 'I'm worried that you're going to cause trouble at our gathering' or 'I'm actually worried about money right now'. Immediately, I didn't need to point the finger at the boys, who simply landed me in these life themes, to feel.

As I surrendered to the idea that sleep was more important than emotional release, I made the time to feel, even late at night. As I let go of the need to be on time, I released my emotions until I felt clearer and ready to get on with my day. The boys reflected this as they consequently agreed to get in the car to go to school or got along with the other children at our homeschool gathering.

If I tried to push through and get on with our day or night, rather than honour my inner state, I always ended up with the opposite result. *For example, when I tried to sleep it off, one of the boys wet the bed and woke me up or* the next morning was chaos. *If I ignored my stress and went to a social gathering with the boys, they ended up in some altercation with the other children.* I was reminded yet again of 'you are it'.

Although it seemed over-the-top to really let it out about a smaller issue, I started to trust, 'I won't have any prodding scenes like that, now that my charge is gone'. Sure enough, the day or night simply flowed. I didn't attract tricky scenes from my inner universe because I was free of that ball of energy. I was in a different vibration and it was like I had changed tracks and gone down a different trajectory of how the day would have panned out, if I had not expressed my emotions.

Of course, on that IGA and mower man day, I could have justified my reactions because of Declan's or the mower man's actions. This type of expression however, didn't reflect self-responsibility. The rising energies within me attracted my reality. What I could control was how I flowed them.

When we own that our external challenges are there to free us of our inner hurts, we play by empowerment.

The rising energies

One day I saw the 'lava lamp' concept! Our emotions rise like blobs of energy, just like the blobs in a lava lamp. Ever-rising and all different sizes, they continually invite us to notice and work with them. They come one by one, like contractions in labour, rather than a continuous stream of rising emotion. We could also see this analogy like the ever-changing patterns of weather, all orchestrated by many factors. The 'lava lamp effect' explains the concept that our unexpressed emotions continuously rise and they attract our reality in the external world. Our reality is not created by what we think about.

> Lava Lamp Effect - emotions we have clocked in the past, continue to rise like packages of energy. These attract the scenes we land in, which make us feel the exact emotion that arises.

The smaller blobs

As with the lava lamp effect, our smaller 'blobs' of emotion, or rising energetic packages, may be noticed when we feel a little bit tender, out of sorts, irritated, sore in any place, grumpy, stressed or more achy than other days. As these smaller blobs rise, they 'cloud' us and make it tricky to express ourselves from our true essence, our light. We may snap at others, respond from fear of missing out or try to control others. Remember, we have been conditioned to blame the feelings we feel on what happens around us. We haven't realised these sensations arise from within.

> True Essence - our unique true nature, which we express when we are not 'clouded' by our rising inner hurts.

The bigger blobs

When the bigger energetic packages rise however, it can feel like we literally are the lava lamp blob! We may experience a lot of pain in our physical body, feel anxious and panicky, get pushed to lose it or feel seemingly unable to feel light again. We can literally feel beside ourselves. It may be just for a day or it may be for some period of time.

In those times of 'I AM THE BLOB!', it's like the blob is so big, we can't see around it. We lose connection to our true essence, the divine.

We see our life through the filter of this big, energetic package. If we don't express it, to shift it, we show up as what the old world may call depressed, low affect, stoic or unemotional. As we saw in the Emotional Blackbox chapter, we lose connection with hope and our life force.

For many however, we are unable to keep it together, no matter how much we try to. For those who do crack, including children, the old world may call this a meltdown, nervous breakdown, panic attack, anger issues, explosive-type, pathological demand avoidance, anxiety and the like.

Some people contribute their less-than-magnetic expression or perceived shadows to the astrology at the time or other justifications such as tiredness, the food they ate, the mosquitos, their menstrual cycle, a diagnosis or any event or actor that has supposedly caused it. Any of these justifications keeps us distracted from simply feeling inwards and the empowered aim of inner work.

'You are it' reminds us to acknowledge that our inner hurts continue to rise as energetic 'blobs' or emotions. Empowerment is to reflect inwards rather than make sense of our reality externally.

Divine timing

It is generally accepted that the universe is in constant expansion. The energetic law of 'we are in constant expansion' reflects this dynamic within our inner universe too. By default, this outwards pull opposes our physical body's inclination to contract and hold onto our unexpressed energies. In other words, whether we like it or not, emotions we have held onto since point zero of our life continue to rise for us to feel. As this energy swirls within us, we attract how the events and people in our external world play out, in perfect sync with the life themes that we agreed to on our soul agreement.

> ### ENERGETIC LAW
>
> 'We are in constant expansion' - the constant outwards pull which opposes our physical body's inclination to contract and hold onto our unexpressed energies.

'We are in constant expansion' reminds us of another part of the game of life that we do not have control over. As with all energetic laws, it is true 100% of the time. It is the energetic pull to ensure that we continue to move forwards with our challenges, rather than back away. By the divine beat of our seed of intelligence, our emotions rise, one blob after another. We must humbly accept that we can choose to feel or will get forced to feel.

The origin of our lava lamp

The energetic 'blobs' that create the lava lamp effect within us have been there since point zero. It is like the lava lamp was switched on at birth and the first blob was activated to rise for the first life theme we landed in. In divine orchestration, this blob perfectly matched the situation we landed in as we took our first breath. Each of us landed into very different scenes at our birth, of which most of us have no recollection. We all however, expressed our emotion and released this first blob of the lava lamp through our first cries. It may have been a blob of overwhelm, fear, pain or other.

As babies in our era, there were not many perfect births, where the baby felt at peace in their very first scene. Despite this, one thing that worked for us was that we were still in connection with our reflex to flow emotions. You can imagine that as the years went by, we didn't express all of these divinely timed blobs, although they continued to rise. This is one place where we lost track of how to play the game of life by energetics.

Why you want to know about the Lava Lamp Effect

Remember that to play the game of life, The New Way, is to feel. Both the emotional blackbox and the lava lamp effect are energetic concepts that represent the energetic law of 'feeling cannot be turned off'. The concept of the emotional blackbox shows us that we have clocked emotions to the scenes of our past, whether we like it or not. The unexpressed energy sits where our physical body is tightened. The lava lamp effect then shows us that these stagnant emotions will forever rise in perfect order, as an invitation to feel them, prodded by our challenging external scenes.

In the Life Themes chapter, we saw that we can find our soul lessons as we feel these emotions. The upcoming Monkey Mind Nets chapter will go through what happens to our character's expression if we don't feel the 'blobs' as they arise. The Titanic chapter will show us why it can take some emotional release before we see bigger changes in the external.

It is important to continually remember that we have been conditioned to suppress our feelings. The lava lamp effect however, reminds us that these old unexpressed energies are still there, as we feel challenged by our day to day scenes. Of course, it is a practice, to feel safe and willing to feel our emotions. Remember that our seed of intelligence places us in scenes every day that will magnetically raise our charge, so we can feel it and release it. It invites us to find our way back to inner peace.

We are not in control of our mood

As we see that our inner universe has a changeable 'energetic climate', just as the weather changes all day long, we can also consider that how we feel emotionally is actually out of our control. We can think that we create our happiness through our thoughts and view on life. We must consider however, that at any given moment any disaster, out of our control, can instantly change our mood. *For example, we receive a phone call that a loved one has passed away.*

In my story, when Declan bought the Lindt chocolate, I could have told myself to "pull it together, there are worse things out there". The very next divinely orchestrated scene however, where I saw what the mower man had done, insisted that I stayed with how I truly felt on the inside. When a blob of a certain emotion arises, we must get honest, to honour 'what is'.

> *Our inner universe can be seen like the weather. The weather constantly changes, no matter what time of the day or night. It can be sunny, dark or anywhere in between.*

If we don't release the blobs

As we have seen in this chapter, our unexpressed energies continue to rise as opportunities to feel them. We also saw in the Emotional Blackbox chapter that if we don't release the charge of an energetic package as it rises within us, our physical body constricts around it and we change our behaviours.

Our unique soul agreement even lists the life themes of 'what it feels like to hold my unexpressed emotions in certain types of places in my physical body'. *For some, they tense around their throat as they sense a big blob of sadness. That then pulls their shoulders in, which eventually gives them a stooped posture. For some, they tense their head area as old anger blobs rise up and they end up with migraines. Others tense the smaller muscles around their nose or forehead, when they feel subtle blobs of an emotion like disgust or frustration, which results in sinus issues.*

> *We have been conditioned to suppress our emotions because it is the portal to be able to connect with our divine seed of intelligence and who we really are, which is powerful.*

As we learned in the Emotional Blackbox chapter, we have a trade off if we don't allow our emotions to flow. Below are the side effects that energetically happen if we constrict our emotional flow. That is, we *will* have at least one of these side effects, if we don't get honest with the state of our inner universe, as a 'lava lamp blob' of energy rises. Let's remember our three points of truth.

We may:

* leak this energy at others -more detail in the coming Monkey Mind Nets chapter
* attract challenging scenes in our external reality, which keeps us disconnected from our seed of intelligence
* attract bugs or weaken our cells

In other words, you don't want to hold it together, you want to crack! As we respect the energetic law of 'better out than in', we aim to flow our emotions responsibly.

> *Our seed of intelligence shows us that we are designed to flow emotions. It is the divine timekeeper of our lava lamp effect, which pulls us into matching scenes to make us feel.*

The lava lamp effect guides us to self-responsibility

As I mentored women in their life challenges, we came across 'feeling cannot be turned off', which guided them to own 'you are it'. They were confused or frustrated when they made the effort to meditate, to find their calm. 'Argh Heidi, the minute I walk out of my meditation, my children fight and I'm mad again', they said, as they blamed their children for this problem. The children however, energetically reflected a rising 'lava lamp blob'. The mums wanted to push away these rising emotions because their little old human was told that meditation was their answer to peace and they wanted to make that happen. Their children's behaviour however, reflected the state of their inner universe, 'what is'.

> *Our thoughts are a result of how we feel as our old emotions rise. If our lava lamp is quite clear, we can feel quite amazing about life. If a big blob of old emotion surfaces, we can start to dread life or hear negative self-talk.*

As we go The New Way, we must acknowledge the actual state of our energetic climate rather than what we want it to be. As our energies rise in perfect order, we are guided to do the shadow work and release this first. We cannot hold onto the light if we try to disconnect from the discomfort through practices such as meditation.

As we co-create with our inner universe and release the rising energy, we will naturally find inner calm and won't necessarily need to withdraw from life to meditate. Instead, we receive clarity on-the-go and we *become* peace as we clear our inner hurts. We understand that our children prod us to feel our emotions, as they reflect the energetic climate of our inner universe. We then don't need to fix and change these actors in our reality, which includes many perceived childhood health and developmental issues.

We can easily forget the lava lamp effect that goes on within us and instead see that our actors are the problem. Here is another common scenario I hear from my clients. 'But Heidi, I am so energised when I'm at my job. I'm fine. The minute I enter the house, my partner triggers me and my children immediately send me into a spin'. Again, we can only turn a blind eye to our inner sensations for so long. We *can* enjoy what lights us up at our job. As we saw in Your Actors chapter however, our inner universe constantly attracts specific actors and scenes that invite us to lean into our rising energies within us at any moment. No matter how much our ego would like us to ignore our inner discomfort, the energetic laws of 'you are it', 'we are in constant expansion' and 'feeling cannot be turned off' are always at play. The energetics don't even care if it's our birthday or we are on holiday!

Some mothers claimed that it was their *children's* meltdown and they refused to ruin their high vibe to feel what their child reflected. As these mothers attempted to maintain their calm, they essentially 'split' from their emotional and physical bodies, their point of truth. As a result, their child screamed louder to energetically remind them, 'Mum, I am reflecting your actual inner state'. We will cover the importance of mothers feeling *with* their children and how to do this with Mother-Child Teamwork, in an upcoming book of The New Way series.

The sooner we get honest about how we actually feel, the sooner we are able to read our energetic climate at any moment in the day and do something about it. We allow our children or partner to prod us, to work with the life theme they land us in. We then enjoy our job *as well as* our family. We meditate in far more peace and clarity. Through this process, we begin to see and change our behaviours of victimhood and disempowerment.

We find out what we feel for

Although emotional expression can be seen as weak or even painful, our challenges arise so we can *feel* what we care about, what we chose to stand for in this lifetime. As we feel into our day to day scenes, we connect with our soul agreement, life themes and soul lessons. We literally unfold our concept of truth and identity from a different place than sometimes what our ego thought we were about.

The New Way brings more depth to the concept of values, with the concept of life themes. Values are an important tool however, they don't always link us to the details of our soul agreement. Let's look at both concepts.

Life themes

As we experience a challenging scene in our day, we can name the life theme we landed in. In good timing, we can then feel into our rising emotions. As we do this, we find out what we stand for. We embody how much we feel about a certain theme of human life. These linked emotions indicate who we really are and give us energy to take action as well as courage to express a new part of ourselves.

Here is an example of how I found out what I stood for by feeling.

As I struggled to keep Hayden entertained when he was little, I found myself in the life theme of 'what it feels like to be a mother of a bright child who burns through toys'. When Hayden got into trouble at school, it often stemmed from his angle of the life theme of 'what it feels like to be a child who resorts to crazy behaviours because I am so understimulated'. My lava lamp blobs of frustration arose in perfect timing as the school reported Hayden's bad behaviour. They refused to link it with his understimulation.

I felt the anger of 'what it feels like to expect others to provide a stimulating environment for my child, yet have them turn on me and my son when he misbehaves through boredom'. The more this went on, the more my anger, frustration and eventually sadness came up. I found out what I stood for. The anger and sadness turned to passion in what I wanted to yell from the rooftops, 'We need to work harder to tune into what our children are about and provide them with opportunities to bathe in these interests. Curriculums and even well-meaning, adult-designed activities just don't cut it!'.

That is what I stood for. Even just a year before this, I had no idea that it would be something that I would feel such passion for.

What we stand for often surprises us. I was next amazed when I realised that I stood for the children who craved screen time, to be supported by their parents. I had been conditioned to value natural environments, face to face contact and to do something with your hands rather than through a screen. As a mother however, I learnt that my Hayden was drawn to technology. His seed of intelligence pulled him towards a screen wherever he was. He excelled in coding and even gaming. When I didn't honour the pull of his seed of intelligence however, Hayden started to respond with angry and disrespectful behaviours towards me. Before long, I was forced to either understand Hayden's pull towards technology or lose his heart connection with me.

What I wanted for Hayden was ego-driven as it did not honour his connection to his seed of intelligence's pull. Through this experience, I realised how much I prioritised heart connection with my child. So I went through the painful and emotional process to let go of what I thought was best for my child. When I saw the cost of parent-child relationships in my work, my passion then grew to honour all children's soul paths. I saw how we need to honour the child's seed of intelligence when it indicates it wants to explore a certain life theme, in *all* its facets, dark and light. Our children's path is not perfect but we can honour their soul agreement and bring unconditional love.

As I embodied my mother role, I also began to stand for how important it is for us mothers to honour the tug of our seed of intelligence too. We cannot just give way to our child's seed of intelligence without feeling into our own. *At times, I had to check in with the amount of time Hayden spent gaming. My seed of intelligence always indicated when he took it too far as I started to feel desperation or frustration.* We will look at this further in Mother-Child Teamwork in the coming books of The New Way series.

> *Our emotions, divinely connected to our soul path, help us to realise what we feel strongly about.*

Our life themes and what we stand for are borne from our challenges. As we land in challenging scenes and feel through them, we change as a person. As we continue to feel through our recurring life themes, we find the passion to do something or to speak up. The more we feel, the more we stand for a growing number of life themes. The specifics of these, support us to know ourselves in detail and to talk from a quiet power about them, rather than a need to fight for them.

> *We need to feel, to connect with what we stand for on our soul agreement.*

Common challenges that women are invited to feel into and take a stand for are:

* to have community - from the life theme of 'what it feels like to have little support with a young family'

* to have children who know themselves - from the life theme of 'what it feels like to have shy or people-pleasing children'

* to have children who are received for their uniqueness in their community - from the life theme of 'what it feels like to have others judge my child' or 'what it feels like for my child's gifts to slip through the cracks at school'

* to have men who are confident fathers - from the life theme of 'what it feels like to have to encourage the father of my children to connect with their children'

Values

Values are a powerful tool to begin to tap into what we stand for. The concept of values is to make changes to our life so that we stand behind what we value. As we saw with our seed of intelligence however, is that it pulls us to the scenes that we need to experience. We don't always get to live by what is important to us just when we choose to!

Sometimes we are pulled into the seasons of our life where we do *not* experience our values, such as when we value family harmony but we play out family challenges. Our seed of intelligence does this so that we can feel *how much* we yearn for the opposite. Instead, if we pathologise the scenes we land in, we may feel that we have failed or need to distance ourselves from the actors. It appears that they caused the problems that go against our values.

Here are some examples of how we can name what challenges us and use our emotions to say 'yes' to what we yearn for.

* Maybe we feel that we need to separate from our partner if we have continued arguments. Instead, we can see the invitation to firstly feel our life theme - 'what it feels like to not have a harmonious, respectful relationship with my partner'. Then we use this emotion to yearn for and insist on the opposite.

* Maybe we feel that we need to get a diagnosis of autism or pathological demand avoidance for our child, who constantly brings resistance to our family's daily scenes. Instead, these scenes invite us to feel 'what it feels like to experience challenging scenes with my child everyday'. Then we can yearn for and insist on the opposite.

As we do the inner work on these life themes, slowly but surely we find more respect and harmony in our inner universe, which begins to get mirrored by our actors in the external. We don't necessarily need to divorce or diagnose, which of course, is difficult to believe when we play the game of life from old conditioning. We will go through this in more detail in the chapters on The Cone, Yearnings, The Rainbow and The Titanic.

> *As we embody our life themes we find out what we feel strongly about, what we stand for. Values are a word we can claim but may not have embodied in every sense of the word.*

Although we may intuitively choose our values, it is also possible to choose them from an ego point of view. That is, what we'd like it to be. We are often taught to identify our values through a more intellectual approach, to *choose* them. On the contrary, with life themes, we can only find what we stand for if we *feel* for them, which we know energetically links us to our soul agreement. We cannot see everything that we stand for on our soul agreement, although many values we choose *do* link with the life themes we will continue to embody.

Values can also represent 'something I like the idea of but when it comes to the challenging times to truly embody it, I turn away'. Sometimes we don't truly live by the values we say we are about, in every circumstance. *For example, a mother may claim that respect is one of her values. She expects her children to respect her with certain expectations. Yet in certain ways, she doesn't respect her children's or partner's voice, the pull of their seed of intelligence. These actors reflect that she doesn't respect her seed of intelligence either. This may look like children who talk back to her, make fun of her or don't help out enough.* It brings up the concept of 'respect' from older generations and how they expected respect but didn't necessarily embody respect. Sometimes, the values we choose link back to our conditioning and how we were parented. This has nothing to do with what we individually stand for and will 'come to' on our soul agreement.

> *When we have embodied the particular life themes we stand for, we are more respected, heard and believed.*

Values is one word that is an umbrella for countless related life themes. *For example, let's use the value of 'support'. A woman who values support may seek support for herself as she employs a cleaner at home and encourages her husband to cook at least once a week. Perhaps she even supports others as she encourages them in their work.* She knows 'what it feels like to support myself in the home' and 'to support others in their business'. There are many other life themes around support however, that she may not realise or even have on her soul agreement to play out. *For example, perhaps she doesn't support her children emotionally because she also doesn't support herself emotionally. Perhaps she doesn't support her husband to follow his seed of intelligence, that guides him to drink alcohol or explore tricky friendships. Perhaps she doesn't have support for her own business.*

> *We are more successful in life, when we shift towards what we yearn for, rather than expect that we can create our life perfectly.*

As we go The New Way, we humbly accept that we are only 'about' what we have embodied at any one point in time, 'what is'. In this process, we come to all sorts of views on life that we did not dream that we would stand for. We must first respect the lava lamp effect within us, which invites us to *feel*, so that we can connect with our soul agreement and purpose.

In a coming book of The New Way series, we will go through how to do our inner work by tuning into the energy of four of our 'bodies' - physical, emotional, mental and spiritual. These four bodies are powerful in roads to shift our inner universe and pull our 'weeds' out by the root. In the meantime, we must honour and respect the concept of 'you are it' and the energetic laws that encompass it.

Summary

* Our lava lamp effect began at birth.

* Emotions arose to land us into scenes that made us feel this matching emotion.

* The aim is to express these rising emotions.

* We began to disconnect from our 'lava lamp blobs', as we were conditioned to suppress these energies.

* Our physical body constricts where the 'blobs' end up, and we disconnect from our divine true essence.

* As we feel our emotions again, we link back to our soul agreement and what we said we would stand for in this lifetime.

To explore…

As you wake, notice how you feel. Notice any physical sensations or emotions within you. Put your finger on the muscles that hold this energy. Say out loud, 'I feel x'. Now go about your day. Pay attention to every scene and how each one makes you feel. Your challenging scenes will likely make you put your finger on the very same place and announce the same emotion. This is where your latest 'blob' of emotion has arisen for your attention.

Monkey Mind Nets

...you behave from your rising emotions...

2014

As I mentioned in the first chapter, I had my overnight awakening at an 'Energetic Anatomy of a Yogi' workshop in 2013. Paul spoke about our ego self and also referred to it as the monkey mind. I studied every behaviour of myself and others from hereon in. How did my monkey mind show up? What did this look like?

I sensed my ego, or monkey mind, show up when I expressed myself in repelling ways. I felt it when I yelled, complained, stewed, pursed my lips or lectured my boys. I didn't want to express myself like this, but it was nearly impossible to avoid these behaviours at times, particularly as big emotions arose within me.

In the heat of the moment, I snatched. Before I realised it, I huffed. As I got really provoked, I said things to Anthony that I regretted. Sometimes it was just really obvious when I wasn't my true self. The energy of my own shadows was revolting, yet it was driven by my inner hurts, which deserved my heart.

Paul created a personalised meditation for me to listen to every night for 21 nights. I did a lot of inner work. I released what it felt like to have hurt others and also to have been hurt. I dissolved many crusts from my heart night after night. From this clearer place, I began to change the way I reacted to my children's challenging behaviours. I could see when they reacted from a place that wasn't their beautiful true essence. Their challenging behaviours had the same repelling energy about them as the monkey mind energy I spied in myself. I hadn't seen my children react from this monkey mind place before because I had been blinded by my own monkey mind behaviours. Heartbreakingly, I had grabbed them, lectured them or given out consequences. As I acted from my own monkey mind, I had only perceived their shadows but not their inner hurts that drove this.

Hayden, at around three years old, behaved from his monkey mind often. He ran away from me, he threw tantrums and he acted impulsively. It grew to a crescendo where I saw Hayden's self esteem weaken by the day because of everyone's reactions to his monkey mind behaviours. Myself, Anthony, daycare staff and other adults had told him off, given him time out, taken away privileges and so on. His posture and behaviour reflected his shame and life theme of 'what it feels like to be naughty and a nuisance'.

One day, when Anthony reprimanded Hayden in some way, I realised, 'He can hardly help it. He just clocked Declan on the head because his anger is inescapable. He has so much anger from so many life experiences already and rightly so'. I said this to Anthony. I then turned to Hayden and explained what I saw myself, 'I know you didn't really want to hit Deccy. Your monkey mind came in and took over when you got angry that he broke up your Lego, hey? It's like your monkey mind threw a net over you to make you act that way, from your bubbling emotions'.

Immediately, Hayden softened in relief that I saw this! Finally, I was on his page instead of against him and his behaviour. I continued, 'your monkey mind comes in and tells you to do some stupid stuff when your emotions rise up, right? I know it's hard to stop. I grab your arm with force when I get so mad that you are about to run away on me. My monkey mind takes over too'.

With that, I cried and cried for all of the children who are blamed for their emotional reactions of which we have been taught to label, diagnose or respond with 'ugh, I don't love you when you show up this way'. I cried for the children from every generation who grew up with the idea that they *are* their monkey mind behaviours and have lived in shame ever since. I then felt the surge of emotion as I realised how much I blamed so many actors in my life for their monkey mind responses. I eventually found compassion for myself when I realised, 'Wow, there are so many times I have responded from my monkey mind because I haven't afforded *myself* the opportunity to release my underlying emotions'.

From that day on, I passionately reminded my boys when their monkey mind stepped in, whilst I called myself out too. I reminded them, 'This is not your true self! Your monkey mind threw a net over you to virtually make you act that way. There is an emotion that wants to be seen underneath'. Then I worked to tune into how they felt.

After a while, Anthony pulled me up. 'This type of talk makes them think that they can get away with anything if they blame their monkey mind'. It was true. As they inevitably showed up from their monkey mind, they even told us, 'it was my monkey mind'. Declan easily got this concept by the time he was three years old. So I added in the clause, 'We all have control over our monkey mind. It can be really hard. But we do. When we let our emotions out, it's *much* easier to do'.

As I worked with more families, I naturally introduced the 'monkey mind' concept. I called it a 'monkey mind net' to name how we behave from our unexpressed emotions. When our emotions swirl within us, our monkey mind energetically throws a net over us every single time. It causes us to act in a certain way, so we don't feel these rising inner sensations or 'lava lamp blobs'.

The nets could be:

- behaviours and choices
- words or tone of voice
- postures

> Monkey Mind net - a disempowered type of expression that we are virtually forced into, if we don't express our rising emotions.

The Monkey Mind nets

Let's look at examples of all three types of monkey mind nets. All of these nets are behaviours which distract us, so we don't feel the rising energies within us at the time. We may or may not be aware of these emotions within us, which drive the monkey mind behaviour. If we don't express ourselves through this net however, we then start to feel the energy swirl within us. That is, if we don't constrict around it or leak it at someone, we have no choice but to feel the burn within us.

Example monkey mind behaviours and choices in children and adults

- 'The snatching net'
- 'The dobbing net'
- 'The sucking my thumb net'
- 'The judging others net'
- 'The hiding behind mum's leg net'
- 'The "I don't have time to eat/go to the toilet/do something for myself/do my inner work" net'

- 'The living vicariously through my child net'
- 'The focusing on keeping everyone else happy net'
- 'The avoiding responding to someone because they have made me feel an emotion I don't like net'
- 'The focusing solely on physical health issues in my family and avoiding emotions net'
- 'The helping my child/partner but feeling resentful net'
- 'The researching anything and everything net'

Example monkey mind words and voice tones in children and adults

- 'The "I hate you" net'
- 'The swearing net'
- 'The complaining about my issues hoping they will join me whinging too net'
- 'The "what part of this don't you get?" tone of voice net'
- 'The "I'm not up for this" & walk away net'
- 'The "I'm better than you" voice net'
- 'The lecturing net'
- 'The heady voice net'
- 'The sarcasm net'
- 'The "something not so great has happened but I'm okay with that" net'

Example monkey mind postures or how we hold ourselves in children and adults

- 'The jaw pushed forward net'
- 'The shaking my head as I talk at someone net'
- 'The hip to one side net'
- 'The hand on my heart, solar plexus or forehead net'
- 'The sway back/pigeon toes net'
- 'The speech issues net'
- 'The lip pursing/biting net'
- 'The rolling my feet outwards net'
- 'The closed lips smile net'
- 'The belly hanging out net'

As we name these behaviours, we can make light of these nets. Look at all of the different ways we can express ourselves as humans! The energetic concept of the monkey mind net is also child-friendly, which makes it easy for parents to communicate with their children about the concept. It gives us all a way to remind our children *and* ourselves, that we are not our monkey mind behaviours.

We can learn to split and notice the two parts of our being, our true essence and our monkey mind. Our true essence behaviours are when we feel our true self, which is powerful and magnetising to others. On the other hand, when our monkey mind is at play we know in our hearts, there is something to be felt underneath. Sometimes it can be a very fine line to know if our reactions are from our true essence or our monkey mind. Sometimes our monkey mind acts from our 'spiritual ego', which parades as the light.

Our ego, monkey mind and 'little old human self' are all the same concept.

The spiritual ego nets

Whilst we have resorted to the same types of monkey mind nets since we were little, there has been a surge of behaviours that have been touted as 'high vibe' and 'heart-centred' in the new age spiritual world. As we will see in coming books, both the mainstream and the new age spiritual worlds continue to turn away from the power of emotional expression. It is clear to see when someone does in fact feel emotions, by the three points of truth - monkey mind expressions, physical body issues and challenging scenes with their actors.

Here are some examples of 'spiritual ego' nets that still distract from feeling.

* 'I'm okay with that'
* 'they are the energy vampire'
* 'they're not touching my high vibe'
* 'the cool and "I'm woke" tone of voice'
* 'the smile of pride and superiority'
* 'the few calm breaths'
* 'love and light emojis to cover my rising emotions'

Releasing the nets

I explored how I could free myself from my monkey mind nets in much more detail. I realised that as soon as I released my emotions, I no longer expressed myself from the particular monkey mind net.

Here are some examples of how I reverted to my true essence expression as I released my emotions.

* One time, a friend made me feel frustrated. Immediately, my monkey mind threw the 'stewing net' over me. I played out this net, as I refused to express myself through the 'ranting net' and moan to another friend. Instead, I lay awake at night with my unreleased charge or noticed my lack of presence with the boys the next day.

    When I got honest about how I felt however, frustration rose up. I allowed myself to cry tears of how I was misunderstood. Immediately after, I felt calm and didn't stew any further. I no longer cared about the whole scenario as I had released the blob of energy that had arisen. There was also no need for a monkey mind net to distract me, as there was no further trapped energy within me. Without the charge, I was able to be present, see clearly and talk from my heart about this person. I shifted within so that

I could express myself from my true essence. Every time I stewed about anything else from hereon in, I took it as a clear sign to honour my emotions.

* Often, I started to lecture my boys when they did something to upset me, a monkey mind expression. If I remembered to drop into the emotions that they made me feel and release them, I could simply get to the heart of the matter with them in a much calmer way. In reflection of 'you are it', they responded with much more respect too!

As I continued to release my emotions, the nets of ego fell away. I started to unwind from the pull to gossip, slump, rant, call names, control mine and other people's paths, compare myself, laugh when I didn't find it funny just to make someone feel comfortable, go to places out of fear of missing out and more. It all changed the instant I released the emotion that had caused my monkey mind to throw these nets over me. People either connected with me through more respect or bowed out of my life, in reflection of my monkey mind nets that fell away. Of course, I am not finished, as there are always more nets from different angles to be released.

As long as our lava lamp effect rises old energies, we will continue to have monkey mind nets thrown over us. The more we work through the blobs, the less ego we express ourselves from.

As I became less connected to my ego, I began to change how I expressed myself for the better. I was more confident to speak my truth, to do what felt right to me and to be honest with myself in all areas of my life. I began to find my true self, in what I call my true essence. The more I released my emotions, the more sneaky and subtle nets of ego fell away too.

> Disempowerment - To blame people or external circumstances for your reality and how you feel rather than recognise that you can change what you don't like if you show up in different ways. To respond and react from your inner emotional charge through blame, rather than shift within and express yourself from this calmer place. To give your power to others as you seek your answers from them.
>
> (There is no shame in disempowerment. We all play from disempowerment as we take steps towards more and more empowerment.)

Why you want to know about the Monkey Mind nets

We all show up from monkey mind nets, whether it's our posture, words, behaviours or voice tone. It is simple. We either express ourselves from our true essence or from our monkey mind, in every scene of our day. When a lava lamp blob arises, we *will* express ourselves from our monkey mind, if we don't express this emotion at the time. If we express the rising emotion, we clear the 'blob' and then connect back to our seed of intelligence, which guides us to express ourselves from our true essence enlisted on our soul agreement.

> *Our true essence unfolds as we do the work to clear the rising energies that prevent us from true expression of our soul.*

We are up to our eyeballs with unexpressed emotion

Picture your lava lamp as within you. If you don't regularly express your emotions, you can see it like the inside of your lamp as quite full. The energy of these rising 'blobs' has to be dealt with. Our monkey mind actually helps us to deal with the backlog of unexpressed emotion within us or else we might go insane from the chaos or pain of it. We feel just a tiny bit of what our ego covers up. Our monkey mind throws a net over us to block or distract us from feeling this rising emotional energy.

To block and distract us from our rising emotions, the countless monkey mind nets may:

* *tense* around the rising energy with our muscles, fascia and tendons, like when we purse our lips
* *leak* the rising energy behaviourally, like when we rant or snatch
* *distract* ourselves so we don't feel this rising energy, like when we eat or seek more gratitude

Here are some more monkey mind net examples.

Tensing

* 'The toes squeezed together net'
* 'The tight shoulders/hunching net'
* 'The tight jaw net'

Leaking

* 'The ranting/venting net'
* 'The lecturing my children net'
* 'The making perfect choices for my child net'

Distracting

* 'The phone scrolling net'
* 'The alcohol, eating chocolate or other vice net'
* 'The adding more and more on my plate to keep busy net'

Whether we leak it, distract ourselves or both, our physical body always tenses around any unexpressed energy, as we saw in the previous chapters. When we express ourselves from a behaviour that leaks energy, we release just enough so we don't truly lose it. There is still more unexpressed energy from the rising 'lava lamp blob' however, which our physical body has to manage.

> We express ourselves from our ego every time an emotion arises within us and we don't release it. Yes, this is many times in one day. No, we are not meant to ever express ourselves perfectly.

Noticing our monkey mind expressions

We must remember it is a practice not to judge ourselves when we do show up from our monkey mind expressions. We have been conditioned to behave perfectly, how society prefers. We shame and defend ourselves or blame limiting beliefs, diagnoses or self-sabotage when we don't. In fact, our expression relates to energetic laws. *Our behaviours are an energetic response to our divinely orchestrated rising emotions within.*

It is also a practice to notice when and how we express ourselves from our monkey mind. As with 'you are it', our actors energetically invite us to claim self responsibility when they prod us. That is, when our actors make us feel displeasing sensations within us, this is the time to notice how we respond from our monkey mind and work to release this energy. If we focus our attention on our actors, we miss the opportunity to spy on our particular type of monkey mind nets.

Here is an example of the emotion that drives our monkey mind behaviour.

Perhaps we don't realise that one of our go-to monkey mind nets, when our partner parents less-than-perfectly, is to act from superiority. We get distracted by our partner's behaviour, and hence, we don't realise our own monkey mind expression of 'you are doing this wrong, I know better'. The emotion underneath our superiority reflects 'what it feels like to be a mother watching my child get hurt by my partner when I can see a better way'.

It is often the actors in our external reality that draw our attention to our own monkey mind expressions. In response to the state of our inner universe, they respond as energetic puppets with displeasing responses, such as resistance, hurtful comments or silence. When an actor in our external reality expresses themselves from a monkey mind net, it is an invitation to check in with our inner state and whether we firstly expressed *ourselves* from a monkey mind net. We cannot expect our actors to stop their monkey mind expressions if we hold onto charge ourselves. As with 'you are it', we must go first.

> *As children, we are conditioned to point the finger when someone does something we don't like, rather than notice what we first said or did from our own monkey mind.*

Understanding our own monkey mind responses

As we tune into the sensations of our inner universe, we start to realise why we act from our monkey mind nets. Some examples might be :

- we yell at our children because of our rising inner sadness at constantly being 'on' as a mother,

- we tense our shoulders because of the ball of heartbreak that would arise if we didn't clamp down on it,

- we don't form our own true opinions because we are scared we might create heart-palpitating conflict with our loving partner's truth.

Our monkey mind nets can be loud and obvious or sneaky and subtle.

> *A simple way to recognise when we disconnect from our inner universe and thus our inner power, is to spy on how we express ourselves.*

In the name of self-responsibility and empowerment, our monkey mind nets or behaviours are important clues that remind us to honour our inner universe. It is disempowered to consider another person's behaviour or a challenging scenario as justification to act from a monkey mind net. It is empowered to feel first and then respond.

Here are some examples of times to own our monkey mind expressions.

- *When our child won't put on a jumper because we perceive that it's cold, we are not justified to act from the "I'm your mother and do what I say" net'.*

- *When our partner doesn't help out in the house, we are not justified to express our frustration through the 'complaining about my partner to anyone who will listen net'.*

- *When we are afraid to be seen for our gifts, we are not justified to play by the 'I keep my successes to myself net'.*

The temptation to act from our monkey mind behaviours is something that can be stopped as we feel the emotion that drives them. As we feel and then speak up about it, we express ourselves more and more from our true essence instead. We will go through this in more detail in a coming book of The New Way series.

Understanding our actor's monkey mind responses

Not only do we respond from our lava lamp effect, but our actors respond from theirs. It is like everyone is a walking lava lamp. We collide into others with energetically matching 'blobs' to literally raise the energy within each other. This is essentially a good thing as we realise the need to flow our inner hurts and particularly if we all practise self-responsibility!

As we saw in the Emotional Blackbox chapter, even if an actor says they aren't emotionally affected by a challenge in their day, they *will* respond from some type of monkey mind net, if in fact a 'blob' of emotion did arise at that point. Of course, if the actor has landed in any challenging scene, this indicates there indeed was a rising blob. This goes with the energetic laws of 'feeling cannot be turned off' and 'we behave from our rising emotions'.

As explained earlier in this chapter, whether we like to admit it or not, if we don't express the emotions that arise within us, as they surface, we will do something to leak some of the energy, to distract ourselves, and everyone around us, from it. If not, our physical body will simply tense somewhere to 'keep it together'.

ENERGETIC LAW

'We behave from our rising emotions' - as an emotion arises within us, we will behave from a disempowered expression.

Whose energy is it?

As we saw in Your Actors chapter, if you feel it, it's within you. Many people insist they pick up on other's energy. This avoids the energetic law of 'you are it'. If you felt it, this other person interacted with you in divine timing, to raise the lava lamp blob that arises within you. At the same time, the actor also has a rising emotional package, hence you both collide in 'it takes two'.

Some people also tap into past life experiences and wonder how to work with this. The New Way brings everything back to the energetic laws that allow us to play the game of life most efficiently. That is, to get to the heart of the matter, clear our vessel and find our soul lessons, we need to work with our divinely orchestrated experiences from *this* lifetime. Let's look at this further.

If we become aware of a scene from a past life that we were in, we can notice the life theme we experienced then. We can then match it to where we have experienced this *same life theme* in this lifetime. Our emotional blackbox recorded the emotion we felt from *this* lifetime so that we can make sense of the corresponding sensation within our inner universe. *For example, you may become aware of a past life where you were more important than your father. If it's relevant for you to work through, there will be a life theme you have experienced in this lifetime about 'what it feels like to have more power than my father' or something similar.* From here, we can work with our inner sensations on this very life theme, to find our soul lessons. As we come to these lessons, we can then take inspired actions in our external reality of this life. To get lost in the details of a past life is yet another monkey mind net, which distracts us from feeling.

To play the game of life, we simply need to explore the life themes we land in, all day every day. We don't need energetic readers. We don't need to know past life details. We only need to be prepared to notice and feel responsibly.

Claiming compassion and self-responsibility

As we begin to nurture our own rising energies, we foster compassion for ourselves and our experiences. With the energetic law of 'it takes one to know one', the more compassion we have for our constantly turned on lava lamp, and corresponding monkey mind behaviours, the more we have compassion for the monkey mind responses of others.

> ENERGETIC LAW
>
> It takes one to know one - when we see something in someone else, light or dark, we recognise it because it is within our inner universe too.

We may complain about the challenges in our life, yet our challenges are the reminder to play the game of life, The New Way! Often, our challenges come from an actor who behaves from their monkey mind. Perhaps they yell at us, are over-giving, forget to communicate with us and so on. We must remember that our actors respond from the state of our inner universe. Often, we have already shown up from a monkey mind net ourselves.

Here is an example of when we can spy our monkey mind expression in hindsight.

Let's say you did a favour for your partner and they didn't say thanks. They showed up from the 'I don't bother to say thanks' monkey mind net. Energetically, this must be in response to a monkey mind expression of your own.

You realise you played out the 'jumping in to help out when I don't have the energy' monkey mind net. Your partner's disrespect for you, ultimately reflects your disrespect for your own energy. This is our opportunity to own 'you are it' and also how it feels to have acted from this monkey mind net and receive this response. It will bring up feelings.

You are it. If you don't like when your children resist you with rigidity, consider where you have been rigid with them. If you don't like when your friend tells you what to do, consider the opportunity to trust you already know the answers yourself. If you don't like how your partner won't support you, consider how you can support yourself even more so. You can do this!

> *Our actors' monkey mind behaviours are in response to our own monkey mind expression from a previous scene.*

Finding your true essence

We have been taught what 'bad' behaviour is and even what 'good' or 'heart-centred' behaviour is. Much of this is conditioning and we copy it without question. There are many ways however, where we are unknowingly trapped under and behave from a monkey mind net. We continue to give our monkey mind a role to cast nets, until we shift the rising energies within us. When we do this, we shake our monkey mind expressions, and instead, find out how our unique true essence *wants to be* expressed.

Often, we have created our identity from behaviours that aren't actually our truest expression.

Here are some examples of how we may have turned out to be the opposite of our true essence.

* *Perhaps your true essence is about loud and fun expression however, you were shut down for this as a child.*

* *Perhaps you were taught to always say the right thing, however, your true essence is about expression of some tricky truths.*

* *Perhaps you were conditioned to make sure everyone else feels good about themselves, however, your true essence is to explore 'honouring my soul first'.*

Here is an example of when we do what we think is best however it is emotion-driven.

* *Perhaps it seems like the right way forward to urge your children into earth-based activities, to create with their hands out in nature. If you have to convince one of your children into it however, it may be because their seed of intelligence wants to create digitally instead or has any good reason not to go. If you push them to go, you express yourself from the monkey mind net of 'I want to interfere with your path so that you become what I think you should be'.*

  Ultimately, it was a monkey mind response to avoid the discomfort of your own rising sensations. The discomfort may have been worry that your child won't be balanced in life, if they don't get out into nature. It may have been frustration, that it is too hard to take one child and not the other. It may have been embarrassment, as you worry how other mothers who attend the nature play will judge you.

* *Perhaps you tell your children to behave for your new neighbours. It is impossible, as eventually they fight out on the lawn or tell one of the neighbours' children that they can't play. Essentially, your children reflected your rising emotion of embarrassment. Your monkey mind slipped the net of 'try to control my children's behaviour', so you didn't have to feel this emotion as a mother.*

The first step towards more authentic expression is to notice when you act from a monkey mind net. Your actors remind you to search for your monkey mind expressions when they respond to you via theirs. Become an expert on your go to nets.

If we try to convince our child that they will like the nature play, we unknowingly disrespect our child's seed of intelligence and what they are drawn to or repelled from. We will surely receive a monkey mind net response from our child in reflection of our monkey mind expression. As we express ourselves from our monkey mind towards our children, the heart connection between us is then weakened.

> *The New Way invites us to humbly spy on our countless monkey mind nets that we still express ourselves from, so we may turn human disempowerment around.*

As we express ourselves from our true essence more often, not only will we interact with others in a brighter, different way but we will be called to explore more of our inner magic. We have a treasure chest of gifts within us, which waits to be explored. For most of us, we are distracted by our inner chaos and how we express ourselves from our monkey mind nets and rightly so. We have a huge backlog of unexpressed energies within our inner universe. Unfortunately, without clearing these, we only ever explore the gifts at the top of our treasure chest.

Here are some examples of how we may spend our days in distraction of our gifts.

* *Being* soul-tired
  We respond from monkey mind nets of 'don't do that, it will give me more work', 'why can't you help out?', 'I think I'll just sit and scroll' or 'I don't have the energy for that'.

* *Managing physical, emotional, mental and spiritual health issues*
  The cost to our four bodies as we hold onto our unexpressed energies means that we must deal with the daily effects of illness, headaches, 'hormonal' issues, sore back, emotional heaviness, anxiety, tiredness, being unclear in life and so on.

- *General monkey mind nets*
  We spend time and energy as we point the finger at our actors, research the answer to our children's issues, ignore our own issues or put more and more on our plate, to distract from our inner work.

- *Distracting storylines*
  We write off a lot of time to play out the bigger scenes designed to crack us, such as a car accident, a trip to emergency, divorce and so on.

Although it would be great to fast forward to explore our gifts, we *must* go through these tricky scenes, as they reflect the inevitable rising lava lamp blobs. If we don't feel 'what it feels like to be going through…' our particular challenges, then we miss the opportunity to connect back in with our true essence. If however, we continue to feel as these scenes prod us, we begin to unravel the layers of ego that keep us distracted from more and more of our gifts.

Once we begin to shake the monkey mind nets of our ego, we realise the amount of untapped potential we all sit on. We must get honest with how we feel, to connect with our unique true essence's expression. Most humans don't get honest about how they truly feel because of their fear of feeling, and also, the knowing that they might then have to act on this and speak up.

Our gifts

As we begin to 'pick up' and play with our gifts at the top of our treasure chest, we see other gifts below. The end result is like a toddler at the treasure chest. They pick up the first gifts they see and explore them until more gifts catch their eye. They toss the first gifts over their shoulder to reach for the next ones. At some point, they may go and pick up the gifts on the floor and explore them further, before more gifts in the treasure chest catch their attention. Perhaps by the time we finish our timeline here, our treasure chest will be somewhat empty, with our gifts thrown everywhere, like we had a good time with them! Of course, we will likely never empty that treasure chest either.

Summary

* As humans, we all behave from either our monkey mind (ego) or from our true essence (soul).

* As we feel our emotions, we see the monkey mind responses from which we have expressed ourselves since we were young, to protect us from the fear of feeling.

* As we release our emotions, we release the monkey mind 'net' which forces us to express ourselves from our ego.

* If we don't continuously spy and dismantle our monkey mind expressions, we inevitably express ourselves from our ego, which robs us of our true essence and soul path.

* Our actors will continue to respond from monkey mind nets until we identify our monkey mind expressions and release the unexpressed emotions within us.

* Our ego can parade as a 'spiritual ego', which justifies certain expressions as heart-centred, more perfect/pure or 'the right thing to do', in place of our true soul expression in its imperfections.

To ponder on ...

From the monkey mind net examples in this chapter, which monkey mind net did you see yourself in? Next time you notice yourself caught under that net of expression, check in with how you honestly feel underneath. It's okay to be vulnerable.

Snow Globe

...when it's time to explore the Heart energy,
our emotions surface whether we like it or not...

2022

A lot of women approached me for mentoring support because they were upset at how they leaked their emotions on their family. They talked about their overwhelm with life and those moments where they couldn't help but explode with certain actors. They felt ashamed at how they expressed themselves, particularly when everyone around them seemed to have it all together.

I saw the concept of the 'snow globe'. Like in a snow globe that's sat on the shelf for a while, the energies that lie stagnant within us, begin to swirl. It is like someone has shaken a snow globe inside us, and we have no choice but to do something with these energies. When we feel this, we know we have moved into the season of life where we are to explore the Heart energy, our emotions. We will go into more detail on seasons of life in the corresponding chapter.

I explained to my clients that as we grew up, we explored the Earth energy. Part of this was to keep it all together, to be the rock, often for our parents. For many, this was the Earth energy in the shadows. That is, 'to keep it all together, I must turn away from my emotional reactions'. We now know by default, this means to turn away from your true essence.

For those who kept it together, their physical body and behaviours masked their rising energies, as we have seen in previous chapters. Many have since ended up with physical ailments, as the physical body took the brunt. Most have not realised the monkey mind expressions they took on, which have since formed part of their personality.

> Snow Globe - your energies swirl to be expressed as you land in your time to explore the Heart energy, as a child or an adult.

The more we choose not to respond from our monkey mind expressions, the more we feel our rising emotions. The more we relax each muscle in our body, the more we surrender to the rising emotions. The result can feel chaotic in our inner universe. Women report that they feel volatile, nauseous, teary, overwhelmed, shaken, hopeless, overheated, hormonal, fatigued and even anxious or panicky. Despite this, they resonate strongly with the call to feel.

Due to the strong conditioning we grew up with, to keep it together, it can feel foreign to feel our big energies rise. These inner sensations may remind us of negative responses from others, when we had a tantrum or simply cried as a child. Our actors may then reflect our doubts of emotional expression. They may insist we pull it together, point out how useless we are when we are emotional and make us feel even more unsafe to express these rising energies.

As we have seen in previous chapters, we have been strongly taught to pathologise ourselves rather than honour how we feel within. This all avoids empowerment, to go within to co-create with our rising energies, to connect with what wants to be seen and felt. Every time we pathologise ourselves, we take sides with the conditioning that 'emotions are weak and a waste of time'.

Why you want to know about the Snow Globe

We all explore our inner universe, in different ways in a different order. As you explore the Heart energy, you feel things emotionally. As you explore the Earth energy, you feel things physically. As you explore the Star energy, you perceive but don't 'feel within'. At any time, you will likely explore a combination of all three energies in many different ways. Each energy has their light and dark sides. We will cover this energetic concept in detail in a coming book of The New Way series. The aim of the game of life is to explore all three energies, somewhat equally, across our life timeline.

Your role in the family

As we consider the state of our inner universe, we must look at the energetic law - 'the family bubble seeks to balance itself energetically'. The more one person explores the energy of Star, Heart or Earth, the more other family members explore other energies in opposition. That is, if one person in the family is quite emotional, adult or child, it is likely that the others are not connected to their emotional body as much. In opposition, others may explore the Star and/or Earth energy more so. Those who are more grounded, attract physical health issues and feel physically, explore the Earth energy. Those who play out creativity, intuition and dissociation from their physical body, explore the Star energy. We will now briefly look at this angle of family energetics, so you can better understand your unique role in inner work. Family energetics will then be covered in more detail in a coming book of The New Way series.

> ### ENERGETIC LAW
>
> 'The family bubble seeks to balance itself energetically' - we exist in opposites in every way, to ensure the energetic entity of the family remains balanced.

Your season of life

Possibly, you are a woman who yearns to connect more with your emotions, however, you feel numb or disconnected from feeling. This occurs when you sense your future, where you will lean into the Heart energy however, you have not arrived there at this point in time. Instead, you may perceive your inner sensations physically (Earth) or even feel disconnected from feeling (Star). There is no need to shame or pathologise yourself for somewhere you think you should be when you aren't. It's simply not time on your unique path. Instead, you can feel or communicate, as with the Heart energy, in any small steps that you feel pulled to. The main practice however, is to encourage those family members whose time it is to explore the Heart energy to feel and speak up even more so.

Perhaps however, it *is* your time to explore the Heart energy. You may sense your 'snow globe' is shaken up because you can barely hold in your emotions. You may leak this rising energy as you yell, huff, lecture or snatch. These behaviours are a clear sign that you are in the thick of your experience in the Heart energy and probably more so than other family members. You are called to focus primarily on your inner work, to flow these energies. This heart work becomes the priority of your days and in time you trust that it serves your whole family too.

> *Despite the benefit of emotional expression, not every family member will be in this season of life all at once. You can support those that are, including yourself, and notice the gifts the others bring from the Star and Earth energies.*

The goodie bag

The thing is, whilst it can seem pretty shadowy to have your emotions shaken up within you, there are just as many reasons to value them. As you release your emotions, you get a 'goodie bag' on the other side. Just about everyone knows the peaceful, clear feeling after you have a big cry. Your physical body thanks you with one less muscle or tendon that has to hold onto that energy for you. You literally begin to find more comfort within your physical body.

As you step into *true groundedness*, you don't need to continually chase external measures to ground you. You are embodied. Your emotional intuition starts to skyrocket. As with the energetic law 'it takes one to know one', you begin to know how everyone feels around you, particularly your children and partner. You respond with more compassion. You become more mentally focused on where you want to go with life, and your spiritual body thanks you with big feelings of fulfilment as you honour your inner universe. It is the ultimate in self care.

The Heart energy

At first, we must deal with the backlog of energies our emotional blackbox has clocked for a long time. This is where most people give up and feel emotional expression has no value. As with the lava lamp effect, the more you express the backlog of emotions, the more you then start to perceive the individual 'blobs'. You also perceive the breaks between the emotions that arise. This is also the same concept as labour contractions, which come in waves. They are designed for you to feel and then to have a break, so that it feels manageable.

It is a test of faith to stay with responsible emotional expression if you find yourself in the Heart energy. It is to remember you gain efficiency and ease with practise of any skill. It is to remember that as you practise mastery of the Heart energy, in divine timing, you energetically invite the next family member to follow suit. You may then explore the Star and/or Earth energy more so.

The Earth energy

Maybe you only perceive your inner universe through physical sensations. Your physical body feels weakness, aches and pains and also experiences physical ailments, from where this energy stagnates. When you explore the Earth energy, it is like the energies within you are settled, like a settled snow globe. These energies have been physicalised or snapped up and even numbed by the physical body.

With your 'snow globe' shaken up to a lesser degree, it is harder to explore the Heart energy, to connect with your rising emotional energies. It can be trickier to interact with others because you are not so easily able to respond from how others feel, in reflection of your unfelt emotions. Whether you feel these emotions within you, your lava lamp is still most definitely 'switched on'. It continues to surface emotions like your heart continues to beat, albeit these emotions can be somewhat pushed down. You may sense that your physical body holds onto this energy by the tension you feel in certain places.

As far as our emotions, we have been conditioned to see that it is better to explore life through the Earth energy, to keep it together. As we have seen however, there is a cost to this. Of course, there are many positives for those whose time it is to explore the Earth energy, such as groundedness, much less care factor and the ability to be 'the rock' for others. If you find yourself here, then it is vital to embrace your season in the Earth energy.

The Star energy

Maybe you don't perceive your inner sensations emotionally or even physically too much. Instead, it is like your soul has disconnected from your body, which pulls you in an upwards direction. This can make you feel busy, unpresent or chatty as you literally exist in your head area. These are some signs that you are in the season of life to explore the Star energy. Yes, your lava lamp is also 'switched on' and you clock emotions via your emotional blackbox too. Your focus however, is more on the gifts of your intuition and creativity.

Like with the Earth energy, those who explore the Star energy will find it trickier to sense others' emotions, when they don't sense their own. The family member(s) who explore the Star energy may even be perceived to be 'autistic' or 'neurodivergent'. As we go The New Way, we simply understand that these members bring balance and gifts to the family whilst they practise mastery of the Star energy. They can still take any steps to feel and/or communicate as they come up, which allows them to integrate more Heart energy..

Whilst the family witnesses their Star and Earth gifts, these family members can support those in the Heart energy to feel and to speak. As we have seen, the more one person embodies an energy, the more they activate the next family member to unlock it too. Don't forget, we often explore one or two of these energies at once. We cannot hurry our family members to move onto a different energy. As with 'you are it', we can only do our own soul path as well as we can! It can help to map out the family bubble once you know who explores which energy.

To find out more about Star, Heart, Earth - what I call our True Essence Profile - scan the code.

You can check off different traits for you and your family members for Star, Heart and Earth in the light and shadows or even take the mini quiz!

Summary

* In certain seasons of our life, we will feel more shaken up.

* There is nothing wrong with us when we are emotional and we do not need to pathologise this.

* The more emotional we are, the more clearly we can notice our monkey mind expressions.

* Many mothers have their snow globe shaken up right now but not all. For those that don't, there will be another family member who may be more emotional.

* Yes, we have bucketloads of tears within us all!

To play with ...

- Which family member has the most emotional energy rising at this point in time?

- How are they (or you) supported to be in the Heart energy by the other family members?

The Cone

...your recurring challenges continue until your soul lessons have been realised...

2019

Anthony and I regularly argued about money or parenting. Sometimes we had a fair gap between disputes and I relished in the peace. My hopes were then dashed when we found ourselves in yet another scene that brought up our chaos. I felt so disheartened.

It seemed like we were on a merry-go-round and the longer we repeated these recurring issues, the more I was desperate to find the way off! I was sick of the disharmony almost more than the issues themselves. Anthony on the other hand felt like we were done for. "What is the point in continuing our relationship when we keep having these same issues?", he asked in frustration. He felt we had failed to make progress in how we dealt with money or parenting as a couple.

I was called to find the positive in how we moved through the challenges and to cheer Anthony on, for the sake of us and our family bubble. This was when I saw it! 'You know, last time we would have argued for longer. We wouldn't have talked for a day. This time we didn't! We still argued but we were more respectful and quickly saw what we needed to see. Every time we have an argument, we always come to *something*. We always come back to our hearts in the end. We are succeeding!'.

All of a sudden, the merry-go-round I saw in my mind became a cone shape, like an upside down ice cream cone. Picture the merry-go-round at the bottom of the cone. Every time you come back around to the 'seam' of the waffle cone, you face the same type of challenge, such as a parenting disagreement or a child who wets the bed. This particular scene is an invitation to explore the life theme *you* find *yourself* in, such as 'what it feels like to have different ideas to my partner on education' or 'what it feels like to have to wake up and change sheets at night'.

Each time you land in the recurring scene and do something to own 'you are it', you travel *upwards* around the cone, like a trail up the mountain. At each challenging scene, a step forward may be to feel your emotions or to find the heart of the matter and then talk to your actors about this. Other steps forward may be to take practical actions to insist that these scenes improve. You may even encourage your actors to release *their* feelings and talk about the heart of the matter from *their* angle. You can take these steps either at the time or at any point afterwards. Sometimes there is a lot of chaos and emotional burn that needs to play out for yourself and/or with other actors, until you are in a place to remember 'you are it'.

> *The heart of the matter usually maps back to the first time you experienced this life theme, often in childhood or early parenthood. It often starts with 'I'm just feeling...' in inward reflection, rather than to point the finger of blame.*

If we don't 'come to' anything when our challenges surface, we stay on the merry-go-round at the bottom of the cone. *An example might be a couple who fight until it blows over or a mother who huffs each time her child wets the bed but does nothing internally or externally to further insist that her reality somehow changes.* If we don't work with our challenges, we continue to land in scenes that nudge us to feel this life theme. On top of this, the scenes tend to get more chaotic, to invite us to crack.

Many women experience multiple challenging scenes in one day, which directly reflects how much rising emotion is there for them to feel. If they do acknowledge, feel or talk about how they feel about their angle of a particular life theme, then they circle up the cone. It takes many, many trips around the cone to reach the top. Throughout the journey and at the top, we come to our unique soul lessons behind the life theme we explored.

As Anthony and I circled up the cone on relationship life themes, we worked to see each other's side and trust that we could solve it. In the process, I often released a lot of emotion to be able to see his side and speak up for mine. We continued to circle upwards and around, until we met with the 'seam of the waffle cone'. This was the point where we faced a challenging scene to do with the life theme we explored. It was all in divine timing and we faced many scenes because we still needed to explore *more* angles of this life theme.

'The cone'

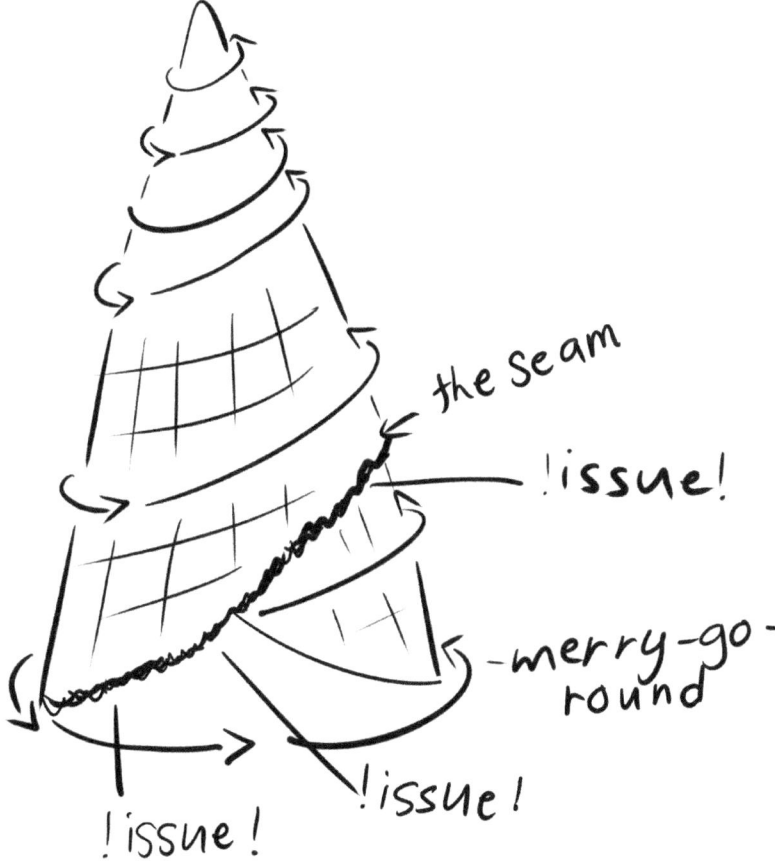

Each time we landed in another challenging scene, we felt the stress as we explored our corresponding rising energies. Despite this, as I noticed the positive changes in our blow ups and what we came to each time, I knew we had travelled up the cone. There was nothing wrong with us as a couple. It was conditioning that told us we had failed if we had rising emotions or arguments. In fact, we had become far more empowered as individuals and as a partnership than we had ever been.

After I saw this cone analogy, I soon experienced what it was like to get to the top of the cone. There continued to be noticeable progressions in how we dealt with our challenging storylines, be it miniscule at times! As we neared the top however, where it was smaller in diameter, the issue reared its head much more often. We literally circled the cone in quicker time, which brought up the root of the 'weed'. We had to stand and face our shadows head on as we explored the root of these life themes. Our inner chaos arose. It got wild. We literally felt beside ourselves and wanted to run and blame.

To blow up this life theme and get off the cone of recurring issues, we had to sit in our disgust of each other, which reflected the matching energies within us both. At that moment, we nearly let go of our relationship. It was painful to be present with our deepest hurts. As we were about to run however, our seeds of intelligence made us reconsider and we tentatively agreed to take each day as it came.

For us, we had come to the soul lessons we needed to and ticked off the life theme in the process. We saw each other in a very new light. We were unattached as we had let go of so much control and codependency.

As we felt good together, then we stayed together. We were no longer bound by co-dependent webs, such as, 'you need to do/say/be like this to win my love and make me happy'. We stood on our own two feet. I saw that we had gone through an 'energetic divorce'. We saw each other without the big blobs of rising emotion. Suddenly, we found respect and a purity of love for each other that we could not have created without the journey up the cone. This reflected the respect and love we had found for our *own soul* through the challenging process. We will cover the concept of the 'energetic divorce' in more detail in a coming book of The New Way series.

> Energetic divorce - an energetic process, that we get invited into, to let go of disempowered relationship patterns. This can and will happen with any of our actors, such as partners, friends, extended family and our children too. You must be ready to see your own shadows, release your emotions responsibly and communicate vulnerably with the other party.

As we ticked off this life theme, it was like the cone collapsed. It was hard to believe it used to be us. I realised I had found humility, self-respect and self-responsibility as I burned through this process with Anthony. Our relationship also displayed these qualities. It was miraculous.

It broke my heart to realise how many couples separated, just as they were about to blow their life theme up. At the top of the cone, it was like they could only see a shadowy fog on the forest path ahead of them. Rather than stumble through the shadows, to the light on the other side, they turned left or right. They felt they had no choice but to split up. The conditioning to turn away from rising emotions ensured that they did not get to see the miracles of an empowered relationship.

Of course, at this point in time, most women are not aware of the possibilities with their partner, if they claim 'you are it'. Where you are now is exactly where you are supposed to be, for very good reasons. Your unique soul agreement may include experiences of life themes around separation and divorce. If you are in this position, you are on the cone to come to soul lessons around the life theme of separation.

Every life theme has a cone

Remember, your soul agreement has countless life themes that you have the opportunity to circle up the cone with. Every life theme you explore has its own energetic cone. At any point in time, you may be further up the cone with some life themes than others. You may be at the merry-go-round on the bottom with some life themes and some you may never finish. This is all perfect for our path.

Come back to the life themes you find yourself in at this point in time. At any moment, you can take note of what life theme you are called to explore. You can take a small step forward to feel, 'what it feels like to be a woman/mother/partner/friend who....'. As you feel and/or speak up about this, even in small ways, you move up the cone. Trust that as you want to run from anyone, you are probably near the top of the cone of a particular life theme. There is magic if you choose to feel the big 'blobs' and speak up to your actors about where you first experienced challenges on this life theme. You can review the Life Themes chapter for example life themes.

The cone analogy helped my clients and myself to have hope that despite a recurring challenge, if we do the inner work, we continue to progress forwards. It also reminded us that it takes time to move through our challenges. There is much to play out before we can tick off certain life themes. Everything is agreed upon in perfect timing on our soul agreement. To stand and face the shadows wins the game of life!

Why you want to know about The Cone

The cone helps you to make sense of recurring scenes in your life, when they challenge you. The minute you spy yourself in a recurring scene, you have two options. You can approach it through disempowerment or empowerment.

To approach your challenge through disempowerment might mean you put up with it, complain about it or try to change others to fix it. We have been heavily conditioned with these responses, which keep us on the merry-go-round of this particular life theme. To play from empowerment however, means that you must shift the energy within your inner universe, to shift your external reality. An empowered response might mean you first honour your feelings and take a moment to release what made you feel sad, disappointed or frustrated. You might then talk up and *without attachment*, invite others to change. If they don't change, you are invited to further explore your inner universe, which takes you even further up the cone.

As you do the inner work, you start to notice the positive changes that come, both within and without. This helps you to trust in your heart that you circled upwards and that one day, you will spiral up and off the cone. Of course there will be days of doubt too. When you do get to the top however, you finally reach the scenes that you yearn for right now. *For example, one day you realise you are able to talk peacefully with your partner about money or perhaps you know you have mastered sleep.*

Playing it out

Whether we like it or not, we face recurring issues in recurring scenes until we 'crack' and feel. Some people believe they don't need to feel their emotions to stop their challenges. Essentially, this can seem true as a recurring challenge may suddenly fade from our lives, such as the child who no longer wets the bed. Whilst the challenging storyline may disappear, the unresolved emotions within our inner universe attract a different challenging storyline instead. Let's call it a 'same, same but different' one. The child may instead go through a period of night terrors or perhaps a different child starts to wet the bed.

Whilst our storylines can seem different, they play out the same underlying life theme, *for ourselves as 'player one'*, that wasn't explored the first time. In this case, it is the mother's life theme of 'what it feels like to have to get up to my child at night' or even 'what it feels like to have interrupted sleep'. The life theme continues.

At each recurring scene, it's not obligatory to feel but simply an invitation to release the energies within us that attract these challenges. Our continued energetic release collapses the cone and its life theme at the root cause. This process creates inner peace and frees our actors from being our energetic puppets. We can get off the merry-go-round of the life challenges we don't like! Conditioning has kept us small to think we just have to put up with our life's challenges or cut and run.

> Energetic puppets - our actors energetically respond via their monkey mind nets if we express ourselves from our own. We free our actors to show up from their true essence, or bow out of our reality, as we express ourselves from our true essence.

We *experience* a life theme when we are an actor in any scene but we don't acknowledge or release how we feel about this. We *explore* a life theme, often at some point in the future, when we get honest about how our soul felt about the experience. To explore it is to talk about it and release our emotions. Children show us what it is to *explore* a life theme on-the-go when they have a tantrum or burst into tears then and there.

Here is an example of how we continue to attract storylines that match scenes we never truly *explored* the first time we *experienced* them.

Hayden was a sleepless baby. He didn't go to sleep without a lot of work and also didn't stay asleep for long. (I now understand that his unsettled behaviour reflected my unexpressed emotions from his birth). Anthony couldn't take more of the load as I refused to look at bottle feeding. Energetically, it was clear that it was Hayden and I that had to play out this life theme.

For me, it was the life theme of 'what it feels like to be exhausted as a new mother, with a sleepless baby, with little hope'. By the time Hayden was seven months old, my desperation took us to a sleep school. There, I experienced the life theme of 'what it feels like to hand my son to nurses, who told me what to do in order to get my son to sleep' and also 'what it feels like to do something I don't feel good about'. Disappointingly, we continued to struggle for years with sleep issues. Finally, Hayden grew up and started to sleep well, very well. It seemed like I had ticked off this life theme without any inner work.

The truth is, when Hayden was a baby and throughout these early years, I barely released any of my emotions. I experienced but did not truly explore the life themes I found myself in. During the scenes however, my emotional blackbox clocked every one of my emotional responses. For years and years, these 'blobs' continued to rise to invite me to feel them, as with the lava lamp effect. Instead, my monkey mind mostly threw nets over me to leak it as I huffed, yelled, blamed and more.

Ten years later, we bought a puppy for Hayden's birthday. From Bounty's first night with us, I was anxious about how our new pet would sleep. Sure enough, he reflected this with panicked behaviours without his dog mother.

Whoomp. This reflected the emotions that I had clocked the first nights after Hayden was born premature. Back then, as I lay awake in my hospital bed, I felt extremely uncomfortable to be separated from Hayden whilst he was by himself in a special care incubator.

With our new dog, Anthony and I were not called to have our puppy in our bed. I was forced to face my emotions, as I was separated from our dog, or else react from a monkey mind net, such as the 'talk sternly to the dog' or 'ignore him and he will eventually settle down' nets. I released my tears as I dreaded each night with our beautiful dog and the frustration that I was 'back here with sleep anxiety' again. I certainly moved up the cone of 'what it feels like to worry about my baby going to sleep alone without its mother'.

Before long, our puppy settled down at nights. Despite this, I still sensed my swirling charge as my heart considered that he was surely still frightened to sleep alone. Whether he was or he wasn't, inevitably, I still had more emotion to rise at some point because I could feel it within me.

A few months down the track, Bounty started to wake up and howl when he saw car lights or heard someone out the back of our house. Instantly, I felt the anger rise within me. I was angry I was back here again. I was angry that I couldn't get him to stop so I could go back to bed. My nervous system couldn't take it. I even threatened to give him away as it seemed to be me that was drawn to solve the problem and I just couldn't change it.

I finally allowed myself to feel the same emotions I swallowed down ten years ago as Hayden woke up and howled for many hours of many nights, even after sleep school - the frustration, the helplessness and the exhaustion. Bounty and I were now entwined in this life theme too.

Each night I awoke to Bounty's howl, I felt the charge run through my veins. Whilst he barked, I simply stood and cried the buckets of tears from my experience with Hayden. I never honoured how difficult it was for me as his mother. No one had been able to give me answers to get him to sleep. I had been so exhausted that I couldn't figure it out either. I finally felt peace after I released the 'lava lamp blob' of emotions, and of course, Bounty came back to his bed and slept.

As it often does, my soul lesson surprised me. Like I was adamant I would not bottle feed Hayden, I was also adamant we would not put our dog in a crate. As my tears brought me clarity however, I realised I faced an 'unperfect' path with the factors I had landed into. I had to choose our dog or myself. I released so much that I felt a calm knowing of the next step forward. I knew it was time to try a crate. I knew I would have heart for him in his crate experience. I needed to have heart for myself now too.

Of course, there is light and dark in any path, so you can never truly get it wrong. I still had to feel my emotions as we introduced Bounty to a crate. I then began on a new cone of 'what it feels like to be a mother of a dog, who sleeps in a crate'.

We played out some shadows with the crate experience and it also flowed. In the light, I saw the crate helped Bounty to know he didn't need to be on duty at all hours. After this, I sensed that I had collapsed the cone of 'what it feels like to worry about and get woken up by my child/dog howling in the night'. That was one cone done. Since then, we moved house and realised Bounty didn't have the same barking triggers. He now *has the crate as an option to sleep in, which he does, but he doesn't need to be closed in there anymore either. It was another cone done.*

Allowing divine timing

You cannot hurry up the cone, even if you think you know your direction or what your soul lesson is at the top. You only reach the top of the cone of a particular life theme, and consequently collapse it, as you clear the related charge within your inner universe. This takes a predetermined number of trips around the cone, to land in scenes that raise the charge that you wouldn't access by yourself.

> *There is no direct line to our problems solved. We must wind up the cone and land in scene after scene to do with this life theme, until we have resolved our inner universe and come to our soul lessons.*

We cannot possibly rise and dump all of the energies that relate to a particular life theme on one or even two occasions. Remember, our lava lamp effect has its own divine timing and does not switch off. We cannot force the particular energies of a related life theme to rise any sooner than they are orchestrated to. From this process, let's remember that it is a significant milestone to collapse a cone. It means that we have consciously co-created with our inner and external worlds and this takes as much energy as the length of time we needed to circle the cone for.

We must continue to remember that we look through the eye of a needle at all of the divinely orchestrated factors and timing that plays out in our existence. It took ten years for me to realise that I still held onto unexpressed emotions about Hayden's sleeplessness. This was despite the fact that I had already leaned into some of my immense sadness and desperation from the separation at his birth. I had to go through many reminder scenes and many emotional releases to work my way up the cone. Our dog was to be the final straw, at the top of my cone, to take me to the place of 'no more of this' and to find the answer to collapse it.

Energetically, you can picture yourself on a travelator that goes up the cone of each life theme. All you can do is feel through each scene that you find yourself in, that relates to a particular life theme. Of course, you cannot jump ahead or hurry the travelator. In good timing, your seed of intelligence will pull you into scenes that match the rising energies within you. As long as you feel and/or speak to your actors, or even yourself, during or after each scene, then you travel closer towards the top. The coming chapters of the Rainbow and Titanic will also explain why we have to continue to play out challenging scenes, even when we see where we want to go.

Here are some examples to show how people try to hurry up the cone.

* *A woman experienced a tricky childhood with her mother. Throughout her life, the woman shoved down the emotions of how her mother treated her. She went to spiritual circles and talked about her experience and also released a few tears. From this spiritual world, she learned that she could seek forgiveness of her mother, so that she could move on from her past. One day, she decided that she no longer wanted to put up with the stress of her relationship with her mother and so she called in forgiveness. She claimed she had forgiven her mother and used techniques such as breathwork, to seek calm about this. She convinced herself of this forgiveness as she disconnected further from her actual emotions and through distance with her mother.*

    The woman had started to circle up the cone on 'what it feels like to hold resentment at my mother', from the times when she did release her emotions and talk about it. Her inner universe however, was not done. Her seed of intelligence reflected this with other challenging actors and storylines. Her partner played out mind-blowing storylines, which reflected the same ways her mother had been with her. She pointed the finger at him and used this actor to leak her ever-rising resentment at.

    What the woman didn't know was that many spiritual and energetic techniques to find neutrality, only pull the 'flower' off the top of the 'inner weed'. Her lava lamp effect and matching scenes continued to invite her to embody the rising resentment, which started with her interactions with her mother. She had tried to hurry up the cone but didn't see that a new actor still reflected the same life theme for her to complete.

✴ A mother was told by daycare staff that her daughter's speech issues needed attention. As conditioned by the medical system, she tried to jump the stairs three at a time to solve the issue through speech therapy. Each week as they went to the speech pathologist, the mother and child landed in scenes to do with 'communication'. The child delayed getting ready to go but the mother did not see this as an opportunity to invite communication from her child. Her child's resistance to go was instead reflected in monkey mind nets of 'avoid getting ready for the car net'. On other therapy days, the mother refused to listen to her own intuition as she brushed away thoughts of, 'I don't feel like going out in the car on this cold, rainy day'.

In between therapy sessions, the mother also landed in scenes that invited her to feel 'what it feels like to be unheard by my partner' and 'what it feels like to be misunderstood by a friend'. All of these scenes invited the mother to co-create with how she felt on the inside. They all reflected the theme of 'what it feels like to be unheard and misunderstood'.

The child's speech issues were just one more storyline that reflected this communication life theme for the mother to work through. There were many day-to-day scenes where her child landed in life themes to explore 'what it feels like to be a child who is unheard and misunderstood'. This is where the mother and child could have started to circle the cone on this important life theme for all of us humans to embody. The mother didn't see this because she was more focused on how to fix the superficial side effect, her child's speech.

As the mother tried to hurry a solution through speech therapy, she weakened her heart connection with herself, because she ignored her own intuitive nudges. She also weakened her heart connection with her child, whose soul was never asked if she wanted to go or given the opportunity to say, 'my seed of intelligence has told me that's enough'. Instead, the mother found herself on the merry-

go-round of fights and tension with her partner, her daughter and ultimately, with herself, for decades to come, as they experienced continued communication difficulties.

Yes, as you co-create with your life themes, your inner universe and your actors, you end up on an exponentially more empowered trajectory than if you stay on the merry-go-round. It's just that we have not known how to consciously play the game of life to do so. Many women however, yearn to be in these more empowered places with their more empowered partners and children.

You can take a moment here to consider any of the big life themes that you have explored since you came to Earth. Perhaps it was 'what it feels like to be emotionally suppressed' or 'what it feels like to never be heard for my opinions'. Consider the scenes throughout your life that have landed you into this life theme again and again, perhaps as a child, teen, adult, parent or partner. From hereon in, as you notice yourself in *any* scene to do with this life theme, this is your opportunity to get honest about 'what it feels like to ...' and to feel or communicate to others about this. It takes courage, but you will feel satisfaction and empowerment, as you know, energetically, you are on the way up the cone!

Nervous system responses

As we get to the top of the cone on any life theme, we tend to revert to nervous system patterns. We may go through 'flight', where we face 'that's it!' monkey mind nets. In flight, we may move away from the problem, quit a job or unfriend or break up with someone. We may go through 'fight', where we face monkey mind nets of blame or revenge, to seek justice. In fight, perhaps we take someone to court or insist that someone pays in some way. We may go through 'freeze', where we face monkey mind nets of confusion. In freeze, perhaps we allow someone to persist with maltreatment or we justify displeasing scenes in our life. None of these are incorrect. Often, we have to play out these nervous system patterns until we have done more inner work to release ourselves of the energetic charge that causes them. As we do this, we seek to express ourselves through more empowered means.

As we *feel* our way through however, we begin to respond from a calm knowing instead of from our nervous system and monkey mind's response. Sometimes the empowered answers we come to are to back off, stand up for ourselves or wait to take action. They can appear to be made from flight (back off), fight (stand up for ourselves) or freeze (wait to take action) mode. The difference is in how we feel within, as we know we have connected with our seed of intelligence, from firstly feeling.

As we move through our emotions, we energetically connect to 'what wants to be' on our soul agreement. If we feel a deep peace with our decision, then we know we did not make a choice from our monkey mind. (Watch however that our monkey mind doesn't claim deep peace but is actually disconnected from feeling at all!). As we feel through our rising energies, our soul lesson can surprise us because it can often be what we said we would never do.

We can only come to our soul lessons by feeling.

As you can see, there are many angles of our experiences to feel through. In my case, Bounty helped to bring up 'what it felt like to be a mother of a child who woke me up and howled in the night'. Through other storylines, I have since had 'what it felt like to give my power away as a mother' mirrored back to me, from the initial scenes of a hospital birth and also from sleep school. We constantly land in recurring scenes to explore certain life themes. It is rare to collapse a cone as it can take years to land in divinely timed scenes to explore and feel through each angle of the life theme.

Of course, if we don't feel, then we stay on the merry-go-round at the bottom or at least play out 'same, same but different' storylines of the same underlying life themes. We will go through how to get to the underlying life theme and heart of the matter in a coming book of The New Way series.

It's like birth

The cone comes with a warning! It is like a parallel to birthing a baby. As you reach the top of the cone, you will feel as though you have hit the transition phase of labour. You may cry out any of the following, 'I can't do this anymore', 'that's it, I want out', 'what can I do to get away from this inner pain?' or 'I want to do something to solve this quickly', (I'll take a painkiller or caesarean - and that's fair enough).

Take heart when you go through yet another recurring scene in your life, such as when your children don't listen to you, your insomnia returns or you and your partner fight about parenting or money. Yes, you do need to go within and feel what it is like to have ended up in this scene, if you want to circle up the cone. No, these scenes will not then play out forever.

Your children may reject your attempts to be heard, which is a set up to further pull at your heart strings. Your partner may say the most hurtful comments about your lack of ability to make money, right when you feel sensitive about the topic. You may be so done with being exhausted from insomnia that you literally crack. These life themes will not be new to you. In fact, you become so *sick of* these recurring scenes that you start to seek any answer, so that you don't play out these scenes one more time.

When you feel completely *done with* your recurring challenge, these are the moments to lean into the thunderous emotions and possible flight, fight, freeze monkey mind threats that may come. At the same time that you feel beside yourself, notice a quiet excitement of 'I am at the top of this cone! I can feel it. I'm about to get to the glory on the other side', just as you do when you are about to birth a baby. After the storm, there is calm. You find the actual truth on the other side, because you let go of what you thought you cared about. This is what happened as I felt myself *done with* my dog that wouldn't sleep. I let go of my little old human self's resistance to crate him. You only find out as you go through this squeeze. You realise your soul lessons from your commitment to your inner work.

The 'good' cones

As we have seen, we are here to explore both 'good' and 'bad' life themes. Often, we are motivated to work with our challenging life themes, as we are keen to solve them. Think now to any 'good' life themes you have experienced in your life. For me, the life theme of 'what it feels like to travel the world' instantly comes to mind. I see it is a perceived 'good' life theme however, I then quickly see the challenges I have experienced as I continue to circle the cone. 'What it feels like to have a gastro bug in South America', 'what it feels like to lose my luggage', 'what it feels like to be beside myself in discomfort and boredom on a long plane ride' and so on!

Note, I experienced these life themes but I haven't yet *explored* them all, that is to acknowledge and release 'what it feels like to…'! In good time, I will inevitably experience them again, to explore these life themes and travel up the cone. Will I get to the top of the cone on these travel life themes? It is a real possibility, as we become more conscious of the pollution and negative impacts of travel. I sense I may 'do it to death' and instead learn to travel astrally or make new 'worlds' here at home. It could be anything!

Don't forget, we are not here to tick off every life theme that we have enlisted on our soul agreement. As the universe continues to expand, our work always continues. Simply feel through any scene of your day to find a life theme and get started on how you feel about it. There is never really a 'good' or 'bad' life theme as we always experience both sides.

As we pay attention to each scene to do with a life theme, we see it from each angle. Of course, it can seem impossible to see any light from a very challenging life theme. As a child, your soul may have clocked all of the negative emotions and rightly so. As you later begin to explore these emotions and go on your journey towards the top of the cone, you then start to claim the light on the other side.

Here is an example of how we can find our soul lessons to life themes we first experienced long ago.

Let's take a woman whose needs were not met when she was a child. Her home was very chaotic. She was left hungry and to find a place to sleep on the floor. Her soul clocked loneliness, desperation, hunger and panic. It also clocked emotions such as regret, shock and disbelief that this would be an actual experience here on Earth.

As a mother, she swung the other way and vowed to give her children a beautiful bed and plenty of good food and hugs. When her children wanted to co-sleep instead, she was then forced up the cone. She had to feel 'what it feels like to waste my precious money on an unnecessary, fancy bed'. She also had to face her bubbling emotions as one of her children rejected her hugs. Anger then surfaced as her other child was fussy and rejected her wholesome meals. She tuned into her underlying sadness and allowed the old energies to swirl and come up. She saw that her children were simply the actors who helped her to explore and make sense of her childhood experience.

On the other side of constant and committed inner work, the woman found huge inner peace. As she reached the top of the cone, she was ready to surrender to 'what wants to be' rather than 'what I think my children need'. She didn't want to blame her children any further for their seeming lack of gratitude. She then began to explore the light side of her experience, such as 'what it feels like to allow my children their path... to eat what they are called to and the respect we then have for each other' or 'what it feels like to communicate with my children before I waste time, energy and money on what my inner child actually craves'.

Into the future

Many people remain with their disempowered responses of fight, flight and/or freeze as their emotions rise on a certain life theme, particularly as it involves someone else. This however, results in disharmony with others and destroyed relationships. We cannot continue to run from, fight against each other or put up with disempowered ways. Instead, as both parties see their challenging scenes as an inner work invitation, they start to happily claim 'you are it'. At the top of the cone, they face their shadows and claim inner peace, harmony, humility and respect with the other person. This is the future of empowered relationships with ourselves and others.

Summary

* You are already on a cone for every life theme you land in.

* As you land in a recurring challenge, get excited to know that you have spied a life theme from your soul agreement.

* You can feel into your life themes to get off the merry-go-round and circle up the cone.

* You progress up the cone as you feel and/or speak up about your experience in the challenging scene and/or offer others to feel and speak up.

* Your recurring challenges will show up in x amount of time as you circle the cone. You cannot avoid them nor hurry them.

* Your recurring challenges may include the same actor, various actors or just feature you.

* No challenge is forever, if you do the challenging inner work to get to the top of the cone.

* To energise you, it is helpful to notice the smallest changes of improvement in your life theme as you circle it.

To feel into ...

- What is one recurring day to day issue that you experience?
- Next time you land in any scene to do with this topic, aim to check in with how you feel inside and if you can, feel these emotions. Then, talk up from this place to know you have moved up the cone on this life theme!

Inner Universe

...start here, to make sense of your life...

I hadn't realised how much I had been conditioned to disconnect from my inner sensations as I grew up and instead, I did life from what I saw in my external reality. In my primary school years I noticed what others could do well. I didn't have the dance moves like the girls who took dance lessons. I wasn't able to run like those who won first place. I wasn't confident to go for student leadership like those that did. My identity was created from what I was not.

In my older years, I continued to create my identity from what I looked like on the external, through clothes and makeup. I also focused on others. I listened to everyone and tried to support them with their problems. I made conversation with people about what I thought I should say. I then became a mother where I was forced to shoot down daily challenges, which still forced me to focus on life from my external reality. I had very little sense of an inner world.

2013

It was only as I came into my thirties that I began the journey inwards. I did several years of Bikram yoga when I experienced a dendritic ulcer in my eye. I was too afraid to put contact lenses back in my eyes but I could not give up yoga! So I went with glasses and took them off before class. Immediately, I was forced to connect with muscles I didn't know I had, to stay balanced on one leg. Before this, I succeeded in these types of poses as I used the mirror. When I used my eyes to achieve the pose I wanted to see in the mirror, I didn't realise that I recruited the wrong muscles. Without my contacts and for over a year, I did the yoga 'blind' and became very connected with my muscles, because I sensed rather than saw. I sensed an inner world, where I *felt* it.

At the same time, I listened to a personalised meditation that Paul recorded for me for 21 nights. After I cried every night, I woke each morning with a peace and clarity within me. At my government job that day, the minute someone said something I didn't like, I felt a pang within me. I felt my emotional body talk to me. Each night, I leaned into this emotion, plus whatever else wanted to come up from the past too. I simply released one rising 'blob' after another.

A couple of years later, I realised my inner work journey was not an overnight adventure. I had released much tension and pain from my physical body as I allowed my emotions to flow, however, I was nowhere near done. The space within my skin was not a finite space. It was like a universe in there, forever deepening. I literally felt the vastness of this universe-like space within me, in contrast to what we perceive from basic human anatomy!

The more I was in tune with my physical and emotional bodies, the more I allowed my lava lamp effect to dictate the energies that wanted to rise, without judgement. One day, I felt the dread of a full day of chores ahead of me. I was at the clothesline and allowed myself to cry about 'what about my soul purpose, my fulfilment and happiness?'. As I let the emotions rise how they wanted to, I felt a wave of sadness pour through me. Immediately, I thought of the women way back in my family line and their unrealised potential. As with the emotional blackbox, their souls also clocked emotions, as they put aside their purpose and happiness to 'do what it takes to give their children the best start in life, so that they could be successful'. All of the mothers of previous generations came to me with their frustration, grief and even rage at what *they* had lost, by only being of service to others.

Whose emotion did I feel? The fact that I felt sensations within me confirmed they were mine. I remembered that I clocked them as a child, when I observed mothers who spent all of their energy on their children, family or work, to their detriment. My swallowed down emotions were also from my own experiences where I put the needs of others first too much. This was how my ancestors and I were conditioned to be as mothers. This is not to say there aren't light aspects of the mother role. As a child who closely observed mothers however, my soul pondered, 'but what about you and your joy?', 'what do you stand for?' and 'I'd like to see more of that gift you seem to have'.

Again, I saw the depth of our inner universe, whilst I explored my emotions at the clothesline. If I had blocked my emotions on this topic, I would not have explored this important life theme and the giant inner weed for every mother of The New Way. I would have continued to find myself on the merry-go-round of 'what it feels like to be an unfulfilled mother'.

From this experience, I saw that the root of the inner weed within me, ended in a portal to the family line of energies that have never been expressed on this life theme. This concept reminds us that our rising energies are bigger than our own experience. We must not judge what we feel within. At the same time, we must remember that this energy really does exist within *our* inner universe, so that we can shift and birth it.

> *If we feel it, then it is there to be expressed.*
> *We just need to stay present with our inner universe more than the thoughts in our head that judge these sensations.*

Why you want to know about your Inner Universe

We must go tenderly with ourselves as we honour the cost of emotional suppression. We each have inner work to be done, to the degree that is on our unique path, with the depth of a universe. We must keep the focus within, instead of the external focus to fix and control others, when we don't like how they show up. This is not to say that we don't speak up and insist our actors deal with their own inner charge, as we have dealt with ours. This is a key step as we claim empowerment and invite others to as well. We must also find softness for ourselves as we begin to practise the game of life, The New Way.

Honour your inner universe

As emotions rise, you may hear yourself think, 'don't be so silly', 'that's enough of that' or simply, 'where is the gratitude in this?'. Tune back into the sensations within your inner universe and feel. They might whisper or scream at you with physical body sensations. They might whisper at you or scream at you with emotional body sensations. There may even be a confusion in your mental body or an aching of your spiritual body. Feel.

When the big emotions rise, or even when they don't, honour yourself and the challenging times you have experienced as a soul here on Earth. Remember to allow the unexpressed energies of those who have walked these same life themes to pass through you too. Trust that when the 'lava lamp blob' is expressed, you will feel a lightness or perhaps a tenderness. Honour yourself as you come to an empowered feminine place, where you allow yourself to be vulnerable and to be free of these trapped energies. There, you feel embodied gratitude and positivity.

Is it mine?

As we have seen, what we feel within our inner universe is always ours. Although we play out life themes that have played out for generations, we have always experienced a scar point in our own life. We must start here, although it can be easier to 'feel for others'. The sooner we feel for our own experience, the sooner we become present with the energy that seeks to be released.

As we remember to feel without judgement, we get to the root of our weed and sink into the generational experience of the life theme. We then get to the top of the cone and exist in neutrality but with a heart power on this particular topic.

Playing from your inner universe

Let's look further at why you want to tune into your inner universe and what happens next once you do. There are two important reasons you tune into your inner universe as much as you can, as you go about your day.

1. Your sensations connect you to your agreed life themes - such as *how it feels* to be a homeschool Mum, to get told 'no' by your children, to be a single Mum, to be overweight etc. This guides you to work with the divine on these experiences rather than thrash blindly through the jungle of your day's challenges or give your power to someone else to solve them. Head back to the Life Themes chapter to revise this concept in more detail if you need to.

2. Your sensations are a red or green light as to where to focus your energy best, to move towards most flow. Again, we don't remember the exact experiences we popped on our soul agreement, and hence, our sensations tell us 'hotter' or 'colder' to stay on the tracks. We will look further at how to allow our seed of intelligence to guide us, in the Red and Green Lights chapter.

Remember, we can't control the lava lamp effect. It will raise old emotions we may not have made time for in our day or week ... or life. It will raise them in perfect fashion however, for our soul path. What we can control is how much we tune into our inner universe and how much we consciously work with this divine guidance. Let's look at an example of how it can play out both ways.

Here is an example of how a mother can play out her challenging scene in two ways.

Example 1 - to react to your day with no connection to your inner universe.

One mother rises in the morning and a split second later she feels the heaviness come over her, the dread of her day. Her chest is tight and the back of her neck feels dense.

It's not long before her two children fight over their toys and she hears her monkey mind say, 'this is all I need'. Her neck constricts and she feels the burn within her, as she gets pulled into the scene to try and sort it out.

She huffs as she then tries to get ready for the day. She half-heartedly attempts to come back to a sense of renewed hope. She scrolls on Facebook, as she subconsciously escapes her pain for a little while. She notices a friend's post that claims a view contrary to hers. She purses her lips and squeezes her hamstrings. She hears her monkey mind go into judgement mode.

She starts to tell her partner about this friend's view and he takes her friend's side. The burn rises and she feels her neck tense again. She goes into overdrive as she tries to convince her husband to take her side. Instead, he walks away because he thinks she's made a mountain out of a molehill. She takes a few deep breaths as she tries, in desperation, to change how she feels inside. She hears her monkey mind command her to go and research, to find something she can use, to steer her partner to her view. In the background, she can hear the children up to no good. They laugh and get a bit too hysterical.

The children knock over a jar of honey. This time she cracks it. She yells at her children and she sends them to their room. She huffs as she stays in 'closed heart' mode. She feverishly cleans up, as she huffs at her children's behaviour, so that she doesn't have to feel the hurt in her heart of how she treated them. She wonders why she wakes the next morning in dread of what could happen on this new day, with all of the charge that still swirls within her.

Example 2 - to tune inwards as a priority, throughout your day.

Another mother aims to live The New Way. She wakes up and in her mind says 'Oh no, I don't feel good today. I'd better go easy on myself and everyone else I interact with'. She takes time in the shower to slump her shoulders. She leans into the pulling feeling in her neck and nurtures it with a loving hand as she goes about her morning. She lets go of plans that feel too much and instead aims to nurture herself, even with a cup of tea or a hug with her children.

The children start a fight about their toys. She tunes straight back into her neck. It is sore and it keeps her in irritation mode. She ignores her monkey mind, which tries to command her to go and yell at the children. Instead, she swipes this energetic lava lamp blob to the side, whilst she asks the children if they can do something else so that she can spend a moment with her emotions. Sometimes it works, but today the children ignore her and continue to fight. She has no choice but to sink further into her emotions, as she searches for how she feels.

'I am tired!' she announces. 'I am tired of pulling you all apart'. She realises this directs energy at her children in blame, so she slumps her shoulders again. 'Come here. Let's have a hug and sort this out. I want you to know that I've got some old emotions rising today, so I'm going easy on myself too'. She squeezes her children as she notices her hardness to them and to herself. The swirling energy now pulses at her temples, which causes her to grit her teeth.

Before she even sorts out the toy fight, she is guided to stay with her feelings and to communicate them. By doing this, she stays accountable to her inner work as well as to model this process to her children. 'I am tired because it makes me sad when you both fight. I so dearly want you to get along, and it tugs at the sadness inside me when you don't'. She notices the wobble in her voice as she hits on something.

She searches for the exact reason she would be sad at this. The reflection hits her. 'I am sad because I didn't get along with my brother when I was younger, and I wish it was different'. As she says it, she feels a lump in her throat, and her children drop their heart armour. They put their hands out to her. She feels held and allows her tears to drop. Immediately the pain in her neck begins to lessen, which guides her to continue to find this relief through her tears.

She saw her life theme - 'what it feels like to be a mother of children who don't get along'. She realised where the root of it began. The journey to pull this inner weed out by the root began as she allowed her tears to come. She felt her children's souls support her through their caring eyes and touch.

Her emotional release dropped the energy in the room. The children left her to her inner work and ran off to play. She didn't take too long to let go of some of the backlog of this sadness. As she did, she looked forward to her day, which played out much better, because she could feel her connection back to the divine. She felt energised to co-create a glorious day with her family and she did.

When the mother then scrolled Facebook, it wasn't a problem, because she didn't feel reactive. She was in great spirits when she saw her partner; she and the children had found a fun movie to watch together. Her partner showed empathy, as she relayed her childhood story without so much charge.

Of course, the next day she rose in a better fashion, as she was free of this energetic charge and more connected with the divine. She didn't doubt that another energetic package, small or large, may rise at any time that day. She had the confidence however, to work through it and maintain her heart connection with herself and her family.

You can only imagine how the mother in the first example may tell someone about her day. It would be 'Can you believe...?' stories, rants and disempowerment talk, as she blames it on the kids being tired, her husband who works too much or even the planets. The second mother didn't have the need to tell anyone about her day, as she was free of the stagnant energy that wanted to be worked with. Of course, at any time she was happy to rave about her wonderful day-to-day scenes, which included those scenes that prodded her to find relief within.

The life theme not the storyline

When we become aware of our life themes, we find empowerment as we connect and work with the emotions in our inner universe. When we do this, we don't get stuck on the details of the storyline it took to get us to feel it. Remember, there are countless storylines which get us to explore the same underlying life theme and feel the same underlying emotions. The work is to co-create with our life theme and inner sensations instead of our day to day storylines.

Here is an example of a mother who gets stuck on the details of the storyline and another who works with her emotions.

The example is about how they navigate the challenge of 'being a mother of a child who doesn't connect with other children so easily'.

Example 1. The mother who gets stuck on the details of the storyline.

As her son struggles to make friendships, this mother is invited to notice her inner sensations of 'what it feels like to be a mother of a child who doesn't connect easily with others'. Instead, she ignores her inner universe so that she doesn't have to feel these unexpressed energies. From her unexpressed charge however, this mother gets caught under monkey mind nets, which guide her to try and fix her child's challenges.

As sadness arises, she desperately tries to find different activities to try her child in, to see if he can find a friend. As her anger rises, she makes a fuss about how the school handles the bullying. Next, she senses embarrassment arise, which reflects how she sees her success as a parent. In response to this unexpressed emotion, she removes her child from any place that makes her or her child feel inadequate. She continually spends her days in a state of panic and confusion at how to help her child. Eventually, her helplessness drives her to a paediatrician to seek a diagnosis, so she has something to explain her child's expression.

In the meantime, her unexpressed inner charge results in tricky times with her manager at work and blow ups with her husband. She feels the wretched sense of disempowerment within her as she feels out of control and yearns for more zest for life. Her physical body tells her with a sore lower back and tension headaches.

Into the future, her child grows up with part of their identity as 'I don't connect with others well. I am the problem'. Their shoulders shrug over in protection of their heart. Their chin protrudes forward to protect the stagnant energy at the back of their neck and throat area. They struggle with back issues. They don't know how to move through blow ups around communication issues with their future partner and children.

The mother directs her forever-rising frustration at her husband. She justifies friends who don't treat her with respect. In fact, she leaks her charge at them, as she complains about how her now adult son's partner treats him. Her heart connection with her son is weakened, because he never felt his mother truly feel and understand his childhood experience.

Example 2. The mother who co-creates with the sensations of her inner universe.

Through empowerment, this mother explores each of her challenging daily scenes with her son. She feels 'what it feels like to have a child who has few friends', 'what it feels like to be a mother of a child who is bullied' and 'what it feels like to be told my child doesn't have good social skills'. She maps her rising feelings back to the social challenges she experienced in her life. As she releases her tears and finds heart for herself, she finds compassion for her son. She then trusts him as a wise being who can get through it, and she clearly knows what her next steps are.

As the mother feels through her charge, she diffuses the situation and knows how to take more discerning action. This action is to talk calmly with the son's teacher and to make the space for her son to talk and feel through the tricky scenes that he experiences. She had to do this for herself first as the energetic priority in mother-child teamwork. We will cover more on this in an upcoming book.

As a result, the mother doesn't take action from a place of panic, embarrassment or confusion. Her son then understands that this is simply a life theme that he and his mother are to explore together, which brings up some big emotions. She knows it is not an overnight fix but as she makes peace with the theme herself, she shows her son that it is safe to explore it too.

The mother is also aware that her child's challenges are possibly a red light, to nudge both of them to seek a more aligned community. She takes an honest look at how she feels about those she spends her time with. This gives her a clearer idea of the life theme she is guided to explore - 'what it feels like to not truly resonate with those we call our friends'.

As both the mother and child feel through the themes of loneliness and to not speak up for oneself, they start to land in scenes with more resonant families. These families bring a new environment for them both, to practise more free and safe expression of themselves. Ultimately, there was no reason to pathologise either of them. It was just an exploration of a life theme from a mother and child's angle.

Into the future, the son's connection with his mother remains strong as they practise the game of life together. They feel into any life theme first and then take action from this grounded place. They find more and more inner peace, which is reflected by their relationship with themselves and with others and their physical, emotional, mental and spiritual health.

As you can see, there is a significant difference in how the mother-child relationship eventuates. There is also an obvious difference in how each of them makes sense of their entire being and the reality they create from that. The first example highlights the separation that occurs as we take action from our rising energies. We lose heart connection with ourselves and our children if we don't feel through our experiences. It reminds us that our actors and physical body will continue to give us challenges until we honour our inner universe.

The second example highlights Mother-Child Teamwork, where both mother and child seek to feel and speak about their experiences. It acknowledges the energetic interconnection we have as mother and child in the life themes that we explore and the exponential result as both parties do their inner work. Of course, fathers will consequently step into this teamwork as us mothers go first.

> Mother-Child Teamwork - both parent and child seek to feel and talk about their experiences, to prioritise their heart connection above any daily challenge. Fathers will step into this as we go first.

Summary

* Our inner universe is every sensation we feel within us.

* It holds the unexpressed energies from the challenging scenes of our life.

* As we work with these life themes, we then tug at the root of the weed and open up to flow ancestral energies that relate to these life themes as well.

* As we connect with our inner universe, we seek to connect with others - which strengthens heart connection and connection to our true essence.

To explore ...

- What sensations do you feel within you now?

- Some people just perceive and feel. Some people describe and put words to it. Some people immediately put their hands to where the energy sits. Notice your best way to feel and acknowledge your inner universe.

How to Play summary

Now is a good time to zoom out and glance at the rules of the game of life!

At any time, head to the back of the book to check in with this How to Play summary.

1. You wake each morning and check how you feel in your inner universe.

2. You get honest that these feelings will attract how the scenes and actors show up in your life that day.

3. You check to see if you feel to release any charge that wants to come up, either :

    - then and there

    - later, as the external world prods your inner universe - it may take a good while to master responsible emotional expression

4. You talk out loud to your family and actors about how you feel and own any responses that may come from your inner charge as you get prodded. For example, if you blame, yell, huff or try to control them from hereon in.

5. You honour yourself as you spend even a present moment with the sensations in your physical body or with the emotions as they come up. You connect with your inner universe.

6. You take note of the life theme you play out in these scenes - eg. 'Oh this is what it feels like to be doing it all as a mother' or 'what it feels like to have a child who is too much......' or 'what it feels like to run late'.

7. You acknowledge how it relates to any of your four 'bodies' - physical, emotional, mental and/or spiritual, to shift the energy that rises within you. We'll go into this process in more detail in a coming book of The New Way series.

8. The more you do, the more you receive your 'goodie bag' of open heartedness, clarity, energy, motivation and momentum to move towards your dreams for you and your family, in the small everyday scenes and in the bigger picture. You gain heart connection and respect from those around you as you butt out of their path, own your stuff and work your own soul agreement. From the different energetic state within you, the actors and scenes begin to change in positive ways too.

9. The more you play the game of life in this fashion, the more you leap frog into alignment and flow with your soul agreement and true essence. By default, those around you also begin to swirl into alignment, because you hold a very nurturing and empowered energetic space for them to go The New Way.

The magic is to be present in the moment with 'what is', rather than what we'd like it to be. At the same time, we practise how to stay connected with what our heart really yearns for.

The Tip of the Iceberg

...the little opportunities to feel will become the chaos that forces us to crack...

2018

I didn't realise I had discovered the concept of the 'tip of the iceberg' until I started to use this term to everyone I mentored. They told me stories such as, 'My child won't eat the meal I've prepared, and I feel so much heat and frustration rising'. I explained to them, 'When your child refuses to eat dinner it is the tip of the iceberg. They raise your feelings from themes like, 'I cooked this meal for you, with the last ounces of my energy and it feels like a waste now that you won't eat it' or 'I don't even have the energy to consider what else you could eat instead'. Then we went deeper, back to their childhood and why they might have big feelings about this scene in their day. It was usually something like, 'I was made to eat all of my dinner, whether my body craved that food or not'. This was the heart of the matter. The tip of the iceberg was the day-to-day scene that their child landed them into.

As we know, we all swallowed down emotions the first time we landed in a life theme, usually when we were very young. These energies have sat stagnant within us until our children or other actors put us back into the vibrations of those scenes. Boom, the emotions rise. These scenes and actors are the 'tip of the iceberg' of that particular life theme.

> Tip of the iceberg - the day-to-day scenario that represents and raises the unexpressed energies from our initial 'scar point'. Whilst we do need to address the day-to-day scene, we must prioritise the deeper inner work invitation.

As I worked with this concept, I soon realised that *all* of our day-to-day scenes and the actors that showed up, were the 'tip of the iceberg' to a related life theme from long ago. As we have already seen in Your Actors chapter, don't shoot the messengers! How our actors make us feel is an invitation to connect with the lava lamp effect within us. It could be the day we have computer problems, our newborn cries continuously or we get to a shop just as it's closed. It could be even more subtle scenes, which give us a pang somewhere inside us. These day-to-day scenes land us in life themes that match life themes we have already experienced.

Let's look at some examples of how to take the day-to-day life theme and map it to the matching root life theme. Often, it started by our parents or those close to us, when we were younger.

Tip of the iceberg day-to-day scene	The matching life theme where you've already experienced it and/or done this yourself
Your child makes a negative comment about your appearance.	✻ 'what it feels like to have someone make hurtful comments about my appearance' ✻ 'what it feels like to make hurtful comments to others'
Your child snatches from another child at the park.	✻ 'what it feels like to be embarrassed by the behaviour of someone close to me' ✻ 'what it feels like to snatch'
Your partner makes life choices for you - they book a holiday or sort out your own tax.	✻ 'what it feels like to have someone else make choices / do life for me' ✻ 'what it feels like to make choices or do things for others when they are capable'
A lady makes a judging comment to your children as they walk down the street.	✻ 'what it feels like to have others judge my children' ✻ 'what it feels like to judge others' children' ✻ 'what it feels like to have others judge me as a child'

All day every day, we turn away from these 'tip of the iceberg' invitations. We have been conditioned to 'stop being so silly' when we feel emotions about something that is 'not worth crying over'. The thing is, if we can lean into how we feel about each of our day-to-day scenes, we begin to pull up the root of the deeper weed.

If we allow ourselves to cry over 'spilt milk', we practise how to feel the pain of our inner sensations, whilst the storylines are not so big. We start to become more confident and efficient to feel within, even as we find ourselves in more challenging scenes. As these displeasing scenes arrive, we are more likely to continue to release our emotions responsibly, because we have seen the magic of the process. We are more likely to claim 'you are it' than to point the finger of blame externally or turn away from our 'lava lamp blobs'.

In divine timing, our actors really start to prod us. They invite us to feel where these emotions were first felt, well past the tip of the iceberg scenes that they land us into. This is when we are at the top of the cone. *For example, your child says no to lettuce, which they usually like, and it's your final straw. Your emotional reaction is bigger than what the tip of the iceberg scene warrants. Your child has taken you to the heart of the matter of how you were made to feel by your father, when you resisted a certain food.*

If we dived into the big emotions from our challenging childhood scenes from the very beginning, we would be far more flattened. For some, however, there is not as much practice time before their 'snow globe' is shaken up. The path is to dive straight into this practice, to explore the Heart energy. It is still best to feel through your daily 'tip of the iceberg' scenes, and trust that this will unravel your inner hurts most kindly and efficiently. Your actors are there to prod these inner hurts from you.

Our seed of intelligence rises our old emotions in divine timing to orchestrate the right prodding scenes, of what we can handle. We must remember that every one of our challenging day-to-day scenes energetically prods the 'tip of the iceberg' of our past, deeper emotional experiences. For those that don't realise this, they may blame their actors or make too much of a deal about the tip of the iceberg scenes.

Here is an example of how we may take action on the tip of the iceberg scene, rather than feel into the heart of the matter.

Let's say our child puts on a bit of weight, and we project our emotions onto them through our actions. We cement the weight issue onto their identity. We energetically tell them 'some weight is something to be scared about'. Instead, if we first work through our emotions of our experience of 'what it feels like to notice some extra weight on myself' or even 'what it feels like to have an overweight child', we then respond to our child from a calmer and energetically different place. Our child senses that we trust this is a life theme that they can and will move through, in divine timing. We take action from a different place and we remember to allow our child to simply feel and speak about their angle of the life theme, Mother-Child Teamwork.

Why you want to know about the Tip of the Iceberg

We have been strongly conditioned to be tough and resilient, to completely overlook our inner work opportunities. Our lava lamp effect however, ensures that we continue to attract occasions to flow our unexpressed energies. Although we might say yes to 'you are it', we can't work with every challenging scene of our day. It does however, become more and more evident that we need to find time and space to do our inner work. When we start to spend more time on inner reflection, we spend less time on our external challenges. This is because we resolve them more easily, with less inner charge, or they even start to resolve on their own.

Importantly, after we have done the inner reflection, we must still remember to speak up about the heart of the matter to our actors. As we have seen, we still need to communicate and address the challenging scene as our actor's monkey mind is involved in disempowerment too.

> *We start to lean into our bigger traumas as we practise with the little 'blobs'. Our day-to-day prods are usually less prickly storylines than the bigger memories of where this scar point started.*

As we remember our day-to-day actors and scenes are just the messengers, we don't have to invite such a battle with them. The tip of the iceberg reminds us that the little things that get to us in the day *do* represent bigger hurts, every single time. We can lean into them, rather than dissociate from or justify them. It is empowered to distance ourselves from our actors until we have worked with our own inner charge. This is practice!

We must also remember to allow our children to 'cry over spilt milk' and help them connect with their deeper life theme, of which there always is. Our children intuitively attempt to lean into emotions as they arise, at least until we try to make things better or shut them down. It is our work to notice our reactions to their emotional expression and/or if our child shows underexpression where there should be emotion.

The heart of the matter

At any point after your challenging day-to-day scene, you can connect with and understand why you actually feel these emotions. As you feel past the tip of the iceberg scene, it will always lead to the heart of the matter. This comes back to fundamentally sad points for us as humans.

Some examples of the heart of the matter are:

* 'I'm just tired'.
* 'I've tried so hard, and it's never enough'.
* 'I can't see a way out'.
* 'I don't feel heard and understood'.
* 'the BS never seems to end'.
* 'I don't feel loved'.

As we get to the heart of the matter, we flow emotions more easily. It's as if the tears confirm, 'yes, this is what is *actually* rising in this blob of energy, not that tip of the iceberg scene'. Once we release the tears, we can interact in a more empowered way with our actors. As the charge is cleared, we do and say things from our heart. This can be very different from those who try to *come from* their heart but still act from a place of unresolved charge. As we are more peaceful within, we then talk to our actors with the intention to solve the matter with them, because we no longer have energy to leak at them in arguments.

> *We repair the tip of the iceberg scene from a very different place when we have felt through our rising lava lamp blobs. We don't need to sort it out through our inner charge or believe our external actors are to blame.*

Here are a few examples of how to see the heart of the matter, beyond the tip of the iceberg.

✱   *You cut your child's sandwiches into squares, when they wanted triangles. Before you put too much energy on the sandwich issue, which is the tip of the iceberg, you can head straight to the heart of the matter for yourself and your child.*

As your child has their meltdown, you realise this rising frustration ties in with all of the scenes in their life where they have been controlled and rightly so, they clocked big emotions. This is the lava lamp effect in action. As the big blob from the past arises within your child, the square sandwiches are the final straw.

As you feel your rising charge, you realise you have landed in 'what it feels like to be too tired at my core to make another sandwich'. Your child brought you to your final straw moment of 'I am just so soul tired as a mother'.

The first step is to work through your child's emotions, as well as yours, which will inevitably rise with their tantrum. In good time, as you are both clearer, it will go one of two ways. Your child will not care nearly so much how the sandwich is cut or you will feel completely fine to make a new one. Until then, there is inner charge to be flowed.

★ *Your partner comes home and goes off at you because you left a few dirty dishes around. The dishes are the tip of the iceberg to your partner's rising energies of something deeper, the final straw. Rather than engage with the dishes issue, you can move straight to the heart of the matter, that they, rightly so, should have big feelings about. Maybe you noticed their rising stress that morning, as they talked about an issue at work. As your partner brings up the dishes, you might respond with, 'I sense your stress. Is it more to do with what happened at work?'.*

As you hit the nail on the head, your partner will likely deflate or potentially feel this old charge even more so. You can hold space for this issue, as you bring compassion for why they have this inner charge. This then avoids further argument about the dishes. If you don't engage with the tip of the iceberg matter, the dishes, you won't make yourself a scapegoat for the next time their work stress or any other matter arises.

As you land in this scene, you may sense the rising charge within you. Either then and there, or later, you may release the emotions that rise until you find the heart of the matter for yourself. The heart of the matter may boil down to, 'I don't feel good enough, I was always picked on by my parents'. Your partner landed you into this scene to feel this. You can then use the tip of the iceberg scene to feel your unexpressed energies from the root of the weed.

★ *You feel irritated all day and as you get home, your child accidentally drops a heavy toy on your toe. It is the tip of the iceberg to the bigger energies that arise within you. You won't feel the need to have a go at your child, if you instead sink into the emotions that are now much riper. Perhaps you know what the tears are about or perhaps you don't. Your only aim is to flow the trapped energy.*

★ *You are a homeschooling mum (or not) and your children just won't help out with the daily tasks. As you lecture your children, you remember to go inwards, to find the heart of the matter. 'I'm just tired. I have been since you were born'. As you say this out loud, you realise that your emotions are truly justified. You tell your children stories about why you were exhausted as a new mother with no community, and as a result, your children bring you heart.*

After you clear a fair bit of this emotional energy, you are more likely to appreciate the support and love your children do bring, even if it's just their hugs. Through your clarity, you see them as children who landed in tricky scenes too, such as 'what it feels like to be a child without community or support for my mother'.

From this place of diffused emotion, you address the matter with passion. You announce what you yearn for. 'I yearn for us to be a family team, where we all get in and help out, because we are happy to be a part of this team. I know sometimes you don't feel that way and neither do I. Let's go easy on each other. I would love some help with the washing if anyone feels called'. Without attachment, because you now feel better within yourself, you go to do it gladly. Of course, the children reflect this and come to help and chat too.

With far less inner charge, we don't attract the more challenging storylines, which energetically must then play out, to prod these unexpressed energies. Yes, it can feel like crying over spilt milk, which we have been strongly conditioned against. It saves us however, from explosion point, where we express ourselves through disempowered monkey mind expressions. Of course, it also starts to protect us from and unravel our health issues, as well as repair disconnected relationships.

It is important to remember that if you seek the heart of the matter, you won't need to make as big a deal about the tip of the iceberg scenario. You will avoid a lot of wasted time, energy and money if you make sense of your day-to-day scenes from within first. You can then take action on any day-to-day challenge that calls you, from a centred place. Remember, your monkey mind will instead try to make it *all* about the external problem to be dealt with through worry and emotionally-charged action.

As you work with your inner charge, which the tip of the iceberg scene brought up, you then sail through much more easily with your child, partner or anyone else involved. The tip of the iceberg is your opportunity to start to feel inwards and honour your past stresses, slowly but surely… and kindly. Remember, it is an *unperfect* practice!

Summary

* Don't shoot the messenger - your actors help you pull the deeper weed.

* Do cry over spilt milk - you then don't attract the bigger storylines to make you crack.

* Find the heart of the matter so that you can release the rising 'blob' and respond to your actors from your true essence.

* You do need to address the tip of the iceberg matter, to pull the weed out by the root.

To feel …

Name one of the biggest challenges you have right now.
What is the heart of the matter?

- What is the actual problem that it causes you?

- Name the life theme and spy on where you first landed into this life theme.

- Remember to tell your actors about your scar point, so that they can bring more heart to you.

Seasons of Life

...the harmony is between two poles...

2013

Hayden was very sensitive as a baby and into his toddler years. I was eventually pulled into the world of food sensitivities, as I tried to solve his eczema and 'ADHD' type of behaviour, which nearly pulled the family apart. When Hayden was barely three years old, a dietitian advised us to put him on a strict elimination diet. It became a long journey, as we tried to work out exactly which foods set off his challenging physical and behavioural symptoms. We ended up at a naturopath, kinesiologists, an oracle and more. Just the strict diet alone was traumatic for not only Hayden, at such a young age, but also myself. I sat in a cloud of sadness as we went to birthday parties and other events, where I had to tell him that he couldn't partake in most foods.

The deprivation continued into his early school years, where Hayden was nearly everything-free. It exhausted me to find and bake alternatives so he would not miss out completely. Food sensitivities were on Hayden's soul agreement and they were also on mine, as his Mum. I found it difficult to nurse his heart when he felt deprived. At the same time, it comforted me to know that we had solved his eczema and much of his behavioural issues with the diet.

I soon came to the realisation however, that Hayden's behavioural issues reflected my stress. I had to stay accountable to my intuition on this, because my monkey mind insisted it was just the food, so I didn't have to look at myself. It was difficult to claim 'you are it'.

For some years, I played with this realisation. Right when I felt agitated, stressed or just exhausted within, Hayden's behaviour became impulsive or rough. If he was energetically linked to me however, I questioned what would make him act in tricky ways when I wasn't around. This is where I began to understand Hayden's behaviour in a greater light. He behaved in reflection of *everyone else's* stress too. Again, I had to stay accountable to my own reflections first.

Once I saw that Hayden reflected my inner universe, I felt no choice but to focus inwards. I committed to my own inner work rather than sole focus on behaviour management for Hayden. As I released my emotions and had heart for my stressful life experiences, I then had compassion for the emotions that drove his behaviours. I sought to help him feel and speak about this, which gradually changed his nervous system and reactions. I no longer needed to blame Hayden's presentation when I felt discomfort within myself, although it has not been an overnight journey to accept this! As a result, Hayden started to express his true essence even more so, particularly his intuitive gifts. He had come out from under the shadows of my shadows.

I questioned if food was the culprit at all or simply a catalyst for Hayden to behave from the shadows in reflection of my inner state. I soon felt called to loosen up on what he ate. I wondered if processed gluten free bread was honestly better than an organic oat sourdough. Of course, Hayden had no obvious reactions to the sourdough. We broke free of hard and fast rules and simply went with what felt best around food.

2018

As I relaxed on what I was prepared for the boys to eat, of course the theme of deprivation came up. One Easter, the boys announced they wanted to buy Cadbury eggs with their own money. They had only ever eaten my homemade cacao butter eggs (which were delicious and nutritious!). I begged them not to. I felt the surge of my emotions as I thought about how much energy I had spent, to keep my children clean eaters. Now, they gleefully chose to go to the 'other side', all because other people had made a big deal over these sugary treats. I was angry and sad all at once. As we drove home from the supermarket with their Cadbury easter eggs, I realised a season of our lives had come to an end. I cried as I literally let go of the identity of being a mother of clean eaters. I sensed we were about to enter a new 'season of life'.

> Seasons of life - We flow in and out of seasons of life, pulled by our seed of intelligence, to be sure we experience the countless life themes on our soul agreement and from opposing angles.

Before long, you wouldn't believe the scenes the boys managed to find themselves in. They got their hands on chocolate, lollies, Domino's pizza, fruit juice boxes and other junk-style food they had never eaten. I knew if I stepped in between them and this new season of their life, our heart connection would be at risk. I couldn't interfere with their seed of intelligence, which pulled them to experience all that they had missed out on. I had felt that deprivation with them and hence, I had heart for this.

The harmony is between two poles

That's when I saw the energetic law - 'the harmony is between two poles'. As we experience one side of life, we swing one way. We then swing back the other way in equal distance, to experience the other side, *if* we follow the pull of our seed of intelligence. These energetics are explained by Newton's cradle. You know the five metal balls that dangle from a little apparatus that sits on your desk? You pull back one ball and let it swing to hit the other balls. The ball furthest away then swings in the opposite direction, *in equal distance*. We will soon go through more life themes where you might swing in two different directions.

> ### ENERGETIC LAW
>
> 'The harmony is between two poles' - only once we have played out both extremes, can we settle into the harmony which lies between.

Newton's cradle

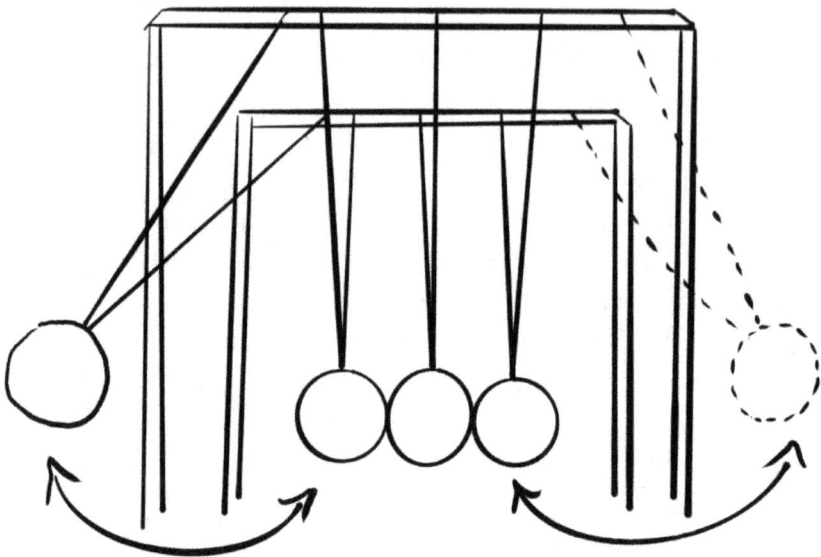

We had swung so far in one direction with clean eating. Now, we literally swung back the other way with our diet and I could feel it. My husband and I soon caved! We played the chocolate game from old memories and tasted some of the different Cadbury chocolate bars we had long forgotten.

As I got honest, I felt my seed of intelligence pull me to have a slice of pizza. I watched from above as our seeds of intelligence called us to experience 'what it feels like to let go and enjoy foods we sneakily do like'. This season suited the state of our emotional bodies at that point, where it soothed us in ways we didn't previously access. It allowed us to eat out, which gave me a break from the kitchen and to introduce our boys to other cultures. Of course, we also embodied the shadows about the particular foods that weakened our physical bodies.

As we explored the shadows of junk food, I desperately wondered, 'Can we go back to cleaner eating now? Isn't that enough?'. I scanned my inner universe without judgement, which clearly leaned me towards, 'Nope, continue. You're not done yet'. It was like rebel energy, the opposite of perfect energy, that we had played out for so long. Off the supermarket shelves, week after week, I brought home Oreos, crumpets, ice cream tubs and more. We mostly only tasted them, but we did it enough to swing that far in the opposite direction. It felt crazy, yet I felt my seed of intelligence's pull. I trusted this path as I came to all sorts of things along the way.

Whilst in that season of life, I realised the light side of sugar. After a certain amount of it, I always awoke the next day with a stiff, sore neck, where the sugar had contracted these muscles. I spent the whole day irritated with my uncomfortable neck, which always ended up in a scene where my actors prodded the emotions out of me. After I had let it all up, my neck then relaxed back to peace. It was like sugar was a key, or just another actor, that raised the next 'lava lamp blob' within me. I was always better off after I released my emotions, both from the discomfort of the sugar effects and ultimately, the rising discomfort within me. As I realised this, I wasn't scared to allow the boys to eat sweet treats. I knew it would end in an emotional release for them, which was a good thing when I played by 'better out than in'. I knew we wouldn't play out this season of life forever. I had stared down my fear of sugar.

As our family explored the two poles of diet, I sat with the idea that there were life themes of light and shadow in any path we explored, whether we chose to see this or not. As we accept this, we become more willing to say yes to the pull of our seed of intelligence. When we believe certain paths are only light and certain paths are only shadow, we are led by our little old human self.

Those who eat cleanly might defend their position, that it's never a good thing to eat junk food, if you can provide better quality food. This can seem very true, if we try to drive the straight line towards health. Perhaps however, we haven't seen the signs of deprivation in our children. Perhaps, our children's seed of intelligence draws them to seek the pleasure of junk-style food as a tool to soothe their heart or even to explore how to fit in with other children. In good time and if it's on their soul agreement, they will explore 'what it feels like to seek foods that strengthen me'. We have to trust this. In the meantime, most of us are still to explore the light and shadow of all types of food, so that we can come to intuitive eating in the middle.

Of course, it is not incorrect to be in either season of life or somewhere in the middle. In fact, some of us will play out the extremes of certain life themes and really swing the Newton's cradle balls. Others will not swing as far in these themes but will play out extremes in other life themes. You only find out your path as you notice 'what is', the scenes you find yourself drawn to.

If we sense that we are invited into the season of life to explore different foods with our children, we can celebrate this with curiosity. As we let go of our little old human's perceived perfect path, we then see the invitations to have fun with life, to spend more time with our children instead of in the kitchen or to enjoy the food experiences we enjoyed as a child, *with* our children. We realise that we will always face factors that prod us and that less-than-healthy eating for a period of time is just another catalyst for our inner work.

Playing by curiosity

If we hold our children back from a theme that is encoded within them, they will most surely seek it out at another point in time. The difference is, when we accept their seed of intelligence's pull, we gain respect from their soul. When we try to veer our child away from a certain path, they play it out anyway, with less heart connection and respect towards us.

> *We can so easily judge the 'other side' of any life theme however, this ignores the fact that there is light and shadow in every path. Either side is not better than the other. It is simply our unique soul agreement unfolding.*

The key is to live life without judgement. We simply ask 'why am I pulled to explore this?' as we follow our seed of intelligence. The more we pull one way in life, the more we are invited to swing back and experience the opposite. As we do this, we exist in compassion for those we judged, who were in fact simply pulled by their seed of intelligence.

I saw how our family was energetically pulled from one season of diet to the other. Like with Newton's cradle, we swung one way, we swung back the other and in divine timing, we started to come to the middle point. As we experienced both poles, I did the work to notice the light and shadow life themes of each side. We had to play out both sides before we could come back to harmony in the middle.

Each of us family members chose a path that explored the two more extreme poles of food, albeit with unique angles of this life theme. We swung from pole to pole because we were connected with our seed of intelligence's pull, more so than the judgement of what our monkey minds deemed as correct.

The harmony in the middle happened when we had explored both poles so much that we had 'done them to death'. The result was when we started to crave foods that were intuitively just right for each of us. They were not necessarily what any guru, health practitioner or conditioning told us was healthy. We were also empowered because we were no longer afraid of junk food.

I reflected on our experience. I saw how we as a society emphasise the benefits of healthy foods for our physical body, yet our emotional and spiritual bodies actually crave some junk to nurture us and actually 'keep balance'! That is, until we have played out both sides in their extremes enough. As we play out both sides, then we can advance forwards with momentum.

On my clean eating path, I tried to be too perfect. I also followed trends and gurus rather than my seed of intelligence. I didn't hear the boys, who were more connected to their seed of intelligence and called for balance much sooner. My penalty was that I played out challenging behaviours with them around food and even hurt my heart as I felt their deprivation.

On the flip side, I honoured our divinely orchestrated path where 'healthy food' served us in many important ways in that season of life. It was *not incorrect* to have explored this or to have taken it that far. Our seeds of intelligence pulled us in that direction so that we could swing back and experience it that much on the opposite. We learned a lot from our experiences.

Although we might think we know what is best, we often have to *explore* certain seasons to realise and embody the soul lessons that await us. Only then, we can come back to the harmony in the middle. We cannot hurry or change our path just because we think we know best. The mainstream and new age spiritual worlds however, encourage 'what is best' as a one-size-fits-all answer, to shut us off from our seeds of intelligence and unique explorations.

> *The balls on Newton's cradle cannot slow, stop or change trajectory. The distance we pull in one direction of life shows us how far our seed of intelligence invites us to swing, to find the harmony in the middle.*

Seasons of life

I noticed our family played out many seasons of life. With food, we swung from paleo to vegetarian and then back to middle ground. We played the school system then unschooled and came back to one boy at home and one at school. We lived close to the beach then moved closer to the forest but haven't found what the middle ground is yet. I expect there will be one.

Anthony, Declan and I landed in a season of life where we played Monopoly Deal with breakfast every morning for over a year. With the seasons of life concept, I said out loud, 'I wonder what will happen, to make us swing back the other way'. Whatever happens will mean we won't play it for quite some time, which will reflect how religiously we played it in this season of life.

When we are attached to something, we can prepare ourselves for a life scene that will come, to shake it up. We will feel motivated to say 'yes' to this new season of life *if* we pay attention to our inner universe. I knew as I religiously went to Bikram yoga for nearly ten years that I would eventually be pulled to have a break. Amazingly, that day came sooner than I planned as we moved house and my energy hit an all time low. Anthony supported me to see how I could make it work, but I knew I was done. Firstly, I felt through my grief, to truly let go. I then explored the light and shadow of life without this practice, before I moved into Tai Chi. I also know my daily cacao drink will get a shake up, because I have swung so far one way with it, yet I can't see what could stop me from this thing that I love. There will be something. I will know when it happens!

As we acknowledge the energetic law of 'the harmony is between two poles', we can start to understand the trajectory of our lives. Once we experience each pole, we then begin to experience the middle ground. Of course, like with Newton's cradle, there is still some movement back and forth as the balls settle with minor pendulum movements, until they find harmony. *For example, as the first ball pulled back, we explored clean eating and then as the ball sailed towards the other side, we explored the opposite pole of junk eating. Before we settled in harmony, just like the balls that needed to settle on Newton's cradle, we went back and forth. We played out shorter seasons of clean eating, such as fasting or eating dairy-free again and then more junk eating, such as all-you-can-eat buffet.*

We can almost predict what is going to happen, particularly the more we pull in one direction with any life theme! This helps us to be more mentally prepared to let go of 'what we think it should be' when our seed of intelligence guides us to explore the other side. As we feel the tug of our seed of intelligence or see it in our family members, we prepare to explore the light and shadow of the other side. Remember, the themes that we play out in the shadows in childhood are in direct proportion to the amount of light we can discover in these same themes on the other side. *For example, the child that keeps everything to themselves will be pulled by their seed of intelligence to eventually excel in open, honest communication with others into the future.*

> *Our seed of intelligence invites us to let go of attachment to all that we hold onto in life.*

If we follow our seed of intelligence and explore the poles in life, we find soul lessons. *For example, I learned that junk food isn't 'all bad' and that I can't instil what I 'think' is healthy eating in my children, if their soul agreement enlists the experience of any food to the contrary.* As we explore the light and shadow sides of our life experiences, we are taught to let go of attachment, embrace change and 'what wants to be', such as with my yoga example. As we hit the harmony point, we are neutral. We know that no path is right or wrong and we can then allow others their soul path, without our ego's interference.

Why you want to know about the Seasons of Life

The seasons of life remind us that balance will eventually *seek us*. You don't have to change your diet, if you feel quite energised and happy with what you eat. You don't have to sell your house that you have had for 20 years, if all the factors still indicate to stay. You don't have to change your child's sport that they are happy with. It is simply to stay open to the fact that we can find ourselves in scenes where our soul path says 'enough of that season, it's time for a change'. We will cover this in more detail in the Red and Green Lights chapter. Don't forget, we often resist the early whispers for change.

The seasons of life guide us to play the game of life, The New Way. The way forward is with flexibility rather than sameness, orchestrated by divine timing. If we fight our child's desire to leave school or the nudges to move house, we can end up in much trickier life scenes. Instead, we welcome our seed of intelligence to rattle us, so that we can see what always wanted to be and will be.

Remember, if you say yes to the pull of your seed of intelligence, you will certainly go on an adventure. You will end up in many life scenarios you never thought you would! Actors around you who remain stuck in sameness will wonder how you upleveled yourself in life. As you accept your divine path, you receive magic and growth. Your seed of intelligence blooms!

> *We want to leap along the lily pads of life, in divine timing and on the heart of the beat. If we rush, race and dive ahead in life, we are in the shadows of the Star energy. If we kid ourselves, make excuses and sit back too long, we are in the shadows of the Earth energy.*

Time for change

You can tune into the divine nudges from your seed of intelligence. You may notice certain scenes, which used to be 'solid' that now start to 'wobble'. *For example, your child, who played soccer religiously for years, comes home one day and mentions their new coach is really strict.* This is a sign that your child's season of life with soccer *may* soon change course in some way. Of course, it is at least an experience to work through, as 'negative change' is always an invitation to practise flexibility and growth. *Another example is perhaps your close friend starts to explore a life theme that makes you feel uncomfortable.* The 'wobbles' of this is good timing to check in with your feelings, which inevitably rise as change starts to occur.

It is helpful to stay open to change and be unattached to all paths. Our little old human self can cling to sameness, where our seed of intelligence may invite us to explore another side of life. Do take notice of any part of your life that is regular, religious or pulled in a more extreme direction, particularly if you sell it as the 'only way to go'. Yes!

Our soul path invites us to embrace humility, where we surrender to our divine path instead of what we think is best. Maybe you are a long-time vegan, homeschooler or seller of a particular product. If you stay open to light and shadow in any path, you *may* hear the whispers to eat meat, the relief as your child explores their wish to go to school or realise a shadow of a product you have invested in.

You may glance back and realise the different poles you have played out in your life. Maybe you had a best friend for a season of your life and then a season without. Maybe you played out life in a busy city and now you live in a quieter place. Maybe you went through a season of life overweight and now you are much skinnier. Maybe you had a season of life where you cared more about others than your own well being and then you were called to focus much more so on yourself. You may be able to spy where you played out both poles and have now found a balanced place in the middle. You would be able to write a book on your experiences!

Balance in the family

You and your partner will often explore opposite seasons of life. One partner might be a money saver and the other more of a spender. One might create with their hands whilst the other creates with ideas. One might explore exercise whilst the other focuses on other areas of their life.

In divine timing, we often finish one life theme as our partner starts to wind up the opposite pole of this same theme. Soon enough, the tables have turned and you find yourself in a scene called to explore the opposite side. *For example, your partner, who used to be a spender, may suddenly be put under financial pressure and start to seek how to save money. As the family bubble always seeks balance, you begin to transition into the opposite season of life around the same time. Perhaps you moved up the cone on the need to save money as you saw the fun time your partner had with it. You then find yourself in scenes to satisfy your inner child, who never got to spend money on what they truly wanted. You become the spender.*

Yours and your partner's seeds of intelligence draw you to experience certain life themes as it maintains balance between you both. Remember, we can't help what our seed of intelligence pulls us to explore. It is useful to have compassion and humility for each other's experiences and know that at some point, we already have or will experience their angle too. We may explore it in very subtle ways, but it will be there if we notice it.

On the contrary, if either partner tries to be on the same page as their partner, when they are pulled to explore the opposite angle, there will be disharmony. *For example, if you are pulled to save money and you convince your partner that they also need to, they will experience inner and outer disharmony, if their seed of intelligence in fact pulls them to spend.* We are supposed to play out the pull of our own seed of intelligence and to understand this in each other.

Of course, there are the typical seasons of life that come to an end, such as when we graduate, become a parent, break up with someone or end a favourite pastime. It is important to remember that we are conditioned to simply face the next day and move into that change. We forget to have heart for the emotions that rise up when change occurs. Every time we notice a season of life end or begin, it is important to honour the grief and other emotions that come with change. We have become a different person because of the experience of the old season of life and embody it even more so, as we free ourselves of any unexpressed emotions.

> *We may think we choose our new seasons of life but from an energetic point of view, we are literally pulled into them. Even if we enjoy the new change, we will have emotions about the end of one season and the start of a new one.*

Summary

* Everything we experience is in a season of life - be it shorter or longer.

* We go back and forth between seasons of life, sometimes exploring the extreme poles of any one theme.

* We can curiously explore a new season of life as we sense change, rather than try to cling to what our monkey mind thinks is best.

* There is light and shadow in every path and so it is just to allow our seed of intelligence to pull us to what wants to be.

* If we don't choose the new season of life that seeks us, we will eventually be pulled into it.

To practice ...

- Notice the seasons that have come to an end in your life. Did you allow yourself to feel the grief and other emotions before you began the next season? Notice the reasons that you were conditioned to simply move on. Remember, it's never too late to feel these ever-rising energies.

Canvas of Life

*...your life at any moment in time,
is a canvas that you can co-create with...*

2018

As I pieced together the analogies that explained how to play the game of life from empowerment, I experienced many scenes in my life that taught me where I could control it and where I couldn't. My family actors really helped me! When I told Anthony that I didn't like what he said, how he behaved or what he chose to eat or buy, I was met with a 'slap in the face' response. Although I tried to tell him how he needed to be many times, I finally realised it didn't work. Anthony didn't change. Instead, I worked through the anger and frustration that arose within me. Ultimately, I felt the sadness that I had to put up with these displeasing scenes in my life.

That's when it hit me. I dreamed of these displeasing scenes being different, better. I had valid emotions to feel as I played out scenes that were the opposite of what this looked like. So I felt my discomfort. I then spoke to Anthony from a very different place, without the charge of 'you need to change, now!' He then responded in a different way. He made changes himself or came up with ideas on how to go about things differently. Sometimes he continued to express himself in ways that displeased me. I knew it was back to me, to feel how it felt to be in the scenes of my life that were not perfectly how I wanted them!

The more I honoured my valid emotions and didn't expect Anthony to change, the more he *did* change because I was less attached. As I released my inner charge, which made me point fingers of 'what I thought it should be', I released attachment. He changed because he wanted to. He opted into it because it was the divine timing for his soul path, led by *his* seed of intelligence.

How could I expect Anthony to change just because I thought he should? My interference made him feel disempowered and that I disrespected his unique soul path. I also realised some partners *did* change for their partner, because they did not have the fire to tell their partner to back off. They also felt disempowered and the disrespect for their unique path.

As I explored how to live life from empowerment, I saw the 'canvas of life'. Each scene of my day was a canvas that I could work with. My overall life, at any moment in time, was a canvas that I could co-create with.

> Canvas of life - each scene of our life is a canvas to continue to notice what pleases and doesn't please us. This practice helps us to keep a balanced focus on all aspects of our life and to remember that we can always change what we don't like.

Some scenes of my canvas were so pleasing, like I had taken the time to have the idea and paint it beautifully with gorgeous paint pens. These were the scenes where I spent days with my boys or when I connected with my body at yoga. Other scenes were finely detailed in black art liner, like the respectful relationship Anthony and I had worked on for so long.

Some scenes however, were like I had taken a paint roller of murky brown paint and just slapped it on the canvas, back and forth, back and forth. These were the scenes where I hadn't been able to give that part of my life as much attention as I would have liked, such as my unloved garden or messy cupboards under the kitchen sink.

Then there were the scenes where I had overdone it, with too much watercolour, pastels, spray paint and then glitter and sequins! These were the scenes where I cooked everything from scratch and spent so much time in the kitchen that I missed certain scenes with my young boys. They were also the scenes where I trawled the internet for answers, when I was desperate to get my son to sleep or to find the right dentist.

After I noticed the better and worse scenes on my canvas, I began to take a zoomed out look at my life more often. I hadn't noticed the murky brown scenes or the over-the-top glittery ones before because I played life ready to simply shoot down the next challenge. I needed to continue to step back and look at my canvas of life.

As I gave the murky scenes some energy, I often just needed to feel the emotions that I had subconsciously clocked about 'what it feels like to not have a beautiful garden or veggie patch'. It was the same thing with the over-loved glittery scenes. I had to feel why I had overdone it. Then I could make peace with and understand the empowered reasons why I had expressed myself like this at that point in time. As I was free of these emotions, I then had more resources to get back to the other scenes I felt called to create and touch up.

Of course, our canvas of life continually changes, just like a garden. I began to master the game of life better once I stood back and saw where I tolerated scenes that didn't please me. Sometimes I realised I needed to erase some parts and start afresh. *One example is when I decided to close the large Facebook group I hosted, called 'Awakened Parenting'.*

I hit a bit of an obstacle however, when I realised that parts of my canvas involved others. This called for me to speak out loud about what I wanted to create. The game of life doesn't allow us to have full control over scenes that involve others. Communication is vital. I could only play out each less-than-perfect scene and explore how I *felt* about it on my canvas of life. After I released my charge, I then came to the heart of the matter and spoke about what I actually yearned for.

Here are two examples of how I invited my actors to co-create a new scene with me.

- *At one point, I announced to my family, 'The reason I go to lengths to get you to come back to your heart and communicate from there, is because I dream of scenes where we have harmony and respect between us all'.*

- *Firstly, I released my frustration that no one heard and honoured my ideas for family outings. I then spoke up to announce that I yearned to have a say too and that I needed support as I explored the life theme of 'not being heard by my family'.*

Most of us forget to speak up about what we yearn for. It is often us women that see our family's direction first. In the meantime, our family patiently waits for us to announce that it is time to review certain scenes on our common canvas of life! You can audit what your canvas of life looks like on any one day and also overall in your season of life right now. Sit with your emotions about it and use this passion to announce to your family what you yearn for.

Why you want to know about the Canvas of Life

To play the game of life means to understand what we truly can and can't change. We were not taught however, how to do this through true empowerment. This is where we do the inner work *and* the external work. The inner work means to feel how you truly feel about the scenes in your life and work to shift the rising energy. As we have seen, when you shift within, you create a better space to talk from the heart of the matter, instead of through charge. The external work means to speak up to others from your heart. To be heard, is to say it without blame or any expectation on others to do as you say. This is the challenge for most of us as we learn how to play through empowerment.

We must remember, we cannot control others. We can only feel our charge as we are pulled into a displeasing scene with them. We can then speak up about how it makes us feel and what we yearn for, even if we are just an observer in those scenes. We trust that in good timing their seed of intelligence will either call them to change, or perhaps they won't show up further on our canvas of life.

Here is an example of how you must insist on a different scene with others on your canvas of life but first, feel through the life theme you have landed into.

We may be upset that our partner continually yells at our child. It is not empowered to tell them, in the moment, what to do or why they did it wrong. We can only find our feminine place, to feel the life theme of 'what it feels like to watch the father of my child leak their charge at them'. It can and will bring up sadness, grief, disappointment, frustration, rage and more. You are it.

As we continually circle the cone with each displeasing scene, we feel more angles of this life theme. Each time we release our rising emotions, we find a bit more inner peace. We aren't so attached to the perfect father storyline. We do speak from our heart, about the heart of the matter - 'I yearn for our family to get along and listen to each other in a safe way'.

Each member is free to adjust themselves, in good time, towards this common dream that they also have deep down. They may not change themselves exactly how we want, but often they will eventually change in different and better ways than we could have imagined. All we can do is feel and speak - heart and throat. They change as we change first. You are it.

> *The golden keys to be able to play the game of life well is to feel and to speak. It begins from the heart and throat.*

On the other hand, if a certain person has no direct effect on us, there is no invitation for us to get involved. *For example, maybe someone walks down the street with a slogan on their shirt that we don't like. Perhaps someone posts something on social media that makes us feel uncomfortable.* In empowerment, we can only feel our inner discomfort and then make changes to our canvas that helps to create a better scene for next time. Often, this is to distance ourselves. To continue to create a canvas of life that pleases us, we may unfollow or unfriend this person or choose different places to spend our time.

We are within our rights to use our eraser on our canvas *at any time*, however there will always be feelings to feel, even if we distance ourselves. We do not have to put up with *any scene* on our canvas. It is just to do the inner work to make decisions from peace rather than to take actions from our fight/flight/freeze monkey mind expressions.

Of course, if we release the lava lamp blob that the actor raises within us, this actor can show up in the same scene next time and we will have far less care. This is of most empowerment, as we are untouchable and don't need to run. With our most tricky actors, this can take quite some inner work to get to this position.

If our actors invite us to have a say, then we can, but we must still work with the process of heart and throat. We must feel through any rising charge first and then talk, or it will be received in disempowered ways. On a platform such as social media or anywhere we have opted into, it is not so much our place to talk up, but to simply opt out and move on.

If a particular person directly affects the scenes on our canvas of life, then we have the right to feel and to speak up about how they affect this particular scene for us. We must find, 'what is the direct effect *on myself* here?'.

Here are two examples of how to explain the heart of the matter to those who affect the scenes of your canvas of life.

- *You may speak up to your partner about how you are affected when they drink sugary drinks. 'When you drink sugary drinks, it is much trickier for me to guide our children away from these too'.*

- *You may talk to your children about how their rough behaviour affects the scenes on your canvas. You may explain, 'When you hit another child, I have to speak up for you. This takes a lot of energy, because I have to deal with my embarrassment that the other parents make me feel, at the same time'.*

We have a right to continue to feel and speak about the scenes that don't please us. If there is a direct effect on our canvas of life, we must not keep it to ourselves, in case we hurt or aggravate the other person. Remember, change does not happen instantly but more through the cone process. We can't hurry the other party to change because our path is not supposed to change overnight either. Our paths are all interconnected. It is our little old human self that is impatient or gives up on others. Eventually, we will have pulled out our inner weed on this life theme, if we focus on our journey up the cone. At that divine point in time, we are ready to step into the more pleasing scene on our canvas of life, the one we have yearned for.

Summary

* It is important to remember to zoom out and see if your focus is balanced across the different aspects of your life.

* It is vital to communicate as you make changes to your canvas of life, because these decisions often involve others and have an effect on their canvas of life too.

* Talk to others when they have displeasing effects on your canvas of life out of respect for your soul's time here on Earth!

To ponder on...

- Which scenes of your life have you put an artist's attention to?

- Which scenes of your life have you left blank or given less attention to?

- Which scenes of your life have you overdone with crayon, puff paint and watercolour?

- How do you *feel* about each of these aspects of your life?

Yearnings

...your inner universe and external challenges show you what you are encoded to yearn for...

2015

Due to his advanced intellectual skills, Hayden skipped the first year of school, prep, to start in grade one instead. It didn't take long before I needed to talk to his teacher about extension. They studied 'sinking versus floating', which he had already extended *himself* on in kindergarten. At that point in our timeline, I remember that I had a random thought about homeschool, although it was a foreign concept.

Two years later, Declan started prep. Literacy began on day one and he resisted it, whilst Hayden was still significantly understimulated. I surprised myself as I talked about the topic of homeschool again. A couple of years later, Hayden was bullied and I struggled as his mother when the staff did not stand up for him. At the same time he was still bored. I spoke out loud to the gifted teacher, 'I'm actually thinking about homeschooling him'. It was probably more of a response out of frustration to what they didn't provide for my boys.

All the while, I hosted my Facebook group, 'Awakened Parenting'. I organised Sunshine Coast meetups and there we met a couple of families who homeschooled. Declan and I saw what it was like for families on the other side. It started to become real. Declan asked me when he could homeschool, even though it still felt like it would never become our reality.

At one point, I tried my hardest to logistically make it work, before the boys started yet another school year. I asked a couple of families if they wanted to share care and then nervously talked to Anthony about this idea. He was resistant, and it just didn't work out with the other families. So the boys started yet another year of school in 2019. I was very disappointed and worried about what was next on the school journey.

Although we didn't know much about homeschool nor was Anthony on side, the idea of it just didn't leave me alone. As I faced more challenges in 'being a mother of a child in the school system', emotions drove me to yearn for my children to be at home with me. Most days it still felt like this dream was unattainable.

As I yearned for my children to be at home with me, Declan also told me at bedtime about his problems at school. Each following day, he was resistant to get in the car. Hayden didn't express that he wanted to leave school, yet I knew that the school system was exactly the opposite of where he needed to be. I felt it in my heart. Despite the traumatic times Hayden had experienced, he resisted change.

Sure enough, it all finally hit the fan in 2019. It was Hayden's less-than-kind teacher. It was the bullying. It was some of the head staff. It was the lack of stimulation. It got to the point where I had released so much charge over the years that I calmly said to Anthony, 'There is not one point in him staying in this place. I can't take him there anymore. I am simply done'.

Anthony and Hayden still resisted the idea. I tried to paint the picture of what it would be like to Hayden. It felt like I had opened the cage door to a lion in captivity, but it didn't know how to accept freedom. I realised that he resisted me, to make *me* talk out loud about what it would be like, to prepare *myself*.

Yearnings seek us

As I spelt out what life looked like without school in it, I realised I had followed a yearning, an idea that *sought me*. Yes, I spoke of the idea. Yes, I pursued it. Despite this, it was hugely stressful to try and make homeschooling happen, as I thought it was my idea and responsibility.

When I considered that homeschooling was a yearning that sought me, I finally considered myself. I resisted it in many ways too. I worried about many angles of it. I didn't choose it. As I realised this, I acknowledged I had put aside my own emotions, so I seemed like the family leader, who was convinced of this path.

> Yearnings - what we dream of is energetically encoded to seek us, not the other way around.

As I accepted that my seed of intelligence had pulled me towards this yearning, I cried tears of exhaustion. I cried tears of relief. I cried tears of doubt. I cried tears that I felt like I was a burden to Anthony and Hayden because I followed this yearning, despite their resistance. I cried tears that I listened to Declan's cries for help and did something about it. I cried tears of grief over what I gave up, namely I had started to write this very book and had to leave it for two more years to even begin.

Despite my intentions, my seed of intelligence had pulled me into 'what was next', the need to get Hayden out of the school system. I knew it was a priority and the rest is history as Hayden came out and realised he will *never* go back. In good timing, I got to write this book too!

> *What we yearn for are the ultimate scenes of having worked through our soul's lessons on our soul agreement.*

Why you want to know about Yearnings

You can see your ideas, dreams and yearnings like messages that come to you, directly from your soul agreement. Like emotions, it is yet another tug from your seed of intelligence, to land you into scenes that ensure you experience certain life themes. We have been conditioned to own our yearnings, with words like 'I've had an idea', 'I think we should...', 'I want to...', 'this is *my* idea' and so on. This stance however, doesn't leave room for our own valid emotions as we take this leap of faith. It also makes it much more difficult to co-create with others. Instead, we are expected to see this idea out ourselves and to be able to manifest the thing via our little old human self. This puts immense pressure and responsibility on us, and it does not honour divine timing and what wants to be.

Whether we push or not, our yearnings manifest at the exact point in our timeline that they are supposed to. It is like we are on a travelator as we journey towards our yearnings and we cannot hurry or avoid it. Instead, we have been conditioned to create steps to our goal and try to make it happen. Those that succeed in this approach, happen to be on their divine beat of time. On the flip side, a lack of success in anything means that we are not quite on our unique beat. We will go through more about this concept in the chapters on The Rainbow and The Titanic.

We have been conditioned to work hard for success and we believe it's the only way. As we learn to let go and live life with more patience, we allow our yearnings to literally come into play. It doesn't mean that we don't have to take action or face fears, but this should take far less energy than we think our dreams should take.

Here are some examples of how our yearnings play out in divine timing.

- *From day one at school, the teachers pushed literacy on Declan and all of the children. It was too much too soon for him, and we spent energy in places that wasn't necessary, to get him to reach their set literacy goals. He resisted this and refused to read. Deep down however, he did yearn to be able to read. Not long after Declan came out of school, without any pressure, he started to suddenly read at a much higher level.*

- *For a very long time, it was a push with my own soul work. I tried to make my mentoring business reach more women than it was ready for. I blamed and shamed myself. I spent too much money on coaching. The day I gave the finger to the universe was the day that I realised, it will all unfold in good timing and so it is.*

Yearnings

Let's take a quick look at some examples of yearnings. Right now or in the past, you may yearn or have yearned for:

* your parents to get along
* your parents to notice you in what lights you up
* a baby
* financial security
* the courage to stand up for yourself
* your partner to be healthier
* a safe person to talk with
* your children to get along
* a piece of chocolate or a coffee
* more restful sleep
* more energy to be the parent you could be
* your connection with your soul purpose

Firstly, we usually notice what we yearn for when we *don't* have it on our canvas of life. Our yearnings appear through our daily challenges. Each challenge flipped, tells us what we yearn for. *For example, when we can't agree on something with our partner, we yearn to be on the same page about the important things. When our children fight whilst on holiday, we yearn to be able to enjoy the time we have invested in. When we struggle with a personal health issue, we yearn for our body to be stronger.*

We can yearn for the big dreams, such as community living or to see the world in a more magical place. These bigger yearnings however, first involve inner work to claim the smaller more personal yearnings. *For example, to live successfully in community, we must be able to remain true to ourselves. We cannot live closer together if we can't speak up for our personal needs or own our unique gifts! We must first work with the shadows of where we people please. We must feel and make peace with how our soul truly feels to put others' needs before ours, since childhood. Our day-to-day actors show up to raise these emotions in scenes where we forget to voice our needs and instead go to please them. The smaller yearning is 'to be able to recognise, honour and speak up for my own needs'. It is a stepping stone towards the bigger yearning to live in harmonious community with others.*

Identifying our yearnings

If we don't notice and work with our smaller yearnings, we see our bigger dreams as unattainable. We get lost in the future of dreaming. Often a yearning comes with a nervous excitement. We feel the grand possibilities of being in this scene. We also, albeit subconsciously, sense the challenges too. No dream is ever achieved without its challenges!

Sometimes, it feels quite obvious when your yearnings call you from your seed of intelligence. A sure sign is when you can't really remember how you got the idea. It's also divine when you can't help but feel emotions when this dream isn't manifested on your canvas of life. You know it's on its way when you are ready to get up and shout from the rooftops as to why it is important. It is easy to own the divine nature of your dream when you feel passionate and can barely explain it. The idea remains with you even when you don't lift a finger on it!

On the contrary, sometimes our ideas can feel clunky. Doubting actors may cause us to justify or explain ourselves, usually when we own the idea too much. The interesting thing is, even when it seems like the 'wrong' idea, an unachievable dream or a self-sabotaging path, it is always divinely orchestrated. There are countless reasons why we are called towards the yearning, not just what we think we want or don't want. Even when we resist our path, we have yearned for it somewhere in advance.

Here is an example of how I did feel 'yes' to my yearning, despite feeling resistance too.

Although I was unsure of how homeschool might affect our reality, I did yearn to have my children home with me and to be free of the school challenges. The more I felt how it felt to be a mother of a child who suffered in school, the more I said 'yes' to this yearning.

Once we started to homeschool however, I then resisted social connection with other families, because the school families had drained me. Also, I had already spent a lot of time with mothers through my work. I always attracted women who wanted to tell me about their family problems! Despite this, I was called to create homeschool gatherings so my boys had friends. This found us more aligned families. I actually enjoyed the company of the mothers, whilst the boys found true connection with particular children. Although I had resisted these social gatherings, they were the manifestation of what I had truly yearned for throughout the school years - for my boys to have more aligned friends and for myself too.

There were many more unexpected paths and soul lessons as we followed the yearning to homeschool. My children became my prodding actors even more so, which brought challenging times for us all. At the same time, Hayden was able to relax and be himself more, as he was finally in a safer place. Declan grew to know who he was in a deeper way and yearned to experience school again a few years later. His return to school was a success and with very few challenges, as we had already collapsed that cone.

> As you follow a yearning, you open the door to a whole new trajectory of life. You then explore that new path in the light and the dark.

The journey

At first, you sniff the winds of a yearning that is yet to come into play. Perhaps you argue with someone and realise 'wow, I actually feel strongly about this point'. Perhaps you jokingly spring something as an idea. Maybe you get excited about it, as you know you will experience it, in some fashion, on your soul path. Maybe you feel quite unsure about this dream and want to close the door on it. As we saw in the Divine Timing chapter, just because you sense it, does not necessarily mean you should take action on it straight away.

> *A yearning seeks us. Our little old human self has been conditioned to think that it is the one that thinks up our ideas, dreams and callings. Energetically, these yearnings come to us, from our divine path of 'what wants to be'. It's on our soul agreement.*

We must remember that our yearnings are 'what wants to be'. Therefore, energetically, scenes to do with this topic continue to play out, so that we become more comfortable with the idea of them, such as our journey until we actually did homeschool. Even if I had not accepted the idea of homeschool, our family would still have been squeezed in some way to take Hayden out of school at the divine point in time. I assumed too much responsibility for it.

As a reminder, the displeasing scenes in our life are the ones that hint at what we will eventually yearn for, *if* we play the game of life, The New Way. Our challenges give us the heads up of our future! Yes, the tricky scenes at the school were my warning of the direction our family would soon head in. Whether we like the direction we are pulled to or not, our seed of intelligence will continue to manifest experiences that force us to face how we feel about our displeasing scenes and take action.

> *Our yearnings seek us in divine timing, whether we actively look for them or not.*

As we get honest and feel exactly what doesn't please us, we energetically say 'yes' to the yearning that seeks us, usually something of the opposite. *For example*, 'We don't have a child in our life and a son or daughter is exactly what I yearn for'. Another example is 'I am sick of being the grumpy parent and realise that I yearn to have fun, like I did before parenthood'. As each displeasing scene arrives and we work with our inner universe on it, we go up the cone. As the scenes get wilder towards the top, we get forced to say 'yes' to yearnings we may have resisted. We may yell, 'I'm so DONE WITH …..!'. We may also proclaim, 'I'm ready to embrace this yearning that has been *seeking me!*'. This matches in with the energetic concept of the cone. As you approach your challenges like this, you also claim 'you are it'.

Here is an example of how you get drawn to see what you yearn for.

Let's say your daughter is a fussy eater. Energetically, she resists this food, as you resist the unhealthy foods she speaks of. Each time there is a struggle, you feel your emotions of frustration and even anger. As you go up the cone however, you start to land in scenes of desperation, as she noticeably loses weight and pulls away from you.

The desperate feelings drive you to see what you actually yearn for. You proclaim with a sense of knowing, 'I just want my child to be happy to eat!'. The divinely orchestrated scenes have forced you to come to what you need to do. You surrender and allow her the foods she craves. Immediately, she is happy and more connected with you. Although she now eats and is happy, your yearning for healthy children still taps at you, because it will come… in good timing.

Different types of yearnings

When you see the benefits of a yearning that seeks you, it can be easier to face the challenges that come. For the yearnings that excite you, you may passionately prepare to step into this future dream. It still brings up all of the fears and doubts in your way, usually prodded by some of your trickiest actors.

It is usually not too long after the big emotions rise up, that the yearning comes into play. The yearning sought you out, and you played out the scenes you needed to before it could become a reality. You let go of places where you thought it would be different and you felt the emotions surface as you did. You played the game of life, The New Way.

Then there are the yearnings that we find difficult to say 'yes' to. Often, we don't realise we are nervous about a particular yearning, because we try to convince ourselves that we have chosen this path. *For example, until I got honest about how I felt about the yearning to homeschool, I didn't realise I wasn't 100% a 'yes' myself.*

On the other hand, sometimes we actively push away that which we yearn for. *For example, some women push their husbands away or reject the idea of homeschool, even though they do yearn for a loving partnership or their children to thrive outside of the school system.*

Monkey mind yearnings

What about yearnings that never come into play? We have many ideas throughout our life that never come to fruition. Maybe we had an idea to phone our Mum but never got to it. Maybe we had a dream to volunteer in another country, but it never eventuated. Maybe our mother had an idea to leave our father, but she never did. Although these appeared like yearnings too, they were never 'what wanted to be'.

Sometimes we think we yearn for something, but actually, there is a bigger part of us that knows it won't manifest. These types of thoughts, ideas and dreams come from our monkey mind, which keep us busy, distracted and focused on 'what could have been' or 'what we didn't do or achieve'. This is why our ideas are important to be *felt through* before we take action.

Here are a couple of examples of ideas that aren't to be played out at that time.

* *Maybe you have the idea to phone your Mum. First, if you stop and feel into it, you soon feel the tug of your seed of intelligence, to get dinner ready or to respond to your children. The idea wasn't to come into play, at least not at that point in time.*

* *Although you may dream to volunteer in another country, when you get honest about your own financial situation and life circumstances, you sense 'uh uh'.*

It is a waste of energy to try to *figure out* if your idea is a true yearning or not. Perhaps it truly does seem like a monkey mind idea but many years into the future, you do go and volunteer with your grandchild. You volunteer in your own country but you can look back and see that you sensed this yearning long ago. If it's a true yearning, it will unfold but maybe not how you pictured it. If it's not a true yearning, it simply won't. The Red and Green Lights chapter explains more on how to be guided to what is and isn't for you.

As we saw in the Monkey Mind Nets chapter, we can get sidetracked from what is truly important to our soul path. If we don't get honest about how we feel and release our rising 'lava lamp blobs', we attract scenes that easily distract us. We live life without clear mental focus.

Alternatively, our monkey mind, or spiritual ego, may fool us into what we think we want, with convincing arguments. When we need to stay focused on what our heart truly wants, shiny carrots are dangled in front of us, such as invitations to money-making opportunities, social catch ups we can't miss out on, keeping up with others and can't-be-missed collaborations. It is a fine line to know what we truly desire, and where is best to focus our energy at any one point in time. We must *feel* into our ideas and opportunities with discernment. We then must be ready to let go of what our little old human wants!

Monkey mind dreams may make us chase money or possessions. These dreams make us do something for money first, rather than because we love to. This path is not wrong as we all go down these avenues to find our soul lessons in the material world.

Monkey mind dreams may make us seek help for our children externally, when we doubt the power within ourselves as a parent. They may make us feel we have to outsource mentors for our children or find the most prestigious learning opportunities for them. We may overspend our energy as we research the best supplements, professionals or therapies for our children. We forget about our inner callings, or north stars, to simply say 'yes' to health, happiness and true fulfilment, and allow our seed of intelligence to show us the easier path. Again, it is not wrong to explore any of these paths and we need to, to embody our life themes. On this path, we find soul lessons to trust ourselves as parents and to learn how we can help our children with much less time, energy and money spent.

We can trust what our heart yearns for, especially if we feel the fear of a big dream and particularly if we continue to have challenges of the opposite.

As we know, our lava lamp effect is forever switched on. There is always some discomfort to be felt in our inner universe, which is reflected in a challenging life scene. If we only aim to perceive what is good in our life, we unknowingly block ourselves from our yearnings and north stars. It is powerful to feel, and get honest about the displeasing scenes on our canvas of life!

Feeling for your yearnings

It is easy to dismiss your yearnings, even though they will find you anyway! If you don't feel your emotions, you may not know what you truly yearn for or sense 'who you really are'. When you own your yearnings, you are honest with 'what wants to be'. Your family, particularly your children, feel at ease when you claim the path forwards rather than tuck it away. It takes courage to feel for and announce yearnings that seem impossible or like a pipe dream.

As I sensed the life themes of 'what it feels like to be a mother of a child who is pushed into literacy... or bullied', I heard the softest whisper of homeschool. I had to stay open to the how and when. If I didn't, I would have firstly put the homeschool idea to bed because 'I can't, I work part time'. I would have then put it to bed because, 'I don't know how to homeschool' and then 'my husband won't let me'. Instead, I felt the emotions rise up as I faced each scene to do with this topic and how it felt to not have this yearning. This links in with the energetic concept of The Titanic in the following chapter.

When we acknowledge that our ideas, dreams and yearnings come *to us*, we can then afford ourselves the space to feel what it feels like in the light *and* the shadows. We let go of ownership, and instead, communicate to others that we feel *called to it*. As a result, we unravel our little old human self from the responsibility to make it happen. As we announce 'what wants to be', others who may think we chose to make their life difficult can then begin to see us follow our seed of intelligence. If we use the language of, 'this idea has come to me', we can then be more open to co-creation with others.

Co-creating with others

Often, your actors are interconnected with what you yearn for too. *For example, whether he liked it or not, Anthony was energetically tied to the homeschooling pull. Although I accepted the yearning first, he was very much a part of how it would play out for a long time to come. Surprisingly to him, homeschool was also on his soul path.* If we approach our yearnings as more of a team effort, it opens up the conversation for others to voice their aspect. *As I felt it was my idea and that Anthony wouldn't agree, I didn't communicate with him as much as I could have.*

Our actors reflect what we doubt about our yearnings. They may resist us or give us grief about it. This reflects our inner stance, that our yearning is something to convince someone of. The concept of 'you are it' shows us energetically that we are not yet 100% behind this yearning ourselves, if others give resistance. The more we feel how strongly we feel for it, the more we energetically get behind it.

Here are a couple of examples of how our actors reflect where we aren't 100% behind our yearning.

* *I felt like I had to convince Anthony why we needed to take the boys out of school. This behaviour energetically showed Anthony that I didn't trust it would all unfold how it needed to. I expressed myself from the 'convincing' monkey mind net, and Anthony reflected with the 'resistance' monkey mind net.*

* *Let's say a mother accepts her yearning to release her unexpressed emotions, so that she can feel more inner peace. Her children, partner and others start to make comments that hint she is wrong to do this. The mother realises she still carries strong conditioning about the weakness of emotional expression. Her inner doubts cause her actors to act from the 'give her grief' monkey mind net. As a result, she constricts and responds from her monkey mind net of 'keep it to yourself'. She is not yet 100% behind her yearning.*

Allowing it to unfold

As you go through your daily challenges, allow your complaints to guide you to see what you yearn for. The strong emotions you feel throughout your challenging scenes then become about your yearnings, instead of a reason to complain. As you shift this energy within, you pull your dreams closer.

It's important to remember, you land in the scenes you yearn for. You don't create them. Your little old human self can't think up the scenes that your seed of intelligence can miraculously orchestrate!

Here is an example of how to allow yourself to land in your miraculous answers.

A mother has children who are fussy and who refuse her healthy meals. Their physical body symptoms and behaviours reflect their health issues. She could research healthy recipes that hide vegetables. She could look at supplements or particular foods she thinks will make them get better. She could spend a lot of money on a practitioner. She could bribe or trick them to eat cleaner foods that may support their physical body.

These approaches, particularly without consultation of her children, ultimately bring other costs and may not even hit the nail on the head. The children may feel deprivation or even a lack of respect from their mother as they feel her interference on a soul level. She may also be off track on which healthy foods her children need, unique to their needs. Through her approach, perhaps she doesn't address what her children's emotional, mental and spiritual bodies yearn for either. Her monkey mind isn't able to create exactly what her children need through research or advice.

If this mother goes The New Way however, she plays with 'you are it' first. She surrenders to her inner universe whilst she makes sense of 'what it feels like to have unhealthy children and be helpless about this'. She faces many scenes where she feels what it feels like to 'not have healthy children' or 'not know the exact answers to help them'. Her children make sure she feels 'what it feels like to yearn for healthy children, however it happens'. We will cover this in detail in the coming chapter, The Titanic.

In good timing, the mother's children end up in their own unique version of health. By divine encounters with others, the mother learns about the benefits of certain foods she had previously judged. These foods contain exactly what the children needed physically or possibly emotionally, mentally and spiritually. The expensive supplements they refused to eat, remain in the cupboards, whilst one willingly eats endless amounts of passionfruit and the other celery. At this point, greens are not their medicine as much as everything that meat and sweet foods bring them. The exact supplements they need also fall into their lap and the children are energised to have them.

One child's eczema clears up as the mother works on her matching life themes that make her 'feel irritated'. The dark circles under the children's eyes fade in good time as the family is okay to not know what the answer is. The other child's impulsive behaviour changes immensely as the mother continues her inner work and releases her inner chaos.

Through this journey, the mother honours how much she distracted herself from the whispers of her own seed of intelligence. The more she eats with discernment herself, the more she opens the energetic door for her family members to do this even more so too. They are happy to respect each other's path and know the right answers fall into place, if we follow our seed of intelligence. The mother's little old human self could not have researched her way to the unique answers for each family member.

Of course, we are never in perfect health as we continue to change and seek balance. Some of the symptoms may play out for another ten years, whilst other symptoms may clear as the mother allows her children's seed of intelligence to seek its own medicine. The mother continues to yearn for health but this time through 'what wants to be' and for all family members, instead of over-focus on her children, from her monkey mind.

Go within to find direction

At this point, let's come back to why our rising energies are vital to connect with. As we embody the feelings within us, we are strongly reminded of what is important to us. *For example, if we allow ourselves to be present with the exhaustion of motherhood, on the other side we may get clarity of 'I need to make a start on creating the community I dream of myself' or 'I'm going to talk to my husband more about the loneliness of doing it all myself'.* The more we do this with different scenes of our lives, the more we find the direction our seed of intelligence pulls us towards, or what I call our north stars. We receive internal and external hints, nudges and synchronicities which allow us to create miraculous endings to our current life challenges. This is covered more so in the coming Red and Green Lights chapter.

> North stars - the different directions our seed of intelligence aims us towards.

Summary

* What we yearn for is not our idea.

* We will have feelings about our callings and are allowed to feel them.

* Sometimes what we seek for our children is what we yearn for ourselves too.

* It is not our sole responsibility to make our yearnings happen.

* Deep down, we all yearn for the same types of things - safety, being loved and celebrated, harmony, fulfilment and peace in our days.

* Often, us women are the visionaries that sense the yearning and need to call it and lead the family along. Sometimes we kick and scream as we get pulled too!

To ponder on...

In the coming week, notice the recurring themes of the scenes that challenge you.

- What do they tell you that you yearn for?
- Deep down, how much do you yearn for this?
- Have you allowed yourself to feel your emotions about this?

The Titanic

...we must face what is not, before we become the version of 'what is'...

2018

Through the cone analogy, we saw that it takes a predetermined amount of time to move through our challenges. What about when you've seen the change you want to make and know where you want to go? Now what? How long does it take to change course?

Well, at one point in my early mothering journey, I realised I hadn't spent enough time with my children. I declared, 'Tomorrow, I'm getting up and I'm *going to* connect with them'. Of course, it came straight from my little old human self who wanted to be in control of the scenes of my day and to achieve my monkey mind goals.

The following day, I got up and announced to the boys, 'I'm spending more time with you today!'. They looked at me and then silently got back to their toys. Driven by my unexpressed emotions about 'what it feels like to realise you've missed quality time with your children', I persisted and tried to make it happen. 'Deccy, let's play a board game today', I announced. Again, he looked at me and as he played with his animals, he responded, 'Not now. I'm playing here'. My little old human was slapped in the face. I had decided to make more connection with them! Surely, they wouldn't turn me down?

I walked away and did my inner work. I processed, 'what it feels like to finally decide to spend more time with my child… and to then have them reject me'. I couldn't make it happen. As I kept sight of this calling, I looked for more opportunities. Each time I tried to connect with the boys, whatever hadn't been processed in my inner universe came up. The boys rejected me for their friends, their toys, a TV show, their Dad and on and on. I took these times of rejection as opportunities to process how I felt about this life theme. As I freed myself from the desperation to chase them, I happily spent my energy where it flowed more easily. I chatted with Anthony, cleaned up the house, focused on my work or even the dog! It was a clear example that 'what wanted to be' was actually *not* time with my boys that day.

Eventually, as I continued with my yearning to have more quality time with the boys, I found myself in scenes where we connected! I didn't plan it, the scenes just showed up as I did the inner work and continued to insist on my yearning. *For example, the show on Einstein's life appeared on Netflix. Next minute, Hayden and I happily watched it and chatted about it in detail. Down the track, Hayden asked me to buy the Monopoly Deal card game. Declan and I loved it the most and played it together for hours.* I didn't go out of my way to 'think' of an activity and chase it down. These scenes found me.

I still yearn for more and more scenes for my boys and I to connect. I also yearn for the scenes where we will co-create with our gifts in the future too. With only inspired action, I humbly wait for these scenes to find us.

We are more likely to continue to insist on our yearnings if we move through the emotions that would otherwise cast the 'give up on this' monkey mind net.

The moments we try to make something happen because we 'have an idea', we must remember to pause. As we have seen, this yearning will come and so much so that we can trust it is on our soul agreement. We all sniff the winds of our yearnings well before it is meant to align perfectly. This is so we can do the work, in order to meet it as that newer version of ourselves, at the exact point in time and space that it wants to be. Our seed of intelligence starts to attract scenes that help us to consciously see this north star.

A north star comes into our sight when we realise exactly what we yearn for.

As we see the course we want to align with, it is like we are the captain of the Titanic. We look over our shoulder and realise the direction we need to go. Could we change the direction of the ship to align with our new direction instantaneously? Of course not. We have to go through the motions to turn the ship, which involves wild weather, to go against the current trajectory. Once we are aligned with the exact direction, the ship can then progress forward in a straight line with more ease. This is like when the path flows once our yearning has manifested. *For me, these were the scenes where connection opportunities literally dropped into the laps of myself and the boys.*

> The Titanic - we must face what is not, before we become the version of 'what is'.

As I saw the analogy of the Titanic, I realised how many people gave up on their callings because the winds got wild as they veered the ship to their north star. It seemed like their attempts to move towards their yearning had not worked. The women I mentored reported, 'See? It doesn't work', as their children continued to resist their meals, their hugs or their attempts to create peace between siblings. Their partners still did not listen to them or help out in the home.

To be that newer version of ourselves, we have to play out many scenes of what it feels like to *not* have this yearning first. This is part of the journey to find ourselves in the more pleasing scenes. This matches in with the concept of the journey to the top of the cone. We must face a predetermined number of scenes of 'what it feels like to *not* have my yearning' before we reach the top of the cone and finally align our ship with the scenes we yearn for on our canvas of life.

Why you want to know about The Titanic

It is vital to understand that the shadows come up before your yearnings come into play. That is, you must work with your lava lamp effect and corresponding life theme cone to face what it is like to *not have* this yearning. The game of life literally asks, 'how much do you insist on what you'd like on your canvas of life?'. It requires you to face your emotions of frustration, despair and every emotion, until they become passion and the full force power of 'I mean it'.

Stay humble on the path to what you yearn for. Understand that it will come into play at a certain point in time and space but not because your little old human self decides to make it happen. It is so useful to remember that this path may take longer than you'd like but as long as you are prepared to work with your inner universe, *it is a finite path*.

The shadows must rise before our yearnings can come into play.

As you steer the ship, you face emotional scenes, to make you let go of what actually doesn't matter to you. You will then find the heart of the matter, what you truly yearn for, beyond what your little old human thinks. As you are unattached, 'what wants to be' starts to come into play.

Here are some examples of the heart of the matter you may come to, whilst you steer the ship.

- I don't care so much about whether my family sees me cry, I just want to find my inner peace.

- I don't care that my partner doesn't get my soul work, I just want him to have respect for me as I follow my heart.

- I don't care about what my child learns or where, as long as they stay connected to their own true essence and know who they truly are.

You can expect your yearnings to appear like the sunrise. It won't necessarily be obvious or all of a sudden. You may not be able to pick the details of how it will come into play. One day, you will just find yourself in a scene and call out, 'This is it! I've landed in my yearning!'. It is miraculous.

Summary

* As we know what we yearn for, we realise a north star.

* We then face x number of scenes where we *do not* have our yearning.

* These are not a sign of failure but an opportunity to shift our inner universe, to find out how much we *feel for* our yearning.

* As we have shifted enough inner charge, our yearning starts to drop in.

* We become the newer version of ourselves, which is embodied in this new scene.

To explore…

Think about your yearnings and all of the scenes where they haven't come into play yet. *For example, when someone mentions a holiday and you remember travel hasn't come to you yet, or your children fight and you feel your yearning for sibling harmony.*

- Which scenes are you panicking about? The ones you feel will never change…

- Check in with your true inner state - allow yourself to feel 'what it feels like to not have this yearning in my life yet'.

Use these emotions to get behind how important your yearning is. Announce this to your family!

The Rainbow

...allow your yearnings to show up in good time...

2019

As I explained earlier, once I realised mainstream speech pathology was too superficial for me, I decided to study health coaching to add to my resume. After a year, I was ready to start my own business, The Healthy Caterpillar. I took leave from my speech pathology job because I could, but I was sure I wouldn't go back.

I then began my season of life to *embody* my soul lessons about money. I had no idea how difficult it would be to run a business or rely on myself to make money, rather than a wage. As I started, I froze when I tried to figure out how to put myself out there. Instead, I distracted myself and created my website from scratch. I also spent more money on online social media marketing courses.

My Anthony often reminded me. 'You've got to make some money. You have to find clients.' I didn't make it work, and I ended up back at my job about six months later. I felt ashamed that I wasn't able to 'make the money'.

The truth was, I actually did attract some clients. Pete Evans even offered me a job to work as a fussy eating health coach in his paleo world, but that's another story. It all just wasn't 'quick enough'. In fact, quick success wasn't on my soul path full stop!

Meanwhile, I was given two-and-a-half years before my speech pathologist position was due to become redundant, to make way for the National Disability Insurance Scheme (NDIS). The countdown was on to make my business work, and I felt the pressure. Every day, I went to work with a faint cloud of stress over me.

Throughout the following years, I tried it all to bring financial success to my life. I practised Emotional Freedom Technique (EFT) and tapped every day with EFT guides on YouTube. I took a free two week challenge in a Facebook group to throw out many belongings, to make energetic space for money. I paid $20 to download someone's manifestation process that told me to write out my goal to make money about 500 times. I spent the last dollars I didn't feel that I had on the Lucky Bitch book, to learn what I had missed about how to make money. I took free sessions from beautiful souls that tried their approach to dissolve my 'limiting beliefs' on money. Nothing took off. The tiny wins and even the slow dribble of clients that came towards me made me realise that these types of approaches were not my medicine! Did they even truly work for anyone?

The day came for me to leave my speech pathologist job. My divine path gifted me a redundancy package. This gave me space to breathe as I stood on my own two feet in my business again. By this stage though, the cloud above me loomed much closer and I tried not to feel the dread and panic that I felt within my inner universe. I made a little bit of money but not enough for my family.

Lo and behold, about a month later, a beautiful woman contacted me. She was a mother who does what it takes for her family. She told me she wanted to employ me as a speech pathologist for her children, with her NDIS funds. She found a loophole to employ me, without being registered with the NDIS. 'No!', I cried. 'I'm not registered. I cannot work under the tight speech pathology scope anymore'. She explained that with the NDIS, she was free to employ whomever she wanted as an 'unregistered provider'. She insisted, until I told her that I'd look into it.

To be paid by the government yet again was not what I wanted it to be; however, I understood this divine invitation. I would be able to meet the communication goals for this family, my way, and get paid as well as others who had studied this profession too.

Anthony was excited and congratulated me. I didn't see the 'congratulations' part though. 'I didn't do anything. She rang me. It literally fell into my lap! I'm almost angry. All that time I tried and tried and it obviously wasn't my time back then. It's my time for more money to come to me, in this way, right now'. I had chased clients ahead of 'my time'. In hindsight, I sat present with the fact that I had wasted so much precious time, energy and money on this dead pursuit.

From hereon in, I saw the fact that we can't hurry our way through so called 'limiting beliefs' or anything our little old human self wants to make happen. I had always known that I was worthy of the money. I always maintained that I deserved to earn more than mainstream speech pathologists as I brought *much* more to a family, if they were ready.

I also knew my physical body held onto old shame about money and unworthiness, *from when I grew up*. These speech pathologist scenes were the tip of the iceberg of 'what it feels like to not have enough money'. I had to release the corresponding emotions of that life theme and where it first started, to step into what I knew I deserved. Although I knew what I deserved, I couldn't hurry the scenes that would prod this charge from me, like we saw in The Cone chapter. They had to arrive in divine order, to prod me on this money life theme, from each divine angle.

Through the years, as I searched for money, I spent a lot of time in panic, frustration, stress and more. I released many, many 'lava lamp blobs' of emotion. By the time I received regular money through the NDIS, I had obviously cleared enough to collapse a cone. This cone related to the life theme of 'what it feels like to be unable to find regular income through my business and soul work'.

As I cleared the charge from my vessel, I then saw that it was *all* about divine timing. Most women found it hard to trust my 'new' work, let alone want to look at their own inner hurts, let alone convince their partners that this would be better than regular speech therapy. I had to wait for them to receive my work too. It came down to divine timing on all accounts.

Since then, I saw the 'rainbow'. As we see a new direction we want to go in life, we cannot hurry and force it. It is like we say 'yes' to the idea, throw it up into the air and in good time, it will land, like a rainbow. It might happen in a week. It might happen in a month or ten years. We cannot control when this scene will land in our lap or the 'rainbow' will arc back down.

> The Rainbow - as we have an idea, dream or calling, it rises up into the air and follows the arc of a rainbow, that lands it in good timing - minutes, days, weeks or years from now. It is a waste of energy to hurry it.

In the meantime, we can only clear our inner charge and take inspired action, which is then more likely to be from our seed of intelligence. As with the Titanic and the Cone energetic concepts, we meet the rainbow at the other end. This upgraded version of ourselves lands in a brand new scene of our lives exactly when it was orchestrated to. At that point, we have embodied the life theme of what it's like to *not have* what we yearn for. We never need to push or force it to happen, just as we never need to force a baby out, ahead of the divine timing of its birth!

When I first started my business, I saw the direction I wanted to go. I yearned to have plenty of clients and money flow towards me. From then on, my only role was to move forwards, as with the Titanic energetic concept. Every scene that appeared, when I didn't have clients and/or money (and there were many), were my invitations to release 'what it feels like to not have clients and money'. I embodied it from many angles until I landed in 'what it feels like to have clients but still be paid by the government'. I shifted internally and by default, my external reality shifted. I still had to embody many angles of life themes around clients and money. These worked out as I did my inner work, and in divine timing, the rainbow 'dropped more pleasing scenes into my lap'.

Why you want to know about the Rainbow

You may easily know how you want to improve your life. You may decide :

- I'm going to get my children back on healthier food.

- I'm going to make an effort to spend more time with my children.

- I'm going to aim for a date night each week with my partner.

Although you know what you yearn for, you are not actually in control of when these yearnings will play out successfully. As some will say, the 'when' and 'how' gets taken care of by the divine. When we play from our little old human self, we usually try to make these scenes happen and of course, we rise the emotions in us when they don't pan out.

Some mothers literally tell me, 'I've tried it all with my children. They are fussy and can't be helped'. The thing is, they tried for a few scenes in their daily life, but it wasn't the divine timing for the result. Perhaps these children would never eat what she thought was healthy. Perhaps these children needed to eat comfort foods for the next ten years and would realise how to be healthy in their twenties or forties! Perhaps she needed to realise that she had disconnected them from their intuition, as she had technically interfered with their soul path. These realisations and matching successes don't happen overnight. We need to surrender to our own feelings as we let go of how we think our children should be.

Sadly, many mothers give up on their yearning for sibling harmony, healthy eating, time with their partner and even time for themselves or any other callings. They take it personally that they can't 'make it happen', like they have failed. They don't realise these unsuccessful scenes are simply their invitation to clear the charge of 'what it feels like to *not* have this scene I dream of' first.

We *gently* move forward and insist on where we want to go, despite the scenes that don't work out. We only take action when we receive clarity from feeling 'what it feels like to not have this scene that I yearn for'. It is a waste of our precious time, energy and money to try to make it happen, which we know is driven from our ego or monkey mind. *With the dinner time example, the mother may continue to offer many food options or just ensure that she joyfully eats exactly what she feels like, as she focuses on what she can control. She doesn't ignore the inner feelings that rise as her child refuses to eat how she thinks that they should.*

As we let go of when the outcome will happen, we have less expectations. We also then have more resources to say 'yes' to more yearnings. We know they will all land in good timing, like with the rainbow energetic concept.

As you go The New Way, continue to say 'yes' to your dreams and cast them into the air so they can follow the arc of a rainbow and land in good timing. You may say 'yes' to healthier eaters, present time with your children, date nights with your partner, time for your artwork, more energy to garden, the ability to notice more of your children's gifts, more discernment with money, holidays, the right factors to grow a community and so on. Of course, it won't all happen tomorrow. You simply say 'yes' and move forward gracefully, rather than with force.

As you now know, the rainbow on each yearning will drop in divine timing. It will not be a path of ease. You will continue to land in scenes where you don't have what you yearn for. Even though you might agree with the energetics of the rainbow, you will find that your little old human self still has expectations of when certain dreams should eventuate and how they should look.

Remember that the point of your displeasing scenes is to raise your inner charge. As you express the full spectrum of emotions in what you desire for your future scenes and continue to speak up on what you insist on, those scenes that haven't manifested yet, come closer and closer.

Take the time to flip your daily challenges. What do you yearn for? Insist on your yearnings. Work through the doubts of your worthiness. Feel what it feels like to be here on Earth without them. Trust that they will come as you follow the energetic rules of the game of life.

Summary

* You can't hurry your yearnings into being.

* It is a practice to go within and do your inner work as you wait, rather than take wasted action.

* The longer your yearning takes to drop in, the more inner work and related life themes there are to explore - it is a big one on your path.

* Expect miracles and the right actors and opportunities to drop into your lap.

* As we play the game of life in this light, we don't expend nearly as much time, energy and money and instead, we have time to slow down and enjoy 'what is'.

To sit with..

Know that you yearn for certain things because they are on your soul agreement.

* Where do you push, force and/or chase things to make them happen for yourself and your family?

* Who has conditioned you to feel you must achieve what you wish for and on a certain timeline?

* How does it feel to notice what you yearn for and trust it will play out?

Red and Green Lights

...your divine path always gives you hints internally and externally...

2019

I learned many soul lessons as I explored 'being a mother of a child in the school system'. As I approached my final scenes of 'being a mother of my Hayden at school', I started to see the concept of 'red and green lights'.

The school announced a lunchbox challenge. Everyday, each child scored a point for their class if they had a litter free lunchbox. The class that got the most points at the end of term would win a pizza party.

The thing was, I had made litter free lunchboxes for my boys since their first day of school, so this was nothing new for us. The other thing was, Hayden was gluten and dairy free and wasn't able to eat standard pizzas. I braced myself for how it would pan out if his class won. Throughout the challenge, Hayden resented that he had always taken litter free lunches and now they offered a prize that he couldn't partake in. He wanted to take packaged food to sabotage the results.

Yes. Out of about 30 classes, his class won. There was no mention of Hayden or the other child, who couldn't eat these pizzas, as they celebrated the class' mega efforts. I emailed the deputy principal, who was our contact after all of our challenges, to explain the situation. His response of, 'oh well, maybe he could order a salad' raised a blob of rage within me. Hayden didn't eat salad nor was it celebratory food! The deputy principal ignored my email suggestions of hot chips or sushi, that were close by, for Hayden and the other child. I couldn't bring myself to cater for Hayden because the school had decided on this prize, not me. For seven years, I had provided food alternatives to birthday cakes and the like. I felt my exhaustion.

If I hadn't already processed enough anger about the school system, this was the final purge. I had 'kaleidoscope eyes' as I squeezed my jaw, eyes and fists. Hayden and I then got upset together about yet another scene of rejection for him at this school, which was essentially another hit of rejection for me as his mother too. Eventually, I found some peace on the other side of some big releases.

I saw it. Since Hayden's first day at school, I had banged my head on a brick wall. There had been 'red lights' all over the place. I sensed them internally through my feelings. I had seen them externally through the challenges Hayden had copped over and over again. I had even ignored the green lights of when things felt right and easy, such as on the summer holidays, where we were free to follow our own agenda and be under no one's rules or curriculums. As I saw all of the scenes that had hinted 'you're going the wrong way', I realised these scenes had been like guideposts from my seed of intelligence. I then saw them as red, green and yellow lights.

> *Red lights say 'uh uh, dead end, wrong way, go back, you're further from the best path you can take at this point in time, for yourself, your family and everyone you have an effect on'.*

I also tenderly realised I hadn't been ready to see the green lights. The actors and scenes at school *helped me* to release the massive blobs of stagnant energy I had swallowed down when I was young. They were the emotions of 'what it feels like to be kept small at school… and to see injustice there'. I had to go the 'wrong path', to firstly see the shadows, to release my rising energies, to find inner peace. As I felt inner peace, it was easy to crave for and see the green lights.

> *Green lights say 'yes, you're closer to the best way your uniqueness can have a lasting effect on the Earth and allow you to feel all the positive adjectives as a reward'.*

Without nearly so much charge, I decided to write back to the deputy principal to tidy up energetic ends. I emailed him with, 'I've realised I expected too much of you and the school system compared to what I expect for Hayden. All of these challenges have motivated me to homeschool him even more so now'. Of course, he changed schools the following year and I never heard back from again!

Why you want to know the Red and Green Lights concept

The aim of the game of life is to allow 'what wants to be' and to accept 'what is'. To help you with this, your seed of intelligence gives you red, green, and even yellow lights, all day long, through your detailed daily experiences. Internally, the red and yellow lights are like warning lights, which feel like uncomfortable bodily sensations. Externally, they show up as displeasing scenes in your daily life. These signals direct you towards the life themes you agreed to explore. The green lights, of course, feel like much better sensations within and much more pleasing scenes in the external.

> Red and Green lights - this energetic concept guides you back to 'what is' and 'what wants to be' by internal and external signals.

Let's look at examples of how red, green and yellow lights show up. We will start with yellow lights, the more subtle signs and then we will take a look at red and green lights.

Yellow lights

Yellow lights remind us 'there is a knot to be worked with here'. They look and feel like little issues in your day and may be a sign not to pursue the particular path. A yellow light may also indicate there is something to work through, so that we *can* continue on a smoother path. If we don't work with the yellow lights, they will end up as red lights and more chaos in our lives.

Here is an example of a yellow light where it was simply a 'knot' to be worked through.

Declan was drawn to woodworking from a young age. I put out feelers to find a class for him. Finally, a wondrous woman opened a woodworking sanctuary for children. Declan was in heaven. A few months into it however, Declan came home and mentioned he didn't like how the teacher spoke to him. This was a yellow light, like a glitch in the path that had previously flowed so well for him. He didn't want to do anything about it but before long he also told me he didn't want to return the following term.

I could see the issue with his teacher wasn't necessarily a sign to jump ship, which is often a 'flight' response when we don't know how to feel through or speak up about an issue. Declan however, was ready to let it go and quit because he didn't want to bring it up with her. I tried to convince him he needed to sort it out, however, energetically, I saw 'off me, back to you Mum' - his resistance reminded me that it was my path to talk to the teacher. I needed to experience one more scene of 'what it feels like to speak up for my child, to create better scenes around them'. I didn't want to do it, but I knew this woodworking opportunity was too good to simply walk away from.

I spoke to Declan's teacher and it was the moment where I knew her response would either mean we were happy to stay or happy to leave! She responded with, 'Thankyou for telling me. I never want my students to feel uncomfortable and I wasn't aware I made him feel this way. I will change'. Immediately, Declan and I felt relieved and their relationship has continued with respect for years now.

In this case, the yellow light simply hinted there was a knot to sort out. Often however, a yellow light is a warning to do a gut check and switch directions. Yellow lights can feel like slightly uncomfortable sensations within and 'not the best, but not the worst' outcomes in our external reality. Yellow lights can be easy to justify or to completely miss. They become the elephants under the rug that we have unknowingly turned away from. The more we play the game of life, the more we start to sense the tiniest of invitations to 'explore this knot a bit further'.

When we see a yellow light, we have the choice to pay attention to it and act upon it or we will attract more warning lights. Here are some examples of this.

* *Your child says 'I don't like pumpkin' as you buy it to make pumpkin soup. Yellow light... and the writing is on the wall that you will land in a tricky scene at dinner time until you acknowledge pumpkin soup is not on your child's soul agreement at this time.*

* *You accept a job at the interview even though your stomach dropped when you found out it paid less than you thought or it included a task that you've always said went against you. Yellow light... and the writing is on the wall that you will soon land in challenging scenes, until you look for a different position.*

* *Your child tells you there is a problem with their teacher, one of their peers or the activities at a homeschool co-op. Yellow light... and the writing is on the wall that you and your child will continue to land in further challenging scenes until you speak up to sort out the issue or more likely, until you insist on a better place for your child.*

Yellow lights invite us to see what wants to be seen. Here are some examples of this.

* *Maybe your partner eats healthily with the family but is a little huffy about the topic of 'healthy food'. This yellow light invites you to get honest with the signs that your partner is not truly glad to eat all of this food. It's not 'what wants to be' for them. Their behaviours invite you to allow them their path to*

eat what they are drawn to and to have more conversations about how this can work for the family.

* *You invite your child's friend over for a playdate. The family doesn't reciprocate but you invite the child over a few more times. You notice a slight huff as you do it the third time. This is a yellow light that the energy exchange is not even and an 'uh uh' in 'what wants to be', despite your yearning to have children over.*

* *Your child comes home and announces their friend invited them to their birthday party. Your child then displays their usual anxious behaviours, such as flipping out at something small or changing the topic as you ask them questions about the party. These yellow lights invite you to further explore these not-so-excited behaviours for a birthday party. Your child may need to feel and speak about their nerves to go alone or even make the decision to respect their nervous system and politely decline the offer.*

* *You take your child to a new allied health therapist or paediatrician and they mention the benefits of medication for your child's impulsivity. You feel your monkey mind respond as you nod and smile, because you feel too awkward to share your opposing views on the topic. This is your yellow light that this professional and the service they offer does not align with you and fundamentally this will not change.*

Yellow lights may end up as an obvious red light scene. Here is an example.

Your child is out of energy to do their homework. Their head is slumped on the table. You encourage them, 'it's just the last little bit, let's get it done!'. You help them but they continue to show signs that their energy is not behind the task. They get it done, but the next day they forget to take their homework to school.

Their inner universe had hinted 'that's enough', but they ignored it to please you. As a parent, it is easy to respond from the monkey mind nets of 'parent keen for my child's success' or 'do the right thing'. The yellow light was to work with our child's resistance and why we felt to push them. The red light was the clincher when they forgot to take their homework anyway. In hindsight, you and your child can see that wasn't 'what wanted to be'. They needed to explore 'what it feels like to admit "I didn't do my homework" to my teacher'.

Of course, we can ignore yellow lights for years or decades, which only bring the bigger red lights, so that we play out 'what wants to be'. Here is an example.

You are keen to send your son to the best high school you can. You find a private school with many opportunities and he has many friends who also plan to go there. The only catch is, you aren't sure how you can afford it.

In the meantime, you play out financial stress with your partner. You nudge him to change jobs and he resists you on this. It strains your relationship. You sit frozen in how to make more money in your own business. You carry the burden of shame on your shoulders, that you can't financially make this happen. On top of all of this, you start to homeschool your other son when their school issues become too much for them.

The following year, you and your husband scrape together the money to send your son to the chosen high school. He comes home from school on day one and heads straight to his room. The days go by and he deals with subjects and teachers that don't fulfil the promise of magical opportunities. You know he has a tough time with the other children, but you sweep this under the rug as you are so far down this path now. Through your emotional brain fog and self-preservation, you barely think to ask him if he wants to homeschool because you don't want to entertain the idea of two children at home.

Eventually, your son's health takes a turn. He is underweight and out of energy to do life. The panic at this red light forces you to get honest. Your child's path wanted to be something-other-than-school all along. It was hard to acknowledge this from the start as you wanted one of your children to take the traditional path to 'success' that you didn't feel you were given as a child. Instead, you played out the pain of financial stress, which made you feel like you did something wrong with your business. Your heart connection with your husband, son and even your other child suffered. Your physical, emotional, mental and spiritual health suffered as well as that for your son.

The yellow light was actually the gulp you took when you first saw the price of the school fees. From hereon in, each glitch to do with the theme of 'needing money to fund school fees for what I think is best' was more like a red light. This example reminds us that we all walk down many life paths as we turn away from countless yellow and even red lights.

Can you imagine how different and more harmonious your life might be if you took the yellow lights as warning lights?

Over time, the yellow lights always catch up on you. Most adults these days are soul tired and perhaps don't realise it. If we don't pay attention to the yellow lights, we end up with red lights that eventually make us take a break.

Below are some warning lights. They may be yellow or red lights for you, but this doesn't matter. It is the game of life to notice any warning lights, and to understand the trajectory of these if you don't make changes.

You may have physical warning lights of soul tiredness, such as:

* insomnia
* hormonal issues
* adrenal fatigue
* low immunity
* need for sugar and caffeine

You might notice emotional signs of soul tiredness, such as:

* frequently teary
* stressed, panicky behaviours
* sensitivity to what others say
* flat affect
* inability to cope with any type of stress

You may sense the spiritual warning lights, such as:
- less zest for life, creativity or care factor for anything
- often sighs
- gives up easily

Your mental warning lights of soul tiredness may be:
- easily forgets
- frequent 'um's
- breaks down when unclear of direction
- indecision
- pays attention to others' path more than their own

You may play out practical warning signs, such as:
- the need to stay busy so as not to feel the tiredness
- the need to control the children so they don't create mess or any extra work
- the desire to run from any challenges with partner, friends or family as they have no more resources to face their own inner universe

'What wants to be' is to take a break from what your soul is tired of.
- Some need a break from other people.
- Some need a break from constant pressure to perform.
- Some need a break from monotony.
- Some need a break from constant responsibility for others.

What does your soul need a break from?

If you don't listen to the yellow and red lights and take the exact break your soul needs, you may end up with:

* A bigger health issue or injury that you need to stop life for. Perhaps you needed a break from constant responsibility for others. Perhaps you needed a break from the monotony of your job.

* A sick family member you now need to care for. Perhaps you needed a break from the pressure to perform at your job. Perhaps you needed a break from the rest of your family as you spend alone time with one family member.

* A redundant job. Again, it may give you a break from monotony or from other people or anything else your soul needed a break from at this workplace.

The yellow lights become red lights when we try to create our days from what we want it to be instead of what wants to be.

For some, they notice their inner emotions and constrictions as warning lights. For some, they spy the external glitches more easily. Either way, to play the game of life is to bravely address the yellow lights as soon as we can and surrender to 'what wants to be'. Energetics have spoken when we see a yellow or red light and we can either play by the rules of the game of life or play out more challenges.

Red lights

Red lights are the glitches that show up in the scenes of your canvas of life when you ignore the yellow lights and try to push what you'd like it to be rather than allow for 'what wants to be'. The red light could be an unexpected bill, a car accident, a health issue, a fight between your children or any challenge in your day that you would not willingly paint onto your canvas of life.

Scenes with red lights will make you feel even more discomfort within your inner universe than yellow lights. The red lights invite you to feel these sensations, so you can more clearly see where your seed of intelligence wants to guide you. Maybe you attracted the bill to see that you did have the money to get that massage you yearned for but felt you couldn't afford. Maybe you ended up fatigued and burnt out so you could practise discernment of what you say 'yes' to. Maybe you landed in scenes where your children fought, so you could finally voice with passion, 'I yearn for family harmony!'.

> *We can turn a blind eye to how we feel about our challenges; however, our seed of intelligence will pull us into these life themes anyway, through bigger challenges, to make sure it gets our attention.*

Red lights are invitations from your seed of intelligence to change direction. The sooner you change direction, the less chaotic scenes you will attract. This is easier said than done because we have to let go of what our little old human self is attached to. Often, the life themes of 'what wants to be' present a path that can scare us.

For example, your children wake up grumpy and you later smash a cereal bowl on the floor. These are yellow lights to invite you to question your plans to later take your young children to the museum. What wants to be is actually a day at home where everyone can take it easy whilst they feel their swirling inner universe. This choice would land you on the beat of divine timing for your soul path that day.

Let's say you allow your monkey mind to convince you that you can't cancel plans to meet your friends at the museum that day. It is likely your children will continue to whine, and you will receive more and more invitations to 'abort plans', 'take it easy' and 'seek the more peaceful path for yourself'. These are further yellow lights. Then, maybe your friends arrive and say they're on the tail end of a gastro bug. Maybe your friends have a bad morning and arrive so late that your children are ready to go home by the time they get there. Maybe you don't realise you need to buy a ticket for the museum and it is booked out when you get there. Insert any 'you-wouldn't-believe-it-but..' storyline here! These are red lights and your matching discomfort within confirms this.

Whilst you may see red lights in the scenes you land in, you may also spy them in hindsight. In hindsight, red lights confirm where you played life from your little old human self or monkey mind. They are an 'oof' from your seed of intelligence that alerts you to a not-so-great choice in a prior scene or even decades of your life. You might have pushed, convinced and justified your way to 'what I'd like it to be', 'what's easiest' or 'what is most perfect to me', whilst you ignored 'what wants to be'. Remember, we have been conditioned to seek a perfect life or the one our little old human self perceives is best. It's no wonder we judge and turn away from life paths we perceive as wrong, *even if they call us.*

Here are some examples of red lights to explore in hindsight.

* *Your child decides to take an extra handful of chips, which leaves their sibling with much less. They then trip over and spill the chips over the ground anyway. In hindsight, the child may see they were 'bumped' to remember to be fair and do things differently next time.*

* *The family enjoys a certain board game so much that you decide to buy the extension game. As you buy it, the whole family gets drawn to other ways to spend their time and the expensive extension does not get used. In hindsight, you see that you assumed what each member wanted. From now on, you ask each family member more questions before you buy them anything. You also encourage discussions about any family decision, to sync up with 'what wants to be'.*

* *You take your child to a new homeschool hub. Wires are crossed and the organiser doesn't realise you will be there. She hasn't bought supplies for your child. A particular family arrives with a child that your child doesn't get along with. Eventually, an alarming incident happens to ensure you and your child leave. In hindsight, you see you ignored your discomfort around the homeschool*

hub issues because you wanted to make it work. You felt the pressure to have something organised for your child's week and didn't trust there was a better place for them.

✱   *You realise each time your friend suggests you catch up that you search for a reason to be busy. In hindsight, you realise this non-energised feeling invites you to see that your friend always talks about herself and her problems, with little bother about you. You get honest that when she talks over you, you land in the life theme of 'what it feels like to be unheard'. When she invites you to catch up, you find words to communicate that you simply don't feel energised to.*

Of course, we don't need to classify whether an 'oof' is a yellow or a red light. It is to understand the concept of internal and external glitches as signs to reconsider 'what wants to be'. It is to remember that our seed of intelligence always guides us.

> *Everything is a reflection. Sometimes we see it in the external before we notice it within.*

Life isn't perfect

Of course, our path is not perfect. Every yellow light we miss is also meant to be. Sometimes we need to experience the big, burning red light scene to learn our soul lesson. This was in our soul agreement too.

Here are some examples of the soul lessons we might come to as we play out the red lights.

✱   *Perhaps we continue to insist that our partner learns to love healthy food, until we realise this monkey mind net contributes to some of our partner's expressions of disrespect towards us.*

* *Perhaps we continue to invite our friend's child over until a big rift comes between the two children.*

* *Perhaps we firmly encourage our child to go to the birthday party, until we realise that our child's anxious behaviours at the social event turn children away from them.*

* *Perhaps we continue to take our child to the allied health therapist until we get burnt out in motherhood. As we take non-priorities off our plate, we realise the therapy doesn't provide the solutions for our child that we hoped for.*

We are never wrong in our choices and cannot go down a wrong path. The more we act on the yellow lights however, the less chaos we invite into our lives to ensure we play out 'what wants to be'. Think about how much time and energy is leaked as we sit in indecision or when we stew on our regrets. Instead, we just need to remember to notice the life themes we land in, particularly to move through our challenging scenes.

Green lights

Green lights are also feedback either internally or externally. Internally, of course you may feel excited, goosebumps, heart flutters or just a big 'YES' feeling to any scene in your day. Externally, green lights can be synchronicities where things worked out better than you dreamed of. They are also the things we take for granted that tell us we have done certain parts of our life well. *Some examples are when we have health, energy, inner peace, heart connection for ourselves and with those around us and the freedom to feel and to speak.*

Green lights are not guaranteed to stay. *For example, initially we might feel a green light to take our child to a certain activity but at any time we may feel and see yellow lights instead.* Change is inevitable in the game of life, and hence, we must always be aware of green, yellow and red lights, internally and externally.

Here are some examples of green lights.

* *Your child meets a new friend and you and their mother have a shared interest or grew up in the same area. Green light!*

* *You find a new interest and it happens to be on when you have a free slot each week in your calendar. Green light!*

* *Someone mentions this book to you and it matches up with your desperate question of 'How do I stop a recurring challenge with my child?'. Green light!*

* *You decide to ditch the chores and get out of the house. Your friend rings you that instant to catch up. Green light!*

Green lights are also noticeable in hindsight. They are a wink from your seed of intelligence that you took a path that matches up with 'what wants to be' in a prior scene.

Here are some examples of green lights in hindsight.

* *Let's say the family is in disharmony, and you decide not to go to the extended family catch up. Later that day, you hear a report of a big delay in traffic on the road you were to travel on or you all discover a movie to watch with pertinent messages for the family issues that had arisen. It was a green light to know you made the right call to cancel the catch up.*

* *Another green light in hindsight can just be the feeling of peace and relief. As you say 'no' to someone or something, it can bring up emotions. Yet as you go forth, the relief and inner 'yes' feeling reflects this course of action as a green light. For me, as I made the decision to close my 'Awakened Parenting' Facebook group, I did it with a sense of relief. I realised how much energy I had spent on the group for not enough in return.*

Seeing the lights

All of the red light challenges in our day arrive because we aren't in tune with the yellow lights. There are *always* internal and external yellow lights before red lights. This reminds us of how important it is to take note of 'what is'. Instead, our little old human self loves to guide us to what we'd like it to be, so we miss the subtle signals of our divine path.

* Internally, what do you truly feel within? Do you miss the yellow light sensations?

* Externally, what scenes of your life are not truly ideal? Do you miss the yellow light signs from your actors and displeasing scenes?

As you make decisions each day, it is very interesting to notice your feedback. Did things flow well from that decision? That is, you got a green light. Or did something trip you up? Did you receive tricky responses from your children, partner or other actors in your day? Wherever there weren't obvious green lights, your seed of intelligence flashed you a warning light to check inwards.

Of course, it can be really tricky to see the red or yellow lights because we often have to work through the emotions linked with them. It can be grindingly hard to let go of our monkey mind's plans for us. We also have to have challenging conversations as we change course. Remember, you will feel emotions as you get honest about the yellow lights and accept 'what is'.

Here are some examples of why it is hard to see our warning lights.

* *To see our child's continued school refusal as an increasingly bigger red light to either change schools or leave school is not easy. We know behind these warning lights, there will be change, emotions to be felt and challenges as you speak up as a mother.*

* *To pay attention to the family's financial strain also means there are tough calls to be made, uncomfortable changes for everyone and emotions to be felt about 'what it feels like to make choices because of money'.*

* *It is a big thing to sit with others' suggestions that you look at your stress as a contributing factor to your child's developmental, physical, mental, emotional or spiritual issues. It means you will have to face the elephants in the room and your inner hurts as you let go of the need to fix and change your child.*

Accepting 'what is'

The red and green lights energetic concept literally guides you to come back to 'what is'. Notice your recurring challenges and what it feels like to bang your head against factors that will not change. Notice that you are drawn to these chaotic scenes to have a reason to release your inner charge, not to justify fight/flight/freeze responses.

Here are some examples of why you might be drawn to scenes of 'battle'.

* *When I expected too much of what the school could provide for Hayden, it gave me a reason to release all of my anger.*

* *When your child constantly picks on their sibling, you are drawn into it, so you can release your rising charge.*

* *When your partner leaves their dirty clothes everywhere, you are drawn to nag them, which releases some of your frustrations about life.*

Firstly, dive in and use these scenes to release your rising charge! Then, from the clarity, notice where you can change your canvas of life to more pleasing scenes. *For example, for your own peace, you may accept that you appreciate tidy floor space more than your partner and more gladly pick them up.* It's easy to miss these answers when we focus on what we'd like it to be, just like how I wanted the school system to receive and deal with Hayden well. *Maybe you want your children to get along or to have a tidy home.*

We must slow down so that we can play the game of life by the red and green lights energetic concept. Before we take action on our ideas, we might allow time to reflect, work through any feelings and/or communicate with others. Then we can more likely feel the path of what wants to be. *For example, if you asked your family, 'Should we invest some money into the extension game?', you may have seen the subtle signs of 'uh uh'. Perhaps one actor said 'yeah maybe', or another didn't answer and left. Both responses are certainly not green lights to go ahead and buy it.*

As we have seen, the key to intuitively access 'what wants to be', is to connect with your honest feelings. Does it truly *feel* like a great idea on all accounts or does your little old human want to 'make' something happen? If you still don't know, put the idea aside for a week. You will likely receive more guideposts - red, green or yellow - as to what wants to be. You will also see how your monkey mind feels to wait on something it often wants achieved *now*. When in doubt, talk to everyone involved and really listen to their responses. Stay open to 'what is', the divine answer, not what you would like it to be!

Summary

* Red, yellow and green lights are internal and external nudges towards your best decisions.

* Green lights hint where to continue.

* Yellow lights hint where to change course or feel and then speak up about the issue.

* Red lights hint where you are way off course.

* Our monkey mind distracts us so we don't connect with our inner nudges of discomfort and our less-than-wonderful external scenes.

* As we notice any warning lights, we need to feel through the emotions that our monkey mind distracts us from.

To play with…

- Do you sense your inner nudges or external nudges more easily?

- Do you sense them at the time or in hindsight more easily?

- Play 'eye spy' with your children each day. Notice the external scenes that are glitchy. What do these warning lights tell you all?

Playing Cards

...you can only play the game of life from 'what is'...

2022

Anthony, Declan and I found ourselves hooked on the card game, Monopoly Deal. We played it every morning. In short, the aim of the game is to be the first to lay down three sets of properties, the same ones from the board game. You start with five cards, pick up two cards each turn and must discard to hold a maximum of seven cards in your hand at the end of your turn. There are cards of money and particular cards where you can steal someone's property, a whole set of properties or charge others rent. There are also "just say no" cards, where you can say 'no' to any action card played against you.

The more we played, the more I explored the life themes of 'what it feels like to win the game', 'what it feels like to make a stupid move', and 'what it feels like to forget to play my "just say no" card'! The longer I was drawn to play the game, the more I questioned the connection of these themes with my daily life.

Coulda shoulda woulda

I saw the times when Anthony and Declan played 'coulda shoulda woulda'. When I won, which was clearly not the outcome they played for, they displayed their cards and talked about 'if only I'd had that card, then I would have...!'. They hadn't accepted 'what is'. Instead, they tried to change the outcome in their mind because they could see what needed to happen for them to win. I noted however, those cards *hadn't* come up.

As I pondered this analogy, I realised how many women played the game of life through 'coulda shoulda woulda'. 'If I had more sleep, then I would be a better parent.' 'If my partner helped out more, I'd be happier.' 'If my partner was more accepting of my soul work, then I'd be able to move forward with it better.' Like the cards that weren't in Anthony and Declan's hands, these factors *weren't* in these women's hands either.

We know the point of life is to accept 'what is'. Of course, we can only peacefully accept 'what is' as we make sense of our emotions that drive the 'coulda shoulda woulda' monkey mind net. It could be frustration at oneself for a bad play, which reflects how we feel about failure in real life. It might be sadness that 'I lost because everyone had it in for me', which also reflects a valid theme from everyday life.

Noticing the cards you hold

Sometimes, I held onto a rent card in the hope I picked up the "double rent" card that you can use as a powerful pair. Of course, often I didn't pick up the double rent card and wasted an opportunity to use the card I actually held in my hand. In my mentoring sessions, I realised how many people played the game of life by this move. They waited and hoped and dreamed about the 'card' they might pick up. I explained to them, 'Play the cards you have in your hand. There is a point where you cannot continue to wait for a card that might not even come in this life'. Of course, there is a fine line as to how long you do wait for a card you expect might show up too.

Here is an example of how mums of fussy eaters learned to play the cards they held in their hand.

Mothers came to me to be mentored about their picky eaters. They wanted their child to be a clean eater. I reminded them of the cards they held in their hand. Amongst other life cards, they held the cards of 'give them more meat, which they want', 'allow them to eat their potato with tomato sauce', 'just give them plain dry toast for breakfast, which they want' and 'insist on a green smoothie for breakfast'.

They quickly realised it was more successful to play the dry toast card and to discard the green smoothie one on their next turn. On top of this, they didn't even hold a 'clean eater' card in their hand! They had too much expectation on their child. As the mothers played some of the cards they held in their hand, they were then able to pick up two more cards on their next turn. As their child ate dry toast for breakfast, the mothers then picked up the cards, 'receive a hug from my child' and 'child introduced to gherkins and cheese on toast by nana'. They played these two cards. Before they knew it, their child was more flexible with more options and they found more heart connection with their child. In divine timing, the 'green smoothie for breakfast' card was likely to show up again too!

> *The more you play the cards you actually hold,*
> *the more opportunities you have to pick up new ones.*
> *Keep an eye on when you try to play cards that you don't hold or*
> *forget to play any of the ones you do.*

Many of us however, haven't realised the cards we literally hold in our hand. Cards we hold in our hand can be:

- what comes easily to us
- what we have time for
- what we can afford
- what does work
- what the whole family is happy with
- what are the next easiest moves towards our yearnings

This is 'what is'. Instead, our monkey mind distracts us, to focus on outcomes that are touted by others, such as the mothers who yearn for their fussy eater to also eat cleanly. What cards do you *actually hold* in your hand right now? What cards do you try to play but don't hold in your hand? Often, these are cards that others hold and try to convince you to play them too.

Accepting less-than-perfect

On the days when I was less-than-present with Monopoly Deal, I was more likely to make a hurried move. It always backfired on me and inevitably, it always cost me the game. I felt my frustration as I knew exactly where I had gone wrong. I likened this to my life. Some days, I was tired, emotional or distracted and hence, I made less-than-mindful decisions. I then felt 'what it feels like to blame myself for a bad choice despite not being in a better position to make a better choice'. Essentially, the factors around me ensured that I lost. Even if I made a much worse choice in real life, I could still zoom out and remember that I am part of a *game* of life.

When I lost the game, it worked out for Anthony or Declan who won that day. Although I lose in some way in my real life, someone else always gains. I energetically cannot play perfectly every day, and this ensures balance across everyone we interact with. We are all interconnected. The cards are always dealt again, and another opportunity to play better is always around the corner.

No one could play your cards any better

Some days I lost round after round. The longer I didn't win, the more it started to appear that I had no skills, especially when Declan and Anthony whooped and cheered as they won! On mornings when I was sensitive, I really felt my rising emotions.

Of course, the game always changed. I was always dealt a great hand eventually. The confidence I played that hand with made me realise there was nothing wrong with my skills. When the cards were great, I played them well. When the cards weren't great, I *still* played them well. My losing outcome didn't mean I wasn't a skilled player despite conditioning that told me so.

I saw the reflection of real life. We are deemed successful in life when we achieve the results we've been conditioned to think are 'successful'. *For example, you are successful when you have a partner, children and a stable job.* On the contrary, we have been taught to think that someone who loses a game or doesn't achieve something easily, doesn't know how to play their 'cards' well. We have forgotten however, that we couldn't play the cards they *actually hold* any better. *For example, the boy that doesn't appear to do well with maths can barely think straight because he lives with domestic violence and eats no breakfast. He is successful to keep it together at school and get any work done with these cards that he holds.*

We must remember that we are always successful with life, no matter what cards we are dealt. No one else could play them any better, given all of the factors you are up against. It is empowered to catch the monkey mind net of 'judging whether I am successful or not' because we are much more skilled at this game of life than we give ourselves credit for!

> *When you think you haven't played well with any part of your life, notice the cards in your hands.*

Finding the root of the weed

One of the trickiest parts of Monopoly Deal was when I continually forgot to use my 'just say no' cards. Another player would take a whole set of properties and even win the game, and I didn't remember the powerful card I held in my hand! I noticed the reflection in my day to day life. It was a season where I forgot I had the choice to say 'no' to the scenes in which I didn't feel completely comfortable. *For example, when a friend asked to come over and I said 'yes' despite my need for alone time.*

The frustration that arose for me in the card game, reflected the rising frustration that my soul felt as I continually put others before myself.

From childhood, my path was to play the people pleaser and at that point, I literally didn't hold a "just say no" card in my hand. Despite this, my soul clocked frustration at that time because I could not honour my own needs. I allowed the card game scene, as well as that with my friend, to prod the hidden sadness within me. I then picked up the "just say no" card for my day to day scenes and began to play it!

Why you want to know about the Playing Cards energetic concept

As we have seen, the energetic concept of 'playing cards' relates to the concept of 'what is'. Many of us know how we would like to show up better. We would slow down. We would give out more hugs. We would manage our stress and emotions better. We would eat more healthily. We would go to bed earlier. What else would you do if you could be a better woman/mother/partner/friend/daughter?

We must get honest. There are so many divine factors that ensure we don't play that perfect character. We are also not here for the perfect fairytale storylines, at least not until we have cleaned up our inner universe. It is time to make sense of the character that we play, which is light *and* shadow. It is time to make sense of the fact that we have an agreed path, with many storylines that won't please our human self.

We can only play the game of life from the cards that we hold in our hand. We have far less choice than we think we do. We can feel through our emotions as our little old human self tells us that we have stuffed up. Then we can more clearly see the cards we hold and know the best moves to make with them. This way, we accept 'what is' more peacefully and leave everyone to their own soul path too.

Summary

- We only hold so many 'cards' in our hand as we play the game of life.

- We may think we can achieve certain things but we must get honest about the cards we don't have - skills, energy, money or support to make it happen at that time.

- We must take the time to notice the cards we are dealt and make peace with the ones we hold.

- The more we use the cards we hold, the more we pick up new ones to play with!

- We are very qualified and successful as 'humans who play the cards of life' that we are dealt.

To play with ...

- Despite what you can't make happen easily in your life right now, what 'cards' can you play well, which you may have forgotten?

- In which area of your life does your monkey mind whip you, for less-than-perfect play?

- Which factors hold you back from better play?

- Put any other actor in your shoes - could they play your hand of cards any better?

The Fairytale

...heaven on Earth starts within us...

As we go through the shadows of our internal and external life challenges, the words often slip past our lips - 'I dreamed of a much more magical life than this'. Some even *remember* the magic they sensed when they were very young, even in traumatic times. It truly felt possible that this experience on Earth could be 'heaven-sent'.

So where is this fairytale that we have sensed? Now that you have read this book, you might have an idea of the answer. It is within us! The more we work with and clean up our inner universe, the more we feel inner peace. The more we feel inner peace, the more we are inspired to continue with this inner work, to make our inner universe feel *magical*.

> *It takes commitment to your inner work, to shift your backlog, to see the magic. It works like a snowball and will pick up pace the more you feel.*

As our inner universe shifts, our external world shifts. We may still make those same dreaded lunch boxes but we feel the excitement for life as we do. This task becomes a joy as we have worked to find out exactly what each child yearns to eat. It is no longer a mindless task or driven by ego of what we think is best. We feel the green lights on our new approach.

Through our soul lessons, we now feel the value of any 'perceived' chore as an opportunity to tend to our home and family with even more love energy. Of course, these tasks feel better because we are straight onto even more joyful tasks afterwards too. Perhaps the next thing we are about to do is to happily snuggle with our children, who look forward to this too. Perhaps we are about to get back to our new found gift and have a play. As we feel the magic within us, we expect every scene on our canvas of life to be enjoyable.

We may still walk in the same forest but now we see it for its divine perfection. We aren't distracted by our inner chaos, which allows the forest to show off its magic to us. We realise how we were numb to the magic around us because we had numbed the sensations within us. No one could have explained the magical lens we now see through.

We may still play out some struggles with our loved ones. By this point however, we have reclaimed respect for our own soul, through our inner work, which in turn has created respect within our relationships. We quickly find compassion for both parties and the magic rekindles. We are now more focused on the magic that we can create together, rather than the question of 'should I leave them?' or 'how can I make them pay for this?'.

We don't worry about the future of the planet. We see the divine orchestration of the world's challenges because we have made peace with the shadows that are not only 'out there' but within all of us. We have taken charge of what we can. We have owned 'you are it'. We patiently wait for others to embody this too. Of course, the light and the dark plays out in divine timing. We are content with 'what is'.

When we create the fairytale within us, we create the fairytale around us. It's like we exist on the same timeline as we used to but the scenes have a very different feel and shine to them. It is because we sense it all from a brand new state on the inside.

The journey towards the fairytale works like a snowball. At first, it feels clunky to play by 'you are it'. It's trickier to connect inwards because we aren't practised and so the results are less evident. The more we shift within, the more we shift towards more magic. As we faithfully roll the snowball forwards, we can make it our mission to notice *every glimmer* of magic around us. This is our payment. Before we know it, our continued commitment rains down on us with the fairytale that we did yearn for when we were little.

As we insist on 'you are it' ourselves, in good timing, our family members step into this too. The whole family bubble becomes more harmonious and the family team steps out into the world in a magical light. As more and more family bubbles lean into empowerment, they can then collide and co-create magically, with other family bubbles. Before this, each family and each individual will be continually nudged back to respect the game of life by 'you are it' and 'what is'.

....

In this book, we have reviewed what goes on energetically for *you* as the Creative Director of your reality as you play the game of life. In coming books of The New Way series, we will look at the following in further detail:

* how to find your unique process to connect with your inner universe and flow your energies

* how to interact with your actors self-responsibly and insist on the same from them

* how to use the power of the family bubble to master each members' challenges and unlock your gifts

* how to use the soul lessons from your inner and family work, to step into your soul work

Glossary of The New Way terms

Actors - the people that show up in and interact with us in our day-to-day scenes, who reflect how we feel within, 100% of the time.

Canvas of life - each scene of our life is a canvas to continue to notice what pleases and doesn't please us. This practice helps us to keep a balanced focus on all aspects of our life and to remember that we can always change what we don't like.

Co-creation - to work with either the sensations within or the responses of our actors or external scenes.

Creative director - the scenes of your life show up according to how you manage the state of your inner universe.

Daily scenes - any moment of your day to day life, like a scene out of a movie with certain actors and certain storylines.

Disempowerment - to rely on others for your happiness and life answers, instead of connecting within.

Divine beat - to land in each scene that 'wants to be' and explore this, rather than pull towards what your ego thinks it should be or to race ahead of time. Linked with Divine Timing.

Divine timing - the perfection of our existence and divinely timed scenes that play out so that we can experience the life themes on our soul agreement - despite our ego's attempt to change this.

Ego - our soul's true expression is affected by our ego which shows up as disempowered behaviours, ideas, beliefs. Also known as monkey mind or little old human self.

Embody - to feel it so much that you can say you have 'been' that - eg grief, a mother, exhausted, a teacher.

Emotional blackbox - Our physical body has recorded our emotions in each scene of our human life, since point zero. It has tensed around and numbed much of the energetic charge we would otherwise feel.

Emotional embodiment - to be present with an emotion, to feel it.

Empowerment - to create the inner state you desire by your own inner work, which links you to all of your answers intuitively and allows for the expression of your true essence.

Energetic divorce - an energetic process, that we get invited into, to let go of disempowered relationship patterns. This can and will happen with any of our actors, such as partners, friends, extended family and our children too. You must be ready to see your own shadows, release your emotions responsibly and communicate vulnerably with the other party.

Energetic puppets - our actors energetically respond via their monkey mind nets if we express ourselves from our own. We free our actors to show up from their true essence, or bow out of our reality, as we express ourselves from our true essence.

External reality - what you see, touch, hear and smell through your senses.

Family bubble - the dynamic ball of energy that interconnects all family members in a family unit. As one member changes, to seek balance, the other members are drawn to change.

Game of life - the human experience which includes aims, rules and how to 'win'.

Golden answer - the option of 'what wants to be' which we find as we tune into what feels right on all accounts. Also called 'our dots'.

Green lights - say 'yes, you're closer to the best way your uniqueness can have a lasting effect on the Earth and allow you to feel all the positive adjectives as a reward'.

Heart of the matter - the underlying problem of our life theme which helps us to see the root of our 'inner weed' and find our soul lessons.

Inner charge - the unexpressed energy, also known as emotions, that feel uncomfortable within us.

Inner universe - what you perceive as emotions and sensations within you.

Invisible magic - the gifts encoded within us that no one externally can teach us to do any better, often not revered at school. Also referred to as 'magic of magic'.

Lava Lamp Effect - Emotions we have clocked in the past, continue to rise like packages of energy. These attract the scenes we land in, which make us feel the exact emotion that arises.

Life Themes - A life theme is an angle of life we agreed to explore, to truly feel what it feels like to be a human who experiences this and to better our external reality through this process, such as 'what it feels like to be Australian', 'what it feels like to lose a friend to suicide' or 'what it feels like to eat a green apple'.

Little old human self - that which makes our choices for us from what our ego would like it to be rather than feel for 'what wants to be'.

Magic of magic - that which we can do well without even trying. Also known as 'invisible magic'.

Monkey mind - that which distracts us from our rising charge with disempowered expressions of physical body contraction. Also known as ego or little old human self.

Monkey Mind expression - a behaviour driven by unexpressed emotion rather than from our true essence. Also called a Monkey Mind net.

Monkey Mind net - a disempowered type of expression that we are virtually forced into, if we don't express our rising emotions. Also called a Monkey Mind expression.

Mother-Child Teamwork - both parent and child seek to feel and talk about their experiences, to prioritise their heart connection above any daily challenge. Fathers will step into this as we go first.

North stars - the different directions our seed of intelligence aims us towards.

Our dots - the options in life that have our name on them, from our hairdresser to what we eat for breakfast to how we sort out a disagreement with someone. Also known as 'golden answers'.

Player one - assume you are the only player in your virtual reality game. Everyone else is a non-player character.

Point zero - the moment we were born and started the timeline of our soul path.

Red lights - say 'uh uh, dead end, wrong way, go back, you're further from the best path you can take at this point in time, for yourself, your family and everyone you have an effect on'.

Red and Green lights - this energetic concept guides you back to 'what is' and 'what wants to be' by internal and external signals.

Glossary of The New Way terms

Scar point - the first time we experienced a challenging life theme and did not completely express our emotions.

Seasons of life - We flow in and out of seasons of life, pulled by our seed of intelligence, to be sure we experience the countless life themes on our soul agreement and from opposing angles.

Seed of intelligence - the intelligence encoded within us, to energetically land us into the experiences we agreed to on our soul agreement.

Self-responsibility - to be mindful that your expressions can leak your rising charge at others and to work to release it without projecting it.

Shadow expressions - any behaviour that is not of our true essence, instead driven by our inner charge. Also known as a 'monkey mind expression'.

Soul agreement - our agreed life path, which includes themes we are to explore, which connects with what we are drawn to and repelled from.

Soul lessons - what we come to, as an empowered outcome of the experience of a challenging life theme. For example, 'no more overgiving to my partner in areas where they actually don't want my input'.

The Titanic - we must face what is not, before we become the version of 'what is'.

The Rainbow - we cannot control when our yearnings will drop in and it is a waste of energy to hurry it.

Soul path - our life path we unravel according to our soul agreement.

Snow Globe - your energies swirl to be expressed as you land in your time to explore the Heart energy, as a child or an adult.

Spiritual ego - spiritually-acceptable behaviours that are still ego-driven, from our inner hurts.

Storylines - the exact play out of a scene, including what each actor said and did, to ensure we feel a life theme.

The void - when one season of our life has come to an end but another hasn't yet started, such as when our child clearly doesn't belong at school but we don't know the next best place for them.

Tip of the iceberg - the day-to-day scenario that represents and raises the unexpressed energies from our initial 'scar point'. Whilst we do need to address the day-to-day scene, we must prioritise the deeper inner work invitation.

True Essence - our unique true nature, which we express when we are not 'clouded' by our rising inner hurts.

What is - the divinely orchestrated scenes of our life that actually play out, which show us 'what wants to be', 'what is' or 'what wanted to be'. These can be quite different to how we try to steer our lives or the parts of our lives that we ignore.

Yearnings - what we dream of is energetically encoded to seek us, not the other way around.

Your actors - the people that show up in and interact with us in our day-to-day scenes, who reflect how we feel within, 100% of the time.

Glossary of the
The New Way energetic laws

Better out than in - our body seeks to expel that which is designed to flow, including vomit, ear wax, splinters, urine, faeces and emotions. There is a cost to try and block that which wants to flow.

Feeling cannot be turned off - We experience emotions in every scene of our day. We don't get to decide what we feel. It is 'what is'. Our physical body records these reactions.

Harmony is between two poles - only once we have played out both extremes, can we settle into the harmony which lies between.

It takes one to know one - when we see something in someone else, light or dark, we recognise it because it is within our inner universe too.

It takes two - we always interact as energetic pairs, to land each other into particular life themes and to feel the corresponding sensations within.

The family bubble seeks to balance itself energetically - we exist in opposites in every way, to ensure the energetic entity of the family remains balanced. As one member changes, to seek balance, the other members are drawn to change.

We behave from our rising emotions - as an emotion arises within us, we will behave from a disempowered expression.

We are energetically connected - we have an emotional effect on each other, which drives change in a ripple effect, if we embody our life themes.

We are in constant expansion - the constant outwards pull which opposes our physical body's inclination to contract and hold onto our unexpressed energies.

You are it - the scenes in our external reality reflect the state of our inner universe.

The energetic laws we explore in each chapter - in order of appearance

* You direct your life from your inner universe - You are it

* Your soul path is encoded within you - Seed of intelligence

* You are energetically pulled to the path encoded within you - Divine timing

* You cannot change who you are - Soul agreement

* Every scene of your day is an experience for YOU to embody - Life themes

* Those in your external reflect what is there to be felt in your internal - Your actors

* Feeling cannot be turned off - Emotional blackbox

* The state of your inner universe dictates everything in the external - not the other way around - Lava lamp effect

* You behave from your rising emotions - Monkey mind nets

* When it's time to explore the Heart energy, our emotions surface whether we like it or not - Snow globe

* Your recurring challenges continue until your soul lessons have been realised - The cone

* The little opportunities to feel will become the chaos that forces us to crack - Inner universe

* The harmony is between two poles - Seasons of life

* Your life at any moment in time, is a canvas that you can co-create with - Canvas of life

* Your inner universe and external challenges show you what you are encoded to yearn for - Yearnings

* We must face what is not, before we become the version of 'what is' - The Titanic

* Allow your yearnings to show up in good time - The rainbow

* Your divine path always gives you hints internally and externally - Red and green lights

* You can only play the game of life from 'what is' - Playing cards

* Heaven on Earth starts within us - The fairytale

How to Play summary

1. You wake each morning and check how you feel in your inner universe.

2. You get honest that these feelings will attract how the scenes and actors show up in your life that day.

3. You check to see if you feel to release any charge that wants to come up, either :

    - then and there

    - later, as the external world prods your inner universe - it may take a good while to master responsible emotional expression

4. You talk out loud to your family and actors about how you feel and own any responses that may come from your inner charge as you get prodded. For example, if you blame, yell, huff or try to control them from hereon in.

5. You honour yourself as you spend even a present moment with the sensations in your physical body or with the emotions as they come up. You connect with your inner universe.

6. You take note of the life theme you play out in these scenes - eg. 'Oh this is what it feels like to be doing it all as a mother' or 'what it feels like to have a child who is too much……' or 'what it feels like to run late'.

7. You acknowledge how it relates to any of your four 'bodies' - physical, emotional, mental and/or spiritual, to shift the energy that rises within you. We'll go into this process in more detail in a coming book of The New Way series.

8. The more you do, the more you receive your 'goodie bag' of open

heartedness, clarity, energy, motivation and momentum to move towards your dreams for you and your family, in the small everyday scenes and in the bigger picture. You gain heart connection and respect from those around you as you butt out of their path, own your stuff and work your own soul agreement. From the different energetic state within you, the actors and scenes begin to change in positive ways too.

9. The more you play the game of life in this fashion, the more you leap frog into alignment and flow with your soul agreement and true essence. By default, those around you also begin to swirl into alignment, because you hold a very nurturing and empowered energetic space for them to go The New Way.

The magic is to be present in the moment with 'what is', rather than what we'd like it to be. At the same time, we practise how to stay connected with what our heart really yearns for.

Acknowledgements

Firstly, I'd like to honour *you* for reading this book! A movement requires a movement of people. Whilst many women 'quote Heidi' to their partners and friends, please remember that if you feel called to talk about or spread the messages of The New Way, then you too, are an important part of this unfolding!

It is 'our work' and will continue to be as we go forth into the future. We will all embody it in our unique ways and so will those we activate too. I am one person, yet the more we sit with the *importance* of these messages, the more we realise how quickly it can spread if we all talk out loud about it, in any way, in our days.

Thankyou for playing!

Acknowledgements

To my supporting actors

Firstly, I must thank my Anthony, Hayden and Declan (and Bounty!). They have prodded me, supported me, loved me, cheered me and held the space for me when I have been at my lowest lows through this book-writing journey. We did this!

Next, to the wonderful hearts that have been my 'first followers' from my fussy eating coaching days, New Children Healing Sanctuary and Awakened Parenting days.

More recently, I must thank every wondrous soul that has taken a step or leap towards The New Way and ultimately, helped me to feel a little less lonely on this cutting-edge path, whilst we make magic in our families. There are many of you.

Thankyou with a big hug to Johanna, Hennita, Bronte, Nikki, Wendy, Kylah, Shauna, Megan, Kelsey, Louise, Meika, Jackie, Bryony, Tanya and Eisen.

As I always say, 'all of us who are going first are leaders'!

Lastly, I will wildly acknowledge myself! Mothers rarely say with their hand on their heart, 'Wow, look what I've done of GOOD in this challenging mother role', and heck, this book 'baby' has been a painful, yet transformative creation!

Come and say 'hi' at my social media channels or discover more at
heidihosking.com

www.ingramcontent.com/pod-product-compliance
Lightning Source LLC
Chambersburg PA
CBHW051418290426
44109CB00016B/1347